REA

372.
Townsend-Butterworth, Diana.
Your child's first

P9-AFX-977

Your Child's

Your Child's First School

•• •• •• ••

A HANDBOOK FOR PARENTS

Diana Townsend-Butterworth

WALKER AND COMPANY
NEW YORK

•• •• •• ••

First published in the United States of America in 1992 by Walker Publishing Company, Inc.

Published simultaneously in Canada by Thomas Allen & Son Canada, Limited, Markham, Ontario

Library of Congress Cataloging-in-Publication Data
Townsend-Butterworth, Diana.
    Your child's first school: a handbook for parents/by Diana Townsend-Butterworth.
        p.   cm.
    Includes bibliographical references (p.) and index.
    ISBN 0-8027-1169-3. —ISBN 0-8027-7358-3 (pbk.)
1. School, Choice of—United States.   2. Early childhood education—United States—Parent participation.   3. Education, Elementary—United States—Parent participation.   I. Title.
LB1027.9.T68   1992
372.973—dc20   91-28326
                                                                      CIP

Printed in the United States of America

10   9   8   7   6   5   4   3   2   1

To
MY CHILDREN, JAMES AND DIANA
MY HUSBAND, DUKE
MY PARENTS, MARJORIE AND BARNARD TOWNSEND

And to the memory of my great-great-grandmother, Mary Alice Machemer Wood, who taught in the first public kindergarten in St. Louis, and to all the Bradley relatives who taught young children in cities and towns throughout the South.

•• •• •• •• •• •• •• •• •• •• •• ••

Contents

•• •• •• ••

Acknowledgments

My thanks and appreciation to all the teachers and administrators in schools around the country who shared their wisdom and experience with me to make this book possible. To Mildred Berendsen, Headmistress, The Chapin School; Diane Irish, Head of the Lower School; Diane Lyon, Director of Admissions; Ruth S. Proffitt, Assistant Headmistress for Administrative Affairs; Frances Bloom, Director of Studies; Louise Henderson, Assistant to the Headmistress; Marcia Bridgman; Harriet Hanchett; Loriel Townsend; and Dr. Tracy Pennoyer. To James P. Jacob, former Director of Admissions, Collegiate School; Esty Foster, Assistant Headmaster; and Nancy Saunders, former Head of the Lower School. To Dr. Stephen S. Clement, Headmaster, The Browning School; Andrew McLaren, Director, Little Red School House; Sister Kathleen Fagan, Headmistress, Marymount School; Reveta Bowers, Director, Children's Programs, Center for Early Education, Los Angeles; Christine Garten, Principal, Lower School, Savannah Country Day School; Ruth Summerlin, Savannah-Chatham County Public Schools; Claire McIntee, Principal, P.S. 94, Queens, NY; Lydia Spinelli, Director, Brick Church School; Mitten Wainwright, Director, Park Avenue Christian Church Day School; Mary Solow, Director, Central Synagogue Nursery School; Alexander Zimmer, Director, and Dr. Margaret M. Devine, Assistant to the Director, Madison Avenue Presbyterian Day School; Dr. Paula Newell, Director, Reformed Church Nursery School, Bronxville, NY; Edith Fulghum, Administrative Assistant to the Macon County Board of Education, GA; Len Berkowitz, Learning Disabilities Specialist, District 4, Manhattan; Sally Taylor, Chapter I Reading Teacher, Aurora Public School System, Aurora, CO; and the teachers at Keene Central School, Keene Valley, NY.

Most especially my thanks to my friends and former colleagues at St. Bernard's School: Stuart Johnson, Headmaster; Courtney Iglehart, former Director of Admissions; Betty Kennedy; Al Kilborne; Rosemary Lea; Jean Leness, Head of the Lower School; Mary Lewis; Pam Loree; Kerstin Rhodie; and Anne Turpin. And to my former colleagues at Columbia University and my friends at Harvard-Radcliffe who gave their advice and expertise.

To Gretchen Lengyel, Alice Goldman, and the officers of the Parents League in New York City who gave me advice and shared resources and information.

To Dr. Stephen Clem, Margaret Goldsborough, Mary Lathrop Will, and Martha Westburg at NAIS; Maxime Scherl at the ERB; Herman W. Hall, Education Consultant; Allan Shedlin, Executive Director, Elementary School Center; Melodye Bush, Education Commission of the States; Dr. Vance Grant, National Center for Educational Statistics; and Dr. Charles O'Malley, former Executive Assistant to the Secretary for Private Education, U.S. Department of Education for their assistance in my research.

To Diana Brewster Clark, Ed.D., Reading Specialist, Teachers College, Columbia University; Edward Davies, M.D., former Director of Pediatrics, Lenox Hill Hospital; Daniel Kessler, M.D., Associate Professor of Clinical Pediatrics, Associate Attending Pediatrician, The New York Hospital—Cornell Medical Center; Stephen Herman, M.D., Adjunct Assistant Professor of Psychiatry and Assistant Attending Psychiatrist, New York Hospital; Nina Lief, M.D., Director of the Early Childhood Development Center of the Center for Comprehensive Health Practice, an affiliate of New York Medical College, and Associate Professor of Clinical Psychiatry, New York Medical College; Ruth Ochroch, Ph.D., Clinical Professor of Psychology and Coordinator of Assessment Training in the Doctoral Program in Clinical Psychology at New York University; Beatriz Rubenstein, M.D.; Lee Salk, M.D., Professor of Clinical Psychology in Pediatrics at Cornell University Medical College; Sirgay Sanger, M.D., Director, Early Care Center, Assistant Clinical Professor of Psychiatry, Columbia University College of Physicians and Surgeons for their professional wisdom and assistance.

To Betty Bradley, Lyn Chase, Eleanor Elliott, Beth Glass, Anne Laumont, Lucinda Longstreth, Frances Maffett, Marjorie Mueller, Gretchen Nicholas, Catherine Pasymowski, Alexandra Preston, Jane Roy, Phoebe R. Stanton, Peter Strauss, and Catherine Taylor for their help and assistance.

To Dr. Daniel S. Cheever, Jr., President, Wheelock College; Sheila Hanna, Assistant Professor of Early Childhood Education, Westchester Community College; Joan Halpern, Director, Radcliffe Childcare Center; Kathe Jervis; Dr. Mary S. Kelly, Adjunct Assistant Professor, Remedial Reading, Teachers College, Columbia University; David Mallery, Director of Professional Development, NAIS; Tina Naddeo; Dr. Corinne Rieder, Secretary of the University, Columbia University and former Executive Vice President and Dean, Bank Street College of Education; Betty Schwartz, retired Director of Curriculum Development, Livingston Public School System, Livingston, NJ; Robert Seaver, Vice President, Communications, The College Board; Natalie Shainess, M.D.; Cyndie White, Harvard University Center for Parenting; and Sara Wilford, Director, Early Childhood Center, Sarah Lawrence College for reading my manuscript so thoughtfully and carefully and sharing their impressions with me.

I also send my thanks to all the parents who so openly shared the joys and misadventures of their children's early school experiences with me.

And finally my thanks go to my agent, Robin Rue, for her belief in my work and for her continuous and enthusiastic support. To Mary Herbert and all the people at Walker for guiding *Your Child's First School* through the pitfalls of production and publication. To my publisher, Beth Walker, for her patience and support. And to my editor, Stephanie Egnotovich, for her wise insights, astute editing, and invaluable assistance in helping me shape this book.

Introduction

*Let's declare that—during the decade of the 90s—our goal will
be to have all parents become full partners in the education of
their children.*

ERNEST L. BOYER, PRESIDENT
OF THE CARNEGIE FOUNDATION
FOR THE ADVANCEMENT
OF TEACHING

Before I was old enough to even think about going to school,
my father took me for walks over the hills behind our house.
Sometimes in March when there was a taste of spring in the air,
our expeditions would take us past a field where children were
playing softball. I would stand tugging at my father's hand as
the children dashed around, yelling and leaping into the air after
fly balls, lunging for grounders, or sliding into second base on
their stomachs. Their shirts always seemed to be hanging out
and their faces were smudged with dirt. I wanted desperately to
be out there on the field with them. My father would stand for a
moment watching. Then, turning to point at the buildings behind
the field, he would say, "This will be your school in a few
years."

My parents didn't need books or educational consultants to
help them decide where or when I would start school. There
wasn't a lot of choice. School started in first grade in Troy, New
York, and you had to be six by December 1 to go. My parents
didn't spend weeks visiting schools and comparing them. They
sent me to the school within walking distance of our house.

Starting your child in school in the 1990s is far more complicated. As an educator, I watch parents making choices every

day—choices that our parents never even dreamed of making. First as a teacher, then as head of a junior school and member of a private-school admissions committee, and now as an educational consultant, I have worked to help parents understand and deal effectively with important choices in their children's education. As an academic adviser at an Ivy League college, I saw the results of some of these choices. And, last but not least, as a parent I have made choices for my own children. In both my professional and personal life, I am continually aware of the need for the accurate information and intelligent guidance that enables parents to take full advantage of the exciting new options in education whether they are considering public or private school. And it is this information that I want to pass on to you.

When I began my research, it was with the intention of writing a book that dealt solely with readiness for early childhood school. Most of the research on readiness centered on readiness for kindergarten or first grade. Many researchers focused on readiness for reading rather than on the more global sense of readiness for all of the social, emotional, physical, as well as intellectual challenges of early childhood school. As I reviewed current research and talked to parents and educators across the country, I became increasingly aware of additional needs and questions of parents in the 1990s. I interviewed parents, grandparents, teachers, admissions directors, heads of schools, and principals. I also interviewed superintendents, professors of education, pediatricians, psychologists, child psychiatrists, and, of course, children themselves. The book grew in scope. No longer was it just about readiness. Readiness was but one of the many questions parents had. The book was no longer only about early childhood school. Children do not attend early childhood school in a vacuum. Early childhood school is followed by the early years of elementary school, sometimes even literally in the same school. When parents choose an early childhood school, they are often also making choices about the elementary years and beyond—sometimes without knowing it.

Many of the four-year-olds whose parents I interviewed had already been in either early childhood school or daycare. Some of them had been in semiformal group settings since shortly after birth. Were they ready for these experiences? Who knows. Readiness for early childhood school and its effect on middle-class children has been largely uncharted territory. As an educator I have come to appreciate the enormous importance child psychologists and educational researchers place on the early childhood years. Research documents the benefits children from low-income families derive from enriched day-care experiences, with studies showing that children from economically deprived backgrounds who attend Head Start and other quality early childhood programs have better attendance records in kindergarten and first grade. These children also seem more motivated, tend to have higher grades in elementary and secondary school, and generally have a more positive approach to school. And, subsequently, they are less likely to fail in school, to be unemployed, to have children out of wedlock, or to commit crimes. My own experience in the classroom supports the conclusion that carefully chosen early childhood schooling can enhance a child's readiness to learn.

As we become increasingly aware of the benefits of compensatory early childhood education, many of us believe that all children, rich and poor alike, can benefit from the experience of early childhood school. Parents, however, have less choice at the early childhood level than they can expect later on. Many of the quality public programs have restrictions based on parental income levels, leaving the majority of parents to choose between private and religious alternatives. Choice may be limited further by work schedules and a parent's need for full-day programs. In order to give our children the experiences that will enable them to thrive throughout their school years, both socially and academically, we need to be aware of the choices that do exist and know how to use them wisely. That is what this book is all about.

Making choices, especially choices that concern our children, is not easy. Despite ever-increasing research on individual differences in learning style, there seems to be no real consensus on the best school environments for different types of children. We are left wondering whether we really are choosing the best early childhood educational environments for our children. We may even question whether we have the right to decide to keep our two-year-olds at home if we can afford to send them to school—whether there are still alternatives to early childhood school for our children.

New parents have come to me over the years for advice on

their children's education because they believe that my experience and background enable me to offer an inside view of schools. The parents I counsel know that I speak to them as a professional educator, but they also realize that as a parent I understand their concerns as only one parent can understand another. As a teacher and administrator, I interpreted for parents what the school was really saying to them about their children and helped them learn how to become partners in their children's education. This book had its genesis in these discussions.

The parents I interviewed for this book are all busy people. Many of them work long hours. When they aren't working, they want to be with their children doing the things that are important to them as a family. These parents do not have time to spend hours in the library poring over research on educational options, nor do they have the free mornings or afternoons to sift through "park bench gossip" about which schools are "hot" this year. They deserve more. Parents tell me, whether they have a two-year-old or a six-year-old, that they need someone to give them direction, to show them how to acquire the information they need to find a school that will be a good fit for their children. If they are planning to send their children to the neighborhood public school, they also need information to help them understand how schools function and how they can work together with the school as partners in their children's future.

Today most of us have some degree of choice about where our children will go to elementary school. If you live in a large city, there may be fifty or more schools from which to choose. There are public schools, religious schools, and private/independent schools. If you decide to send your children to a public school, it may well not be the local neighborhood school. Many districts throughout the country have adopted controlled-choice programs modeled after a highly acclaimed program in Cambridge, Massachusetts, that allows parents to choose among thirteen different elementary schools. At the state level, Minnesota approved the first statewide choice plan in 1988. Arkansas, Idaho, Iowa, Massachusetts, Nebraska, Ohio, Oregon, Utah, and Washington have already followed suit and a number of other states have similar plans under review.

If, on the other hand, you are thinking about private school, financial aid packages now make this a realistic option for many families who formerly could never have considered it. Proposals are currently under discussion in a number of states that would provide aid for children to attend the private, parochial, or public school of their choice. If these proposals are put into effect, an ever-increasing number of parents will find themselves evaluating both public and nonpublic school choices. Parents who explore private school options tell me they are looking for the flexible curriculum, small classes, and individual attention associated with private/independent schools. Private schools in turn are reaching out to attract an increasingly diverse population from many different social, economic, and ethnic backgrounds.

You may be considering sending your children to a religious school even if you did not go to one yourself. Some parents are turning to religious schools not only for the religious instruction but because they believe these schools offer a safer and more wholesome environment. And they also like the emphasis on ethics. Religious schools in turn are opening their doors to children of many different denominations and faiths.

There is more to deciding on a school than choosing among public, private/independent, and religious schools. There are large schools and small schools. There are schools for toddlers and schools for elementary-age children. Still other schools, known as ongoing or comprehensive schools, are for children from age three to age eighteen. Some schools are coed and others are single sex. Some are traditional in outlook, while others pride themselves on their nontraditional approaches. Some schools are informal, encouraging children to call teachers by their first names and wear play clothes to class; others are more formal, requiring students to wear uniforms and preface questions with "sir" or "ma'am." There are schools that stress academic excellence and others that emphasize athletics or the arts. This incredible array of schools seems to offer parents every conceivable educational choice in style and philosophy. Making a choice can appear tantalizing or intimidating, exhilarating or confusing as you try to determine what will be best for your own child.

Even though you may not live in an area that offers such a variety of choices, there are still some fundamental educational issues for you to address as parents. Is your child ready to go to school? Chronological age is no longer the sole criterion for readiness. All across the country, I saw four-year-olds taking tests and being interviewed to determine their readiness for kindergarten. Meanwhile, parents told me of their concerns about whether their children could say the alphabet or write their names. Some parents even wondered whether or not they should be trying to teach their three- and four-year-olds to read. Kindergarten and first grade teachers, on the other hand, complained that while some of their students could probably read *The New York Times* or the *Washington Post*, they couldn't take turns on a tire swing, pour juice, tie their shoelaces, or put on their own sweaters.

Educators may deplore the fact that parents looking at a school for five-year-olds are increasingly asking where the seniors are going to college or what their SAT scores are, but to ignore the concerns behind the questions is naive. Consequently, I have elected to write about these concerns, and about all the choices parents are asked to make today in the education of their young children from early childhood school through the early years of elementary school. My research was conducted in a variety of cities and towns across the country, but my own professional teaching experience has been in New York City; hence, many of the quotations and examples I have used, which are drawn from my experiences in the classroom and from my day-to-day discussions with parents and teachers, are from New York City schools. However, I believe that the stories and anecdotes I have chosen to share with you illustrate universal issues and concerns that are relevant to the experiences of parents and children everywhere.

I do not rate or compare schools. Instead I have chosen to try to give you the information and confidence you will need to make your own comparisons in light of your own children's needs. Books that try to be all things to all people wind up serving no one—like the old man with the donkey in Aesop's fable who tried to please everyone and ended up pleasing no one, not even himself. With this in mind I have chosen to impose certain limits. I have included a brief discussion on children with special needs in chapter 4, but the subject of special education is a book in itself and it is not within the scope of this book to discuss it in depth. Rather I would like to point out that much research is currently being done in the field. And many educators feel that it is generally preferable whenever possible to keep children in a regular classroom setting with the teachers working closely with appropriate specialists to give children the necessary help without running the danger of stigmatizing or isolating them. (See the Appendix and the Bibliography for a list of relevant organizations and books.) I have also chosen not to discuss daycare because it has already been widely researched and there are many fine books available to parents. (See Bibliography for recommendations.) In fact, the large number of books on daycare and the relative lack of information for parents on early childhood school was one of the reasons behind my decision to write this book.

I have divided this book into three parts to make it easier for you to find the information you need. In Part I, I focus on the early childhood years, beginning with an exploration of some of the choices and challenges we all face as the parents of young children today. We will look both at the impact of important sociological and economic changes on our children's earliest school experiences and also at the changing role of schools. Next, we will step back to examine some of the key historical influences and trends in early childhood education, as well as current definitions and goals. We will review the basic ingredients of good early childhood schools and discuss what to look for in an early childhood school. I will give you guidelines on choosing the most appropriate school for your child and take you through the admissions process. We will also look at realistic and unrealistic expectations for early childhood school and explore some of the ways our own early childhood experiences exert subtle influences on the decisions we make for our children. I conclude the first part with an in-depth discussion of readiness for early childhood school.

In Part II, we will look at parental choice at the elementary school level and explore the multitude of educational options available in selecting either a public or nonpublic school for our children. I outline some of the key components of all effective schools. I discuss how to look at a school, how to read between the lines in catalogs and brochures to get to the nuts and bolts of what a school is all about—in short, how to find the right fit in a school for your child. We will consider important issues such as curriculum, class size, and teacher quality. We will explore some of the reasons why the school that was right for you may not be right for your child, and we will also look at the question of whether it is preferable for the parent who wishes to combine a public- and private-school education to opt for private school earlier or later. In these chapters you will learn how to get the information you need to make informed, responsible decisions about your children's schools. We then move to the admissions process itself, first looking at some of the different ways admissions decisions are handled at highly sought-after public schools that draw many of their students from outside their districts. Next we will focus on a discussion of private/independent school admissions as I guide you through the different steps of the admissions process, delving beneath rumor and hype to uncover the facts. I conclude this part with an examination of financial options.

In Part III, I focus on you as your child's first teachers. As parents you are the most important people in your children's lives. You play a key role in getting your children ready for school, and in helping them to be successful once they get there. Together we will look at some of the ways you can prepare for the first day of school. I make suggestions on handling separation and explore thoughts on avoiding the superbaby syndrome. There are recommendations on how to help your child feel successful in school, and tips on things to do and things to avoid. I have made some special suggestions concerning ways in which working parents may be part of their child's life at school. I also point out signals that tell parents when something is not right at school. As parents of young children, you will find information and firsthand advice on a range of topics from playdates to parent/teacher conferences to help you become effective partners in your child's education. Finally, the Bibliography includes a list of resources for parents and teachers as well as a selection of books for parents and children to read together.

This book was written for you—the parents of young children. We all care deeply about our children's education. We want to make responsible decisions on key issues that have a significant impact on our children's future. We want to give our children an education as good as, if not better than, the one our parents gave us. This book is about the choices we make as parents and the impact of these choices on our children and our families. It is about deciding to send our children to school at two or to keep them at home. It is about finding the right fit for a child in school, whether it is an early childhood school or an elementary school. It is about helping children feel confident and successful. It is about all the fears and joys of starting a child in school. And finally, *Your Child's First School* is about the importance of giving our children the gift of time, of allowing them to grow and develop in their own way, at their own pace, as we launch them on a lifelong voyage of learning and discovery.

PART I

Early Childhood School

•• •• •• ••
O N E
•• •• •• •• •• •• •• •• •• •• •• ••

Changes and Challenges

We played in tree houses and went on picnics, and read and listened to music on an old Edison Victrola. Our chief organized activity was a weekly visit from grandmother who bundled everyone into her car and drove us to town ostensibly to shop but more realistically to give our mother a few hours to herself.
—A TEACHER LOOKING BACK
ON HIS OWN EARLY CHILDHOOD

More than 6 million American children under the age of six are now in school. The sweeping social, economic, and technological changes of the last decade have made school an increasingly important part of our children's lives at ever-younger ages. We no longer see early childhood school as the luxury our parents did. For many parents it has become a necessity. We know this as fact and accept it. Yet at the back of our minds there may lurk the smallest touch of guilt that our children are missing some of the joy and freedom we like to remember from our own childhoods. We may also fear sometimes that we too are missing out on something by not being there with our children to share in all the experiences of their childhood. Such feelings can be particularly troubling when we try to explain to our parents, in-laws, or other members of an older generation why the choices we are making for our children differ from the choices they once made. I can still recall a conversation I had with my own mother-in-law when my husband and I were making the decision to send our first child to school at two and a half:

"You're not seriously thinking of sending that baby to school? He's not even toilet trained!" My mother-in-law had glanced anxiously first at me and then at her grandson, who was sitting

•• •• •• ••

on the floor trying to build a bridge with his cousin's Legos. "Did your mother send you to school at two and a half so she could spend the day in the library researching a book?"

She was right. I didn't go to school at two and a half or even at three. And my mother wasn't in the library. She was at home reading to me about the latest adventures of Winnie-the-Pooh and Piglet, or watching me zoom around the backyard on a tricycle.

The town I grew up in didn't have a school for two-and-a-half-year-olds. And if you're more than twenty-five years old, yours probably didn't either. Instead, we played in our friends' backyards, and our mothers took turns watching over us. There wasn't really very much we had to do, and there always seemed to be plenty of time to do it. There was time to spend the afternoon fishing for imaginary fish in the stream behind the house, to slay the dragons hiding in the fields, to take a toy wagon apart and put it back together again. There was time just to lie on our backs and watch the clouds float across the sky. One day drifted quietly into the next, punctuated not by schedules and deadlines but by baths and birthdays and family holidays.

As I talk to parents and grandparents across the country, I am constantly struck by the similarities in our childhood recollections. It doesn't seem to matter whether we grew up in California, Massachusetts, Illinois, North Carolina, or New York. We remember a sense of community and a feeling of safety. We recall neighborhoods where we knew almost everyone by name. The houses seemed to be filled with children, and doors were seldom locked. Our mothers often took turns watching our younger brothers and sisters in playpens in somebody's yard while we cruised up and down the street on our bicycles and tricycles. Our parents didn't have to schedule playdates two weeks in advance; we just ran outside to see our friends.

We had a great sense of freedom as children. Our parents didn't worry about muggers or kidnappers or teenagers selling drugs in the local school yard. We had to be home by dark when we were old enough to be out alone, but until then the neighborhood was ours to explore and enjoy.

Many of us remember feeling a strong sense of family. Some of us grew up surrounded by brothers and sisters and cousins. Our mothers were usually around during the day, and our fathers came home for dinner at night with predictable regularity. Often we had a grandparent to take us fishing, teach us how to bake brownies, or lend a sympathetic ear to our troubles. Sometimes there were sprinklings of aunts and uncles and even great-aunts and uncles around as well.

For many of us television was a luxury, and we could watch only on Saturday morning. The rest of the time we played with each other. There were no trips to Toys "Я" Us for the latest Teenage Mutant Ninja Turtle or Batmobile or Nintendo tape. We didn't seem to need so many toys—blocks, stuffed animals, bicycles, and maybe a Barbie doll or GI Joe were enough for most of us. Few of our parents felt pressured to buy the latest "in" toy advertised on the Saturday morning cartoon specials. They seldom felt the need to seek out the most scientifically advanced educational toys guaranteed to promote our small-muscle control or hand/eye coordination. Our parents tended to see us as children, not as future prodigies. They were usually more concerned with seeing that we ate our carrots and washed our hands before dinner than with trying to get us ready for kindergarten.

Sending their children to school at two and a half wasn't an option for most of our parents. A grandmother now actively involved in early childhood education policies remembers that in her day as a young mother, it was considered quite advanced to send a child to school at three. Those who did go to school at that age were usually sent, not to get a head start on the track to success, but because they were only children or lived in isolated areas, and their parents felt it was important that they have some contact with other children their age.

Even though our own childhood was probably never quite the simple, idyllic, carefree time we like to remember, it was not the childhood our children are experiencing today. Things are very different for our children. Rising costs and economic uncertainty have led an increasing number of parents to the realization that it takes two paychecks to maintain a middle-class life-style. Consequently more and more of our children are growing up in two-career families. Many mothers tell me they are in the work force not out of deep philosophical commitment or even a desire for personal fulfillment. They are working for the reason most men have always worked—economic necessity. As a new mother explained to me, "The age of assertive feminism is

Changes and Challenges •• 5

over—it's an absolutely pragmatic thing now—the two paycheck family."

Of course, women have always worked both inside and outside the home. And two paychecks have long been a necessity for many blue collar families. However, the number of children growing up in families where both parents work full-time has increased dramatically in the last decade. In 1980, for the first time the majority of American women worked outside the home. In 1990, 58.2 percent of mothers with children under six, 49.5 percent of mothers with children under three and 49.4 percent of mothers with infants under one were either employed or actively seeking employment.[1] Not only are more women working, the nature of their work is changing. Today women are coal miners and astronauts, bus drivers and university deans, molecular biologists and bond traders, as well as teachers and nurses and secretaries. They are assuming positions of increasing responsibility and leadership. Many women see their work as part of a lifelong career rather than a series of jobs. This translates into longer hours at work—some of them on weekends and evenings—more business trips, and a general decrease in family time. We can't turn the clock back. And few would wish to reverse the course of exciting new career opportunities that have opened up to women in the last decade. We must, however, acknowledge the impact the changes are having on our children from their earliest years onward. One of the most important of these changes is the growing importance of school in our children's lives as they spend more and more of their time there.

Both parents, fathers as well as mothers, are working longer hours and finding themselves away from home more often on business trips. Contrary to predictions about four-day workweeks and a round of golf or bowling in the afternoon, many parents are now working eighty hours per week. Leisure time has decreased 60 to 80 percent in this country since 1973. For many families weekends are given up to chores and marketing, and vacation means a couple of long weekends, not a month at the beach. Time itself is becoming our most valuable commodity. "Eighty-three percent of working mothers and 72 percent of working fathers say they are torn by conflicting demands of their jobs and the desire to see more of their families."[2]

As a result of all these demands and pressures, we often turn to schools to teach our children not only the traditional three

R's but also the kinds of life skills our parents and grandparents taught us at home.

Not only are parents working longer hours, but there are fewer parents around to share the responsibilities of child rearing. One out of every two American marriages ends in divorce. The number of single-parent families has more than doubled since 1970, and one-fourth of all U.S. families are currently headed by a single parent. Two million fewer children were living with both parents in 1989 than in 1980.[3] As joint custody decisions become more common, an increasing number of children find themselves shuttling back and forth between two households. School may provide the only stability in these children's lives. Difficult as it is for two-parent families to cope with work stresses and the demands of young children, it is even harder for single parents, who often feel under pressure to be all things to all people at the same moment.

Nor is there usually an extended family around to help fill in the gaps. Grandparents may be living in an adults-only community in Florida, running their own business, or on a world cruise, rather than sitting on the porch in a rocking chair waiting to take their grandchildren fishing or to help them with their math homework. Aunts and uncles are probably unavailable too, scattered around the world struggling to make a success of their own lives. So instead we again turn to our schools for help as we try to survive without the traditional support systems of family and community.

Over the last two decades, we have moved away from farms and small towns into cities and suburbs. Our houses and apartments are often smaller than the ones we grew up in, and there is less green space around them for our children to dream, to roam, and to explore. We worry that our children will be lonely and restless at home in small city apartments without playmates, without adequate space to play, and without the opportunity to explore new materials. Here, too, we turn to our schools and hope our children will find the opportunities there that we can no longer promise them at home.

We want to give our children the freedom to become confident and independent. We may remember the pride we felt going alone for the first time to the playground or to the corner store for the newspaper or a loaf of bread. We want our children to feel this pride too, but we are afraid. One of parents' greatest fears today is for the physical safety of their children. We worry that the playgrounds and parks and even the neighborhood streets where we once played as children are no longer safe. Our fears are all too real and we find them reinforced every day as we read in the headlines of our local papers about children who left home to do an errand in the neighborhood and never returned, children who were caught in a shoot-out between drug dealers on the way to the playground, children who were hit by drunk drivers on the way home from school. Andrew Stein, president of the City Council of New York, has written that a mother recently said to him, "The most dangerous thing we ask of our children is to go back and forth to school every day. We tell our children: Good morning; pay attention in school; be good. We don't say what is in our hearts: Come back alive; come back to me this afternoon."⁴ Even if we live in safe neighborhoods and send our children to private or parochial schools, the fear is still there in the back of our minds. And increasingly we ask our schools to provide space and activities before and after school hours where our children can be safe.

Our fears for our children's safety are often accompanied by a sense of alienation. We may no longer know our neighbors or the owners of the neighborhood stores. Few of us live in the town where we grew up; some of us don't even live in the same place we lived last year. As we grow accustomed to uprooting ourselves and relocating around the country every couple of years in response to the demands of our jobs, it is increasingly hard to have a sense of community that we can pass on to our children. So we turn increasingly to our schools to give us this sense of community.

Society's economic expectations have also changed for us. In the years after World War II, most of our parents and grandparents expected life to get better and better year by year in small predictable increments. They built a new addition on the house for a family room, bought a new car, and saved money to send us to college. It was the rare middle-class parent who faced unemployment when we were young. Now, in the aftermath of the eighties, when people believed that fortunes could be made overnight, the recession that economists have been predicting has set in, making the future uncertain for many parents. Thousands of American workers have lost their jobs as a result of the restructuring of the steel industry and the growing automation of the automobile industry. And now thousands of financial workers are losing their jobs because of the collapse of the junk-bond market, falling real-estate values, and the S&L (savings and loan) industry bailout. Since the stock market crash of 1987, forty thousand employees have lost their jobs on Wall Street, and the reverberations have had an impact on families across the country. Small businesses have folded, and restaurants and stores have slashed prices or gone out of business. Teachers in both private and public schools see children coming to school in tears, not because they have had a fight with a sibling over the prize in the bottom of the box of Cheerios, but because a parent has lost a job.

Since the 1970s we have seen a growing gap between rich and poor. The total household income for those in the top 20 percent of households increased by 2.6 percent to 46.8 percent from 1980 to 1989. At the same time household income decreased by 0.3 percent to 3.8 percent for the lowest 20 percent of households.[5] Almost one-fourth of American children under the age of six are growing up in poverty. Middle-class children listening to the evening news or walking past homeless families on the street see the difference between rich and poor as a cliff. If a family falls off the edge there is no middle-income safety net to catch them. They fear ending up at the bottom of the cliff on the street. Parents worry too, but they can more easily give names to their worries. They worry about making the next mortgage payment on the house, about the size of the debts they are running up on their credit cards, about paying to get their children's teeth straightened, about being able to afford to send their children to college. They worry about whether they will be able to give their children as good a life as their parents gave them or whether they will become a new statistic in the failure of the American dream. A few worry about their very existence—about whether they will be able to continue to feed and clothe and shelter their families.

During times of economic uncertainty, there can be anxiety and a sense of vulnerability, even in families where parents still have their jobs. Parental feelings and worries are quickly picked up by young children. Parents with children in private school may worry about where the money for next year's tuition is going to come from as they scan the mail for the letter telling them that their children will not be permitted to attend classes until the bills have been paid. Children in turn may worry that they will not be able to go back to school with their friends in September. Overheard arguments about money and partially understood conversations about overdue loans or unpaid bills easily create a sense of insecurity in our children. Children don't leave these worries and insecurities at the classroom door; they bring them inside. And schools must be able somehow to help children deal with their concerns so they can be free to learn.

As society grows increasingly complicated and technological, our children need more education to cope effectively. No longer will a high school diploma guarantee a job paying a decent wage. In the last decade, there was a 10 percent increase in the number of high school graduates going to college. Personnel officers and employment agencies find that college graduates are now often taking jobs that once went to high school graduates. Many people in the business community no longer believe that high school graduates have the training or basic skills to handle available jobs. As Dr. Nan Keohane, president of Wellesley College, said recently, "It is becoming clearer that our educational system is predicated on people having some training past high school to be able to take up the complicated jobs which are increasingly central to our economy."[6]

The quality of our education and the achievements of our students are constantly compared with those of other industrial countries, particularly Japan, and found wanting. Parents and their children have heard the clarion call for a more rigorous curriculum and tougher standards. The sense of competition often filters down to the very youngest student. Five-year-olds say it is important to work hard in school so we can keep up with the Japanese. We have seen a proliferation of classes for the gifted. Some begin as early as nursery school and admission is often based on standardized test scores. This, too, intensifies the pressure on children to perform early and well so they will be able to measure up in a competitive fast-track world.

Like our parents and their parents before them, we want the best for our children. And we have our dreams for them. But partly because we often have fewer children to dream about, the pressures escalate for those we do have. Many are having children later in life and choosing to have fewer of them. Balding and graying heads are now common at parents' days in elementary and early childhood schools. Because families are smaller and have often made considerable sacrifices in terms of both career and life-style to have children at all, parents tend to see each child as an investment. One mother said to me recently, "Since I stopped working, parenting has become my job and my son is my special project." We often feel that each child must be as nearly perfect as possible, and that we ourselves have to get everything right the first time since there may be no second or third chance. We sense that we can't afford to make mistakes with our child's education. We can laugh at ourselves sometimes for taking things so seriously and blowing everything out of proportion when our children, after all, are only babies. We swear that we will never be like other parents we know and let ourselves get caught up in all the craziness about schools. Yet sometimes we still fear, despite all the things we say to ourselves, that if we don't send our children to the right school, if we don't see that they have violin lessons or ballet classes or Little League or ice hockey practice, if we don't get them started off on the right track at the right time, they will find themselves left at the gate before they have had a chance to begin the race.

•• A New Role for Schools

As our society has become ever-more complex and our lives more fragmented, our needs and expectations for school have grown accordingly. We expect our schools to give our children the kind of education that will enable them to get into top colleges and universities. But we also ask our schools to take on new roles—roles that have traditionally belonged to us as mothers and fathers but that we may no longer have either the time or the energy to handle alone. We rely on schools to teach our children not only all the things schools have traditionally taught children but also to teach them everything from good table manners to sound moral values. We ask them to teach our children, as they grow older, about safety, and to tell them about sex and AIDS and the dangers of drugs and alcohol and tobacco, and how to protect themselves on the street. We ask our schools to teach our children self-discipline and how to respond to the needs of others. We want schools to give our children a feeling of stability and help them to develop a sense of community spirit and an understanding of growing up in a complex world. We expect our children not only to start school at ever-earlier ages

Changes and Challenges •• *11*

but also to spend more time there once they start. We need and want longer days, after-school classes, and activities and summer programs. The lines between home and school grow blurry as our children spend an increasing percentage of their lives in school and we, their parents, turn over more responsibility for their moral, physical, and intellectual well-being.

At the same time that we are asking more of our schools, schools themselves are facing new challenges. One of the most acute is the overcrowding that has occurred because of the sudden rise in the school-age population as the children of baby boomers reach school age and the children of our nearly six hundred thousand annual legal immigrants join school rosters. The National Center for Education Statistics estimates an increase of nearly 4 million students in elementary and secondary school by the year 2,000.[7] Some school districts are reopening schools they closed during the declining enrollment in the 1970s. Many are trying to squeeze more students into existing classrooms, and some are finding themselves forced to set up temporary classrooms in trailers or consider year-round school sessions.

Many of the new students will need remedial instruction or other special services. The first large group of children exposed to the ravages of crack before birth are now starting school. Teachers are finding learning and behavior problems for which they have no preparation. School systems in Florida, California, and other states are finding themselves forced to set up special training programs to help teachers cope.

Other students need special language classes and remedial instruction in English. Dr. Harold L. Hodgkinson, director of the Center for Demographic Policy at the Institute for Educational Leadership in Washington, finds that an ever-increasing percentage of the school population comes from minority groups with high poverty rates.[8] In some school districts, English is not a first language for one of every four students. Bilingual teachers are being actively recruited, and many school districts require that reading teachers be certified to teach English as a second language. America has always been a land of immigrants, and the percentage of the population born in a foreign country is actually lower today than in 1901. However, most recent immigrants have come from poverty-stricken countries in Latin America, the Caribbean, and Asia. George Borjas, an economist at the University of California at Santa Barbara, has questioned whether these recent immigrants, who are arriving with less education and fewer marketable skills, will "remain cut off from the greater American culture, raising the toll of poverty and racism."[9]

For schools this means not only struggling to integrate waves of new immigrants into their classrooms but also changing curricula to incorporate the diverse cultural backgrounds of students. The great books curriculum of traditional Western culture no longer reflects the realities of living in an international, multicultural world. But there is no consensus as to what a new curriculum should encompass. Computer literacy is rapidly becoming an elementary school requirement for teachers as well as children. Computers give students access to information and even to students in other schools, enabling them to design and carry out ambitious collaborative projects. Few teachers have the training to use computers creatively, and studies have shown that it can take as long as five years for teachers to learn to use them effectively in their classrooms.

Still another challenge for our schools centers around the ubiquitous role of television in many children's lives. Much has been written about the relationship between violence on television and aggressive play among young children. But nonviolent, well-planned and researched educational programs have also had an impact on classrooms. Children who have cut their teeth on Big Bird and visited Mr. Rogers' neighborhood know things before they start school that earlier generations of children were expected to learn in kindergarten or first grade. As one first-grade teacher in Georgia said to me, "I remember when I started teaching seventeen years ago, half of the first graders couldn't read by March. Now it's March and all the forty-four children in our kindergarten are reading." However, while they may be reading earlier, children are not necessarily reading as well. Researchers at Indiana University have discovered that forty years ago children had a written vocabulary two and a half times larger than children of a similar age today. Other researchers find that middle-class children are reading less than previous generations. Children also are receiving information in a different manner. While former generations of pupils might have been content to spend hours copying sentences from hornbooks and to fill in page after page in workbooks, today's children expect

Changes and Challenges •• *13*

to be entertained while they learn. People in the media talk about condensing information into sound bites and strive to get their messages across in thirty seconds or less. Our children are accustomed to receiving information in quick flashes and then turning their attention elsewhere; they have little experience at spending hours trying to figure something out for themselves. Consequently, their attention spans are often shorter, and they tune out more easily. Good listening is rapidly becoming a lost art. Dull teachers survive less well than in the past. Dull textbooks quickly become dust collectors. But even the books that have enthralled countless previous generations of children have trouble competing in a world conditioned to thirty-second sound bites. And even the best teachers find their students' attention wandering when they try to analyze or probe beneath the surface of a thought. Schools have been forced to adjust their curricula and teaching styles to the needs of a new generation of students.

On another level schools are struggling to cope with complex socioeconomic problems that lie outside the traditional training of teachers and administrators. Teachers are being forced into new roles as social workers and psychologists as they see increasingly angry and troubled children. According to Ronald D. Stephens, executive director of the National School Safety Center, "The age at which youngsters are expressing their anger at teachers is getting younger and younger and the things they are doing are more terrible. In the past it might have been telling a teacher off: now it's using knives and guns."[10] In California in the 1940s the top five discipline problems in the schools were talking, chewing gum, making noise, running in the halls, and getting out of turn in line. In the 1980s the top five problems confronting the schools were drug abuse, alcohol abuse, pregnancy, suicide, and rape.[11] Allan Shedlin, Jr., executive director of the Elementary School Center, a national advocacy, study, and resource center for elementary schools, believes the problems confronting children today are so acute that we should "reconceptualize schools as the locus of advocacy for all children so that they, as the only agency seeing every child every day, can accept responsibility for mobilizing available resources."[12]

Unfortunately, while we expect more of our schools, we are also often able to give them less help in return. As schools struggle with new and complex problems, they are losing us—

the parents—one of their traditional sources of support. Twenty-two thousand teachers surveyed by the Carnegie Foundation said that "lack of parental support" was a problem at their schools.[13] In the past many schools counted heavily on parents as a volunteer labor force—to chaperone field trips, help out in the library, and even work with children on a one-to-one basis in the classroom. Working parents often are unable to take on these duties. They may not even be able to supervise homework every night, read with children on a regular basis, or be available to listen quietly to their concerns. For more and more parents it has become important to look not only at the schools themselves but also at what kinds of parental commitments the schools expect and at the support services and after-school programs offered.

Schools in turn are increasingly reaching out to the people other than parents who play significant roles in children's lives—baby-sitters, nannies, and au pairs. A number of schools have held special workshops to help caretakers get involved in the child's life at school and to give them the training they need to be effective. Many caretakers are now chaperoning field trips, supervising homework, and even attending teacher conferences. Educators tend to view this as a positive adaptation to changes in American family life.

Parents expect more of schools today, but they also give schools less help and are less inclined to grant them authority. Like our children, we are both more and less knowledgeable than previous generations. We may have less hands-on parenting experience, but we have also read more and are more aware of the latest educational controversies and psychological research than our parents were. As a result we tend to expect our children's teachers to know more. If our children are in private school, we are very likely making a considerable financial sacrifice to keep them there, and we want our money's worth. We are less willing to brush off a poor teacher or a dull curriculum as the luck of the draw. We expect the best every year. When our parents were having children, teachers were still generally seen as authority figures. They seemed both older and wiser than our parents. But for many parents today the tables are turned. Parents who delayed having children to establish careers may well be older than their children's teachers—and wiser in the ways of the world. Unintentionally they may cause a teacher to feel awkward or ill at ease. Parents sometimes, in turn, have trouble listening to the advice of someone dressed in a kilt or corduroys who looks like a younger brother or sister. Yet for our children's sake we must listen and learn to communicate effectively. For these very teachers may see more of our children and at times know their needs better than we do.

For some of us schools have become surrogate parents. For almost all of us today, school involves more than learning to read or do long division. It touches on every aspect of our children's lives. We know in our hearts we must choose our children's schools with care, with wisdom, and with knowledge. We must choose them not just because they will give our children an excellent education that may some day enable them to go to an Ivy League college, but more importantly because they will help our children develop the confidence and self-esteem they need to grow up to be decent, caring, and effective human beings who will make a difference in their world. As more and more of our children begin school at ever-younger ages and spend an ever-increasing percentage of their time there, we, their parents, find ourselves confronting questions—questions of when, where, how, and even why—questions that no longer lie within the framework of our direct experience.

Over the years parents have asked me many questions about their children's first schools. A number are asked frequently enough that they obviously reflect parents' universal concerns as they seek to make the best possible decisions for themselves and their children:

1. What is early childhood school, and what can it do for my child?
2. What is the difference between daycare and nursery school?
3. Do I have to send my child to a private early childhood school, or is my child eligible for good public programs?
4. What should I look for in an early childhood or elementary school? How important is it that the school be in my neighborhood?
5. If I don't need daycare, should I look for an early childhood program that runs from nine to five, five days a week, or for one that meets only a few hours several mornings a week?
6. What questions should I ask when I visit an early childhood

or elementary school? What should I pay special attention to?

7. How will I know if my child is ready for early childhood school? How will the school know?

8. What about bonding? Will my children be as close to me as they grow up if I send them off to school at two?

9. What do I do if my child doesn't want to leave me? And what do I do if I don't really want my child to want to leave me?

10. How will I know my child will be safe at school?

11. Can my child get enough stimulation at home without going to early childhood school? What can I do?

12. What do I have to do to get my child into the early childhood school or elementary school of my choice?

13. What should I do if I think my child might have learning problems?

14. What can I do to help my child feel and be successful in school?

15. How involved should I be in my child's school?

16. How should I prepare for a conference with my child's teacher?

17. Will the teacher think I'm a pest if I call to voice my concerns? If the teacher can't help me, to whom do I go next?

18. Will my child get a better education in public elementary school or in private school? And what will some of the differences be?

19. What will private school cost? Is there any scholarship assistance?

20. Is there really a track to success, and do I have to get my child started on it at two?

We wonder whether our children will be different because they started school at two and a half or three. And if they are different will this difference make them more or less intelligent, more or less able to love and be loved, more or less capable of coping with the world? Will early childhood school help our children to be happy, productive members of society, or can it lead to increased pressure and early burnout?

In the next chapters we will examine together all of these questions. Most of the questions are answered in the course of this book. And while there are no simple answers for a few of the questions, I will share with you the results of my own experience and the findings from relevant research studies to give you the information and guidance you need to make your own decisions about the right answers for you and for your child.

T W O

The Roots of Early Childhood Education

Early childhood education begins at home. We are our children's first teachers. We design the lesson plans for our children's early years regardless of whether they are at home, at school, or in daycare. Early childhood education is teaching our children the skills they will need to survive and ultimately to thrive in our world. It is showing our children in our day-to-day lives that we love and respect them. And it is also helping them to learn to love and respect themselves. Early childhood education is passing on our traditions and values to a new generation. It is teaching our children to be a part of our society, to value learning, to have high standards, to get along with others, to be responsible, to share, to be a good sport, to make friends, to work and to play alone and with others. Early childhood education is the way we, and our parents and grandparents before us, have started our children off on the road to self-knowledge, self-discipline, self-esteem, competency, and independence.

•• Historical Influences

Early childhood education and even early childhood schools have been in existence far longer than most of us realize. The ways our forebears chose to educate their children and the roles they played in this education, whether at home or at school, are part of our earliest recorded history. Our curriculum and methods reflect current cultural values, but the origins of some of the underlying ideas and issues can be traced back to the ancient world.

•• •• •• ••

•• The Ancient World

In Greece, Plato (427?–347?B.C.) was already teaching that early childhood education begins at birth. He believed as many parents believe today: that what we say to young children and the stories we tell "shape their souls." Plato was not alone in recognizing the importance of the early childhood years. Aristotle, Plutarch, and Quintilian were among the many philosophers and scholars who spoke out on the importance of the education of young children.

•• Medieval Europe

As we worry that our own children are losing their childhood in the frenetic pace of life in the 1990s, we can reflect that after the fall of the Roman Empire (A.D. 476), the very idea of childhood was forgotten. Children in France and England were hurried out of the nursery, dressed up as adults, and made to assume adult roles. The realities of day-to-day survival took precedence over theories on early childhood education. So many children died in the first few years of life that few parents had the time to develop much interest in their education. And the children who did manage to survive infancy needed to learn specific practical skills if they were to continue to survive. Medieval parents, like many parents today, believed that these skills were best taught by others outside the family. Parents sent sons and daughters between the ages of seven and nine to work for the next seven years as apprentices in other people's homes. In England some parents still send their children to boarding school at a similar age. In medieval times, the sons of tradesmen were taught a trade while the sons of noblemen learned the rules of chivalry and court ceremonies. A few children who were slated for the life of a scholar or priest—like the widow's son Chaucer describes in *The Canterbury Tales*—were sent to school with older brothers and sisters to study religion and Latin. For all children, life was often harsh and difficult, with little time to play or even to dream.

•• The Reformation: Sixteenth-Century Europe

Two important events made political and religious leaders begin to take more interest in children's education. The first was the invention of the printing press in the mid-fifteenth century and the second was Martin Luther's 1522 translation of the Bible. Three years later, William Tyndale's English translation was published, and the King James Version came out in 1611. For the first time the Bible could be read by people other than scholars. (John Wycliffe had actually done the first English translation in 1380, but it was available mainly to scholars because the printing press had yet to be invented.) Luther and his supporters believed that it was the responsibility of individual men and women to read and interpret the Bible for themselves instead of relying on the interpretation of church authorities. Literacy took on a new importance.

•• The New World: Seventeenth-Century America

The Pilgrims and the Puritans brought their Bibles and their belief in the importance of education to America. In 1642, the Massachusetts Bay Colony passed a law requiring parents to teach their children to read. Three- and four-year-old children were taught to read and to say their catechism. Some children were taught by their mothers at home. Others were sent to a "dame school," often run by an elderly woman in her kitchen. In 1852 the first compulsory school attendance law was passed in Massachusetts. Other states followed suit, and by 1918 school attendance was compulsory throughout the country.

•• A Prelude to Early Childhood School Today: Eighteenth-Century Infant Schools

In England in the mid-eighteenth century, men and women left home to seek work in the new mills and factories that marked the beginning of the Industrial Revolution. Many of the workers were parents forced to leave their young children behind at home. A cotton mill manager in Scotland, Robert Owen (1771–1858), became concerned about the plight of the children left behind, often without proper supervision. In 1816 Owen opened an "infant school" called the New Lanark School for the children of workers in his mill. Owen's goals were similar to those of corporate leaders today who open day-care facilities for their employees. He wanted to provide a safe, child-centered environment for the children of working parents. Owen's first pupils were between the ages of five and ten, but before long children were coming as soon as they were old enough to walk and talk. Owen believed, as early childhood educators still do, in the importance of outdoor play and socialization skills. He wanted children to learn to sing and dance and play the fife. He wanted them to learn about nature by going on walks and looking at leaves and rocks.

Owen was not alone in his interest in the education of young children. At roughly the same time in Lucerne, Switzerland, another educator, Johann Pestalozzi (1746–1827), was attracting attention with his warm, caring way of teaching young children. Pestalozzi was interested in child psychology and believed, as do early childhood teachers today, in the importance of matching curriculum and teaching methods to the child's stage of development. Arnold Gesell in America and Jean Piaget in Switzerland would later teach similar beliefs based on their own research with young children. Pestalozzi taught that it was important for children to learn by doing rather than by rote memorization. He also insisted that each child be considered as an individual.

•• The Nineteenth Century: Superbabies

Many of us have come to believe that superbabies are a modern American phenomenon. However, the first superbabies were actually created by an English clergyman named Samuel Wilderspin (1791–1866). Instead of trying to provide young children with a warm, friendly, child-centered learning environment in the tradition of Owen and Pestalozzi, Wilderspin believed in harsh discipline and rote learning. His goal was to prepare his pupils by the age of seven for the next step up the educational ladder. In an attempt to realize this goal, he arranged young children in "tiered infant galleries" and made them respond to his own regimen of books, lessons, and special learning devices. Later Wilderspin toured England exhibiting his child prodigies to parents and curious spectators.

By the end of the nineteenth century, in reaction to the excesses of Wilderspin and his followers, many educators in both Europe and America were expressing concern about the possible adverse effects of too much of the wrong sort of education too soon. Some feared it might cause insanity, others worried about disruptions to family life.

•• The First Kindergartens: The Influences of Froebel, Montessori, and Dewey

Meanwhile in Germany, Friedrich Wilhelm Froebel (1782–1852) was following Pestalozzi's work with interest. While he admired Pestalozzi, Froebel saw the need for a more carefully planned and organized approach to early childhood education. In 1837 Froebel established a school for young children in Blankenburg, Germany. He called the school a kindergarten, or "a garden where children grow like flowers unfolding." The kindergarten focused on children's own experiences. Froebel wanted children to learn through play, and he saw the teacher as their guide. Children were given small objects known as gifts, which included wooden cubes, cylinders, and spheres, as well as balls made of bright-colored yarn. Children were shown by the teacher how to examine the gifts in special ways, then taught exercises and songs designed to train their hand/eye coordination and to focus their attention on relationships between different objects. The gifts also had for Froebel a metaphysical role. He believed that the gifts were symbols of cosmic truths and if used properly they could lead children to an awareness of universal truths.

Two of Froebel's followers, Margaretha Meyer Schurz and Elizabeth Peabody, brought his ideas to the United States by opening kindergartens in Wisconsin and Boston. In 1873 Susan Blow and William T. Harris started the first public kindergarten in St. Louis, where my own great-great-grandmother, Mary Alice Machemer Wood, taught. These early kindergartens had a strong religious component, and children were expected to learn about the unity of God, nature, and the individual. The kindergartens also provided a variety of social services to a rapidly expanding immigrant population, just as Head Start and other early childhood intervention programs do today. Many of the kindergartens were opened in urban slums by religious or philanthropic groups. The teachers were often young women from middle- and upper-class backgrounds who taught in the mornings and spent their afternoons as social workers. Froebel and his followers believed, as do educators today, that the goal of kindergarten instruction should not be just intellectual development but also the social, emotional, and physical care of children.

Maria Montessori (1870–1952), another important advocate of early childhood education, was born about twenty years after Froebel's death. Montessori, the first woman to receive a medical degree in Italy, had been working with mentally handicapped children when she was hired in 1907 by the owner of a tenement in Rome to start a school to keep the children in his tenement houses occupied while their parents were away at work.

The curriculum Montessori developed for the new school was based on her own observations that young children learn best through direct sensory experiences. She created a series of special materials that are still in use today and combined them with real-life activities such as buttoning jackets, sweeping, sewing, and cooking. Montessori's materials are intended to be used in specific ways and in predetermined sequences designed to develop a child's motor, sensory, and language abilities. The primary interaction in a Montessori classroom is not between teacher and child but rather between an individual child and self-correcting materials. The emphasis is on self-directed learning. The teacher serves as a resource to provide materials at the correct level and demonstrate their proper use.[1]

Montessori's teachings attracted a wide following, and Montessori schools sprung up around the world. In the 1950s Nancy McCormick Rambusch founded the American Montessori Society to set standards for the 450 or so Montessori schools in this country. Montessori's teachings remain a strong force in early childhood education. In the United States alone there are more than three thousand private Montessori schools and more than one hundred public schools with Montessori programs.

While Montessori was developing her ideas in Italy, an American contemporary, John Dewey (1859–1952) was stressing the importance of the social interactions between children working and playing together. He believed these interactions had a key role in a child's developing social consciousness. In a Dewey-influenced classroom dramatic play is emphasized, and many of the play materials are open-ended. Unlike Montessori materials there is no one right way to use open-ended materials such as hardwood blocks, and children are encouraged to invent their own ways to play with them. In his writing and in his teaching at Columbia University (1904–1930) Dewey sought to impress on parents and teachers his conviction that for young children school must represent life and that what children do at school has to be "as real, as important and as vital as life at home or in the playground."[2] For Dewey learning needed to be integrated into meaningful experiences rather than artificially broken down into the teaching of separate skills. He believed, as do early childhood teachers today, in exposing children to a wide variety of sensory experiences and real-life field trips to help them to understand their world.

Dewey's ideas became the backbone of the progressive school movement. One of the many offshoots of this movement is known as "the developmental-interactive approach" and is identified primarily with the Bank Street College of Education in New York City. "Competence," "individuality," "socialization," and "integration" are key words for proponents of this approach. Bank Street runs a demonstration laboratory school for children from the ages of three to thirteen. Many early childhood teachers have been trained by Bank Street, and its influence is felt throughout the country.

•• Nursery Schools and Day Nurseries: McMillan and Gesell

Another influence on early childhood education comes from the early nursery schools and day nurseries. The first day nurseries were started in this country between 1815 and 1860 in response to social and economic conditions similar to those Robert Owen found in Scotland and also to ones we face today. Industrialization was again drawing men and women out of the home and into factories. At the same time waves of immigrants were flooding the cities. Mrs. Joseph Hale opened the first day nursery in Boston in 1838 for the children of seamen. Wealthy men and women in other cities followed suit. Most of the day nurseries were custodial rather than educational. They were usually open six days a week, twelve hours a day, and most children went out of necessity rather than choice.

In England similar needs for child care were felt at the beginning of the twentieth century. Studies showed an alarming decline in the health of infants and small children. Eighty percent of the children in the slums of London had rickets by the age of two, and whole neighborhoods were wiped out by devastating epidemics of measles, scarlet fever, diphtheria, polio, and tuberculosis. In response to this health crisis, two sisters, Margaret (1860–1931) and Rachel McMillan (1859–1917), founded a school called the Open-Air Nursery School in the early 1900s, that provided a model for later daycare. From eight in the morning until five-thirty in the afternoon, city children were looked after by an interested and caring staff. Children from the ages of one to six were given three meals, a bath, a nap, a daily health check, and an opportunity for safe, supervised outdoor play.

The McMillan sisters' ideas soon spread to this country with a new concern not only for children's physical well-being but also for their social, emotional, and intellectual development. Nursery schools were started in New York, California, Detroit, Chicago, and Boston. One of the most famous was the Ruggles Street Nursery School in Boston, founded by Abigail Eliot. The new nursery schools were not baby-sitting services like the day nurseries, nor were they the first steps on the track to college. The goal, clearly stated by the founders and teachers, was to enrich children's lives through exposure to new experiences and materials. Children were offered blocks, sand tables, clay, paints, and clothes for dress-up play. It was through play that children learned to solve problems and interact with others. Play was the child's work, but here there were none of the symbolic overtones found in Froebel's kindergarten. "Self-realization," "personal growth and development," and "social adjustment" became key phrases in the nursery school movement.

Many nursery schools were affiliated with universities or research institutions. Some served as lab schools for the study of child development. Others flourished in churches, synagogues, community centers, and private homes. By the 1920s the majority of the children in the nursery schools no longer came from urban slums but from middle- and upper-class homes. They were in nursery school not because their parents needed daycare but because their parents were interested in the new research and theories on child development and because they were aware of the positive effects of early socialization. In 1926 Dr. Arnold Gesell (1880–1961) founded the Guidance Nursery as a laboratory school of the Yale Psycho-Clinic (later known as the Yale University Clinic of Child Development). Gesell's theories and charts on the progressive maturational stages children go through beginning at birth were an important influence on both parents and nursery school educators. (These developmental stages are discussed in chapter 6.) Other universities also opened research centers on child development. Among these new centers were The Iowa Child Welfare Research Station at the University of Iowa and the Child Welfare Institute at Teachers College, Columbia University.

The depression years of the early thirties provided an unexpected boost to nursery schools when the Work Projects Administration (WPA) decided to support the movement as a way to provide jobs for unemployed elementary and high school teachers and nurses. By 1933 there were approximately seventeen hundred nursery schools. WPA nursery schools served mainly working-class families. Middle- and upper-class children usually attended either lab schools with university affiliations or private nursery schools.

•• Child Care for Working Parents: The Kaiser Centers

During World War II, attention once again focused on the needs of working parents, and the Lanham Act provided federal funds for child care for mothers working in wartime factories. Some of these new centers were more concerned with practical issues of health and safety than with child development, but there were also some excellent programs carefully designed to meet the needs of both parents and children. Among the best were the Kaiser Child Service Centers, built by Edgar Kaiser with the help of Eleanor Roosevelt for the children of workers in the Kaiser shipyards. Each center could care for more than one thousand children between the ages of eighteen months and six years. Two child development specialists, Lois Meek Stolz and James Hymes, Jr., were in charge of the centers. Teachers had degrees in child development, and their salaries were competitive with those of other Kaiser employees with college degrees. The centers were open twenty-four hours a day, 364 days a year. They were conveniently located at the entrances to the shipyards, so parents could drop their children off in the morning on the way to work, then stop by to check on them during lunch breaks. The Kaiser centers are often cited as models for work-based early childhood schools today.

•• After World War II: Out of the Factory and Back to the Kitchen

Interest in both daycare and early childhood education faded after the war. In 1945, when the men came home and women were no longer needed in the shipyards and factories, many centers closed. Women were told by ministers and politicians, as well as by educators and child psychologists, that their place was in the home. It was a mother's responsibility to see to her children's early education. This did not mean, however, teaching her children to read at three or to play the violin. The educational emphasis was on the child's social and emotional development. Psychologists and educators often did not seem to have a lot of faith in parents' abilities to know what was best for their children. And mothers were cautioned to stay in the background and not interfere with their children's development.

•• Piaget and Cognition Theories in the 1960s and 1970s

The 1960s brought a new awareness of the importance of early childhood education. But this time, as a result of the research and writings of Jean Piaget, Jerome Bruner, Benjamin Bloom, and J. McVicker Hunt, the emphasis was on intellectual development and cognition. Jean Piaget (1896–1980), a Swiss psychologist who was studying the ways infants and young children think, believed that "environmental encounters" with people, materials, and events were key factors in the intellectual development of children. Piaget looked at children's mental development in terms of four progressive cognitive stages: sensory motor (birth to eighteen months), pre-operational (eighteen months to seven years), concrete operations (seven to twelve years), formal operations (twelve years and up). In each stage Piaget found that children process and interpret information and experiences differently. He saw these stages as partially independent of chronological age and believed that children progress through them at different rates. Piaget criticized the emphasis on undirected play and the bias against cognitive activities he saw in many nursery schools, and his research led to new questions about the interaction between mental development and environment.[3] Benjamin Bloom's work raised similar questions. Bloom studied longitudinal data on child development, concluding that the richness of a child's environment was a key factor in accelerating intellectual development. Jerome Bruner said, "Any subject can be taught effectively in some intellectually honest form to any child at any stage of development."[4]

•• Early Childhood Intervention Programs

As a result of the new research, political leaders began to believe that it might be possible to make a difference in the lives of economically deprived children. At the same time educators were finding that children benefited most when intervention began early, even before kindergarten. The stage was set for Head Start and other early childhood intervention programs.

••HEAD START••

In 1964 the federal government began its first large-scale attempt to use early childhood education as a weapon in the War on Poverty. Head Start came into being under the auspices of the Economic Opportunity Act as a program of compensatory education for three- to five-year-olds whose family income fell below the poverty level. Over 550,000 children were enrolled the first year for a summer program with a federal budget of $96.4 million.[5] Almost thirty years later in 1991, Head Start's budget was $2.5 billion with an estimated enrollment of six hundred thousand children.[6] Over the intervening years Head Start has offered an enriched environment and a variety of activities to encourage language development, reading readiness, and socialization skills. It has also provided a comprehensive group of services to children and their parents, including medical and dental care, nutrition counseling, and parent education. The immediate results of Head Start were apparent early on. Head Start children seemed more interested in learning and had better attendance records in kindergarten and first grade. As they grew older, their grades were higher and they were less likely to drop out of school or become single parents.

Head Start was followed by many other programs,[7] some of which sent specially trained professionals into children's homes to teach parents how to enrich their children's day-to-day environments. Others brought parents together to explain new research on child development and to show them how to adapt the findings to their own lives. All of them were based on the belief that by influencing a child's environment you could influence that child's future.

•• Early Childhood Education Today

When George Bush met with the governors in Charlottesville, Virginia, in September 1989, one of the six goals unanimously agreed upon was that by the year 2000, "All children will start school ready to learn." As parents we may well ask what this means for our own children. We want to know how we can be sure that our children will be counted among those ready to learn.

This is not an easy question to answer. Funding is still a major problem for early childhood schools and intervention programs. In 1988, the United States General Accounting Office estimated the median start-up cost (space, supplies and equipment, planning and administration, teacher training) of an early childhood education center accredited by the National Association for the Education of Young Children (NAEYC) at $48,500.[8] Ernest Boyer, president of the Carnegie Foundation for the Advancement of Teaching, has estimated that it will take $7 billion a year to fully fund Head Start. Despite recent increases in funding, currently only 20 percent of the Head Start centers operate for six hours or more a day, making it difficult if not impossible for many working parents to take advantage of Head Start.

Controversy also surrounds the role of the public schools in early childhood education and intervention programs. Some educators question whether public schools are appropriate settings for the education of very young children. They fear that teachers may feel pressured to teach too much too soon, and will focus on the acquisition of basic skills and cognitive development at the expense of the all-around development of young children. Dr. Edward F. Zigler, director of the Bush Center in

Child Development and Social Policy at Yale and a founder of the Head Start program, advocates a plan he refers to as "the school of the Twenty-first Century." Zigler envisions child care programs for young children in neighborhood schools and says, "Although such preschool programs would include a developmentally appropriate educational component, they would be places primarily for recreation and socialization—the real business of preschoolers."[9]

•• Modern Trends

Over the last decade, as middle- and upper-class families have become increasingly aware of the research on cognitive development and the apparent benefits of Head Start and other intervention programs, some parents, failing to heed Zigler's advice, have begun to look for early childhood schools which they hope will not only enrich but also accelerate their children's development. A few parents even see having a child who reads at two or mesmerizes guests with discussions on Fibonacci numbers or the evolution of the dinosaurs as a kind of status symbol. Other parents believe that early childhood schools that emphasize academic activities will help their children get into the selective elementary and secondary schools that they hope will in turn get them started on the road to success.

Ironically, at the same time that some parents are becoming preoccupied with early academic skills and worrying over ways to get their children started on the track to success, psychologists and researchers are looking towards new modes of learning based on models of "multiple intelligences." Howard Gardner, a MacArthur Prize fellow and Harvard professor, defines intelligence in his book *Frames of Mind* as "the ability to solve problems and create products that are valued within one or more cultural settings."[10] He proposes that there are many different human intelligences, including linguistic, musical, logical-mathematical, spatial, bodily-kinesthetic, and personal. The last involves both the ability to relate to others and to know yourself. In the early childhood years, Gardner believes that "through talk, pretend play, gestures, drawing, and the like . . . youngsters effect an important step in defining what they are and what they are not, what they wish to be and what they'd rather avoid."[11]

Educators predict that it will not be long before every child under age six in this country will spend an extended period in some type of early childhood program before starting formal schooling. Many of these programs or schools may be inappropriate for young children. Some schools may actually inhibit children's natural curiosity and turn them off learning altogether by putting too much pressure on them before they are ready and demanding that they learn things they are too young to understand. Some programs may be so poor that a child's normal growth and development are stunted. A few may pose a threat to a child's health and safety. Some parents seem to give more thought to the credentials of the people who fix their cars and remodel their kitchens than to the training and abilities of the people to whom they entrust their children. Dr. Zigler and other educators believe, and so do I, that the environment in which we place our children "determines in a very significant part the growth and development of the child. If the environment is good, a child will develop well. If it is bad, a child's development will be compromised."[12]

In the following chapters, we will examine together the qualities shared by good early childhood schools. And I will point out key things I have learned from my own experience as an educator and as a parent that you should look for in choosing a school for your children—a school that will foster their natural curiosity and love of learning without robbing them of their childhood.

•• •• •• ••
T H R E E
•• •• •• •• •• •• •• •• •• •• •• ••

The Basic Ingredients of a Good Early Childhood Program or School

A good early childhood program teaches social skills, how to share toys and play together. It stresses physical coordination and develops motor skills . . . it introduces youngsters to the joys of learning . . . an appetite that, once created, carries over into the school years.

—FROM THE NATIONAL
ASSOCIATION OF ELEMENTARY
SCHOOL PRINCIPALS "REPORT
TO PARENTS"

Good early childhood programs or schools are based on the development of the whole child. They provide a safe, nurturing environment that fosters the emotional, social, and cognitive development of children. Good schools and programs recognize that play is fundamental to the intellectual development of young children. According to Ellen Galinsky, director of the Work and Family Life Studies project at Bank Street College, "The preschooler learns through direct experience by doing and acting upon his environment. In touching, tasting, seeking, hearing, experimenting, and playing, the child builds ideas and concepts."[1] As Pam Loree, who has taught young children for nearly twenty years, first in a lab school at Kansas State University, then in Texas, and now at St. Bernard's School in New York City, said to me, "It is attitude, not the acquisition of skills, that is the crucial ingredient of early childhood school. A child who is drilled for certain tasks before he or she is ready won't end up being any smarter. Doing it sooner doesn't necessarily make it any better in the long run and it can be damaging to a child's self-esteem."

•• •• •• ••

It is important for young children to develop a positive attitude about themselves. Countless teachers have told me that they have found over the years that when the children in their classrooms lack a positive sense of self or when they can't get along with others, they are seldom able to learn at an optimal level regardless of how many sight words they can identify or esoteric facts they can memorize. If children are always worrying about whether or not they are really okay or about what their peers think of them, their ability to learn will be affected no matter how intelligent they are.

Good early childhood schools and programs help children develop self-esteem by giving children opportunities to learn about themselves and their world. They provide experiences that will challenge but not frustrate or overwhelm the child— experiences that will help the child develop a sense of competency, that will let a child feel successful. Good early childhood schools and programs help children learn to play together and share their toys. It is here that children begin to learn that different behaviors can be appropriate at different times and places. Children develop a willingness to listen and to pay attention, to focus in on a task and to complete it, to develop expectations, and to set and achieve goals. Children learn many things in good early childhood schools and programs, but the most important thing they learn is how to get along with others and how to function effectively in a group.

•• Early Childhood Classrooms

My research has taken me into many different early childhood classrooms in small towns and large cities around the country. In one of the classrooms I visited, a small boy with large black eyes and shaggy hair was standing at an easel. His clothes were covered with paint. There was a look of intense concentration on his face as he watched the red paint from his brush drip down the paper. In another corner of the room six children were clustered around a table covered with plastic knives, wooden spoons, mixing bowls, and an assortment of apples, bananas, tangerines, strawberries, peaches, and blueberries. The teacher told me that a note had gone home with the children the night before asking each one to bring in a piece of fruit. Now they were all busy scraping, cutting, measuring, and mixing while the teacher read directions from a recipe. The children were making fruit salad for morning snack.

In a classroom in a different city, a boy in a chef's hat is standing in front of a toy stove pouring imaginary ingredients into pots and stirring them up. Across the room two children are sitting at a table fitting together pieces of a puzzle. A small blonde girl with pigtails, red high-heeled shoes, blue beads, and a briefcase toddles purposefully toward a toy telephone. She tells me she is on her way to work but she has to call home first. Meanwhile in the block corner, a boy and a girl have just finished building a spaceship out of hardwood blocks. The boy is filling the spaceship with plastic astronauts. The girl is dictating the words she wants the teacher to put on a sign: "Jennifer's and Michael's Spaceship. Please Do Not Touch!"

In a third classroom in yet another school, I see a group of children sitting on the floor in a circle. A teacher is playing a guitar. The children sing as they help five spiders climb up the waterspout with vigorous hand and body movements. Meanwhile, a boy is sitting on a chair in the house corner in front of a row of dolls. He has a book in his hand from the reading corner. He explains to me that he is a teacher reading to his class. He reads in a loud clear voice with lots of expression. I notice that he is holding the book upside down.

In another classroom in another town I watch a group of children work on a class mural on sea life. The teacher tells me that the previous day the class had gone on a trip to the aquarium and now the children are making pictures of what they saw. One child is busy cutting up small pieces of brightly colored paper. Another is gluing the pieces onto a large sheet of paper attached to the wall. A third is gluing on a design of dried-up macaroni, and a fourth is covering all the glued-on pieces with sprinkles. Next to the mural is a large piece of paper with the name of each child written in large bold letters. Beside the names the teacher has written what each child liked best about the aquarium.

Each of the early childhood classrooms I visited had a wide variety of interesting materials available for the children. In all of the classrooms except the pure Montessori ones, I saw a block corner filled with hardwood blocks of different sizes and shapes, a housekeeping area with a stove and cabinets and pots and pans, a dress-up area, a sand table and/or a water table, and a story corner with lots of big pillows and picture books. I saw easels and paints and markers and clay and other art supplies. In many classrooms there was a carpentry bench and a nature area where the children had planted different kinds of seeds and were watching them grow. There were gerbils and guinea pigs and turtles or other small animals. One of the classrooms I visited had a lop-eared rabbit called Miss Tulip hopping around, and another had a snake called Samson that was being held affectionately by a little girl named Sara. There were neatly labeled bins of small plastic figures and cars and trucks and puzzles and games and beads and pegboards. There were outdoor play areas with climbing equipment and large building blocks. With the exception of Montessori classrooms, where specially developed materials are structured to be used in a specific way and in a designated sequence, most early childhood materials are "open-ended," which means that there is no one right way to play with them. Children are free, in fact encouraged, to explore these materials and invent new ways to use them.

I did not see a work sheet or a flash card on any of my classroom visits: I did not see children memorizing number facts or studying spelling words or puzzling over words in readers. Yet the children were quite clearly learning many things, including mathematical concepts and communication skills and even word recognition. These children, like the children in many of the other good early childhood schools I visited, were all happily involved in age-appropriate activities. They were also all participating in carefully planned early childhood programs. To the uninitiated eye everything in one of these classrooms may appear to be happening by chance, but the teachers have all structured their rooms and planned their programs to motivate children to use the materials they have provided in a positive way. Each teacher knows exactly which concepts and skills are being learned in each of the classrooms I described. As the year progresses the materials will change and the experiences will expand as the children develop new interests and capabilities.

Parents and other adults who have never been trained in early childhood education are apt to see all curricula in terms of reading, writing, and arithmetic. But the early childhood teacher has a curriculum, too, and it isn't focused primarily on the traditional three R's. Curriculum for the early childhood teacher is the planning and structuring of age-appropriate experiences that will motivate students to learn important skills and concepts. But even more importantly it is the encouragement of creativity and intellectual curiosity.

•• A Question of Definition: The Search for a Common Terminology

Early childhood educational programs are known by a confusing variety of names. Sometimes we call them *schools*, and sometimes we refer to them as *centers* or *programs*. Early childhood school, preschool, nursery school, kindergarten, pre-K, infant school, preprimary, first program, learning center, toddler program, Head Start, extended day, and daycare are all names you may encounter. To confuse things further, the names themselves may have different meanings in different parts of the country. Some regions use the term *daycare* to refer to any program for six or more children under the age of six regardless of whether the program is educational or custodial. Other regions prefer to use the terms *preschool, pre-K,* or *nursery school* to distinguish programs with educational goals. *Nursery school* is frequently used to refer to private schools with half-day programs for three-, four-, and five-year-olds. *Daycare,* on the other hand, has traditionally meant full-day programs designed to care for children while their parents are at work. However, many nursery schools are now offering full-day and even extended-day programs. Parents who use daycare facilities are in turn demanding quality care for their children that will foster their physical, social, emotional, and intellectual development. Distinctions between nursery school and daycare are blurring as each evolves into more comprehensive groups of services for children and their families.

Despite the efforts of the National Association for the Education of Young Children (NAEYC) and the National Association of Nursery School Directors to define the field of early childhood education and to convince people to use a common set of terms, the confusion persists. Instead of adopting the NAEYC's preferred term "early childhood school," parents and teachers are still using a variety of different terms to describe a child's first school experience. In an attempt to avoid further confusion, I have elected to use the term *early childhood school* to describe educational programs for children under the age of six that take place outside the home in semiformalized group settings.

•• Types of Early Childhood Schools

When you start to investigate early childhood schools for your children, you will again hear many different names used to describe the various types of schools. Some of the names you will hear are Montessori, progressive, developmental-interaction, traditional, academic, structured, unstructured, open, closed, formal, informal, whole child, total child, child-centered, Waldorf, direct instruction, cognitive, eclectic, all-day. Whatever term a school uses to define its program, it is important for you to find out what that particular school means by the term because, as I noted earlier, there is no consensus on the meaning of specific terms used to describe early childhood schools. One school that calls itself "progressive" may in fact be very different from another school that uses a similar term to describe its program and philosophy. With that word of caution in mind, we will look at some of the approaches to early childhood education generally associated with the more frequently used terms.

••MONTESSORI SCHOOLS••

Schools that operate in a pure Montessori tradition use the materials developed by Maria Montessori in a special way and in a specially planned sequence. The main interaction is between the child and the materials, not between the child and other children or between the child and the teacher. Montessori believed that the teacher's role is to guide children to appropriate materials and demonstrate their correct use. The emphasis is on self-directed learning, and because children of similar ages may be working at different levels, Montessori saw no need to group them by chronological age. Most Montessori classrooms have children from ages three to six working side by side. Montessori believed that children must learn to deal with reality before confronting fantasy. Montessori stories are based on fact, and there is no place for dress-up or pretend play in a pure Montessori classroom. Many Montessori schools in this country, particularly those that belong to the American Montessori Society as opposed to the Association Montessori Internationale, do not adhere strictly to all the original Montessori principles, and instead draw some of their ideas from other traditions. In these schools you may find children using open-ended materials such as blocks and clay as well as the special Montessori materials. You will also see children involved in dramatic or fantasy play.

••WALDORF OR RUDOLF STEINER SCHOOLS••

In a Waldorf school the teacher is the key in the learning process. Rudolf Steiner, who started the first Waldorf school in Germany shortly after the end of World War I, believed that young children learn by imitating the behavior and words of those around them. Here, the teacher is both an authority figure and a source of important information. The children's love and respect for their teacher is seen as the primary motivation toward learning. Steiner believed that children must first gain a sense of their own bodies through play and a variety of physical activities and hands-on experience with various art forms before they can begin to develop their intellects. Steiner also believed that young children experience the world through pictures and movement. Hence painting, modeling with clay, crafts, music, dance, and drama are emphasized, and no academics are taught before the age of six or seven.

••PROGRESSIVE SCHOOLS••

A progressive school, as I noted in chapter 2, is one that is based on the philosophy developed by John Dewey in the early part of this century. It is often referred to as the "whole child" or "total child" or "child-centered" approach. Play is seen as the child's work. It is the medium through which learning takes place and children come to understand their environment. Open-ended materials such as blocks, sand, water, clay, and paint are emphasized, and children are encouraged to engage in dramatic play.

However, the most important interaction in a progressive classroom is between children working together in groups rather than between an individual child and a specific educational material. In the 1950s Dewey's ideas fell into disrepute as many people erroneously interpreted them as advocating permissiveness and aimless, undirected play. Today many educators are taking a new look at Dewey's ideas as they increasingly realize the importance of children's physical, emotional, social, and psychological needs, as well as their intellectual needs. The late

Lawrence A. Cremin, former president of Teachers College at Columbia University, has said, "The return to Dewey . . . may be partly a response to the fundamental changes that education and society are facing, changes similar to Dewey's era. . . . The difficulties of educating everyone are being recognized and confronted, making the solutions Dewey proposed relevant once again."[2] Many schools that do not refer to themselves as "progressive" use the open-ended materials and many of the methods developed by Dewey and other progressive educators.

••DEVELOPMENTAL-INTERACTION, OR THE BANK STREET MODEL SCHOOL••

One of the offshoots of the progressive tradition is the developmental-interaction approach developed at the Bank Street College of Education in New York. *Developmental* refers to the growth and development of children and the increasing complexity of the ways they respond to experiences, then organize and process their responses. *Interaction* refers to children's interaction with their immediate environment. Development is seen not as something that just happens to a child but instead as a direct result of a child's interaction with his or her environment. As Harriet Cuffaro, a member of the Bank Street faculty, says, development comes from "the child's doing, making, questioning, testing, trying, formulating, experiencing."[3] "Individuality," "socialization," "competence," and "integration" are words frequently used to describe the process by which children gradually learn how to use various skills, to make choices, to take responsibility for their actions, and to synthesize and understand their experiences. The key interaction is between children rather than between an individual child and materials. The teacher is also a central figure who creates the appropriate environment to foster learning. The core of the curriculum revolves around social studies, which is seen as an interdisciplinary study of our world and the different issues we confront. The emphasis, in line with the Dewey philosophy, is on solving real-life problems. Concepts are taught through the use of concrete, open-ended materials, as an integral part of the entire program rather than as separate entities. The atmosphere is usually informal and teachers may be called by their first names.

••TRADITIONAL OR STRUCTURED SCHOOLS••

Schools referred to as "traditional" or "structured" are usually based on varying interpretations of Piaget's cognitive theories as well as the developmental stages of Gesell. They are sometimes also called "academic," "cognitive," or "formal." The use of the word "traditional" to describe these schools is in fact somewhat of a contradiction in terms, since "traditional" originally referred to nursery schools in the McMillan tradition in which there was little focus on a child's cognitive development. The schools we refer to today as "traditional" or "structured" are concerned, just as the progressive and developmental-interaction schools are, with the whole child—with physical, social, emotional, and cognitive development. These schools have the same kinds of open-ended materials found in developmental-interaction and progressive schools. They may even use some Montessori materials as well. The rooms in fact often look very similar to developmental-interaction and progressive classrooms. The atmosphere, while still warm and friendly, may seem a bit more formal, and teachers are seldom called by their first names.

The main difference, however lies in the role of the teacher, who tends to be more directive. She or he usually sets clear limits and has quite specific expectations and goals. There are well-defined lists of developmentally appropriate skills to be mastered, such as sorting and patterning, sequencing, listening, following directions, remembering details, and expressing ideas verbally. The children learn the skills through the manipulation of concrete materials, in dramatic play, and by interacting with their environment. However, activities such as finger painting and tracing shapes in the sand are seen by the teachers as reading-readiness activities. Teachers actively encourage children to think and talk about the things they are doing. Children are usually taught letters and sounds as well as shapes and colors. Sometimes schools have a letter or color of the week. If it is *J* week, for instance, children might learn about jaguars, jump rope at recess, make jam, and have jelly beans for snacks. A few traditional schools use work sheets to reinforce concepts.

Some traditional schools use specially developed curricula based on different educators' interpretations of Piaget's theories. One of these curricula was developed by Celia Lavatelli, who believed that while some children make exciting discoveries on their own, others benefit from a more structured approach and need additional direction to develop problem-solving skills and to learn to think logically. In the Lavatelli curriculum, specific cognitive tasks such as sequencing, measuring, and classifying are taught in short ten- to fifteen-minute training sessions. Children may be asked to make a necklace out of beads following a particular pattern demonstrated by the teacher. Teachers are trained to comment on the children's work, to ask questions, and to encourage children to discuss and actively think about what they are doing and why.

Another curriculum based on Piaget's work, the High/Scope Curriculum, is a cognitively oriented curriculum developed by David Weikart, president of High/Scope Educational Research Foundation in Ypsilanti, Michigan. Here again teachers actively intervene and structure children's play to develop cognitive skills. The day usually begins with all the children getting together while the teacher reviews a list of available activities and the children choose among them. After the children have worked on their various activities, they meet again to discuss what they have done, the progress they have made, and any problems they may have encountered. Later there is an outdoor playtime for large–motor skill development—running, hopping, and climbing—and a circle time for more discussion, storytelling, and singing.

Many good traditional schools do not use any one specific curriculum but are really rather eclectic in nature. They have a middle-of-the-road philosophy using what one early childhood teacher referred to as "the tried and true of many different approaches." Rather than adhering to a single specific curriculum, these schools combine what they consider to be the most successful elements of a variety of different early childhood traditions.

••DIRECT INSTRUCTION, OR ACADEMIC SCHOOLS••
In the direct-instruction approach most activities are initiated by the teacher, and the children's role is to give the required response at the appropriate time. Direct instruction is loosely based on some of the programmed learning theories of the late behavioral psychologist B. F. Skinner. Stimuli, response, and positive reinforcement are all key components of Skinner's

theories. DISTAR, one of the curricula sometimes used in direct instruction, was originally developed by Carl Bereiter and Siegfried Engelmann for use in Follow Through, an intervention program for economically disadvantaged children. DISTAR provides children with up to an hour and a half of direct instruction each day. Children are taught to read phonetically—first learning sounds through constant repetition, then putting the sounds together to form words. They are also drilled on simple number facts and taught to count by rote. This whole approach, which brings back memories of Wilderspin to some of us, is highly controversial. Douglas Carnine, a professor of education at the University of Oregon, has said, "Some kids, particularly disadvantaged kids, may come from unstimulating homes—they may never be ready. If they don't get an academic orientation in kindergarten, they may never grow into successful students."[4] Other educators such as David Elkind, a psychologist at Tufts University and author of many books on the education of young children, feel that highly structured direct teaching approaches can cause children to become rote learners, inhibiting their natural curiosity and desire to learn and hampering their sense of initiative and independent problem-solving abilities.

•• Making a Comparison

A number of research studies have sought to compare different types of early childhood schools and their effects on children in elementary school and beyond. Proponents of the Montessori method believe it encourages children to work at their own pace and build on their own knowledge. On the other hand, a recent study by Rheta DeVries, director of the Human Development Laboratory School at the University of Houston, found that "Montessori preschool children scored substantially lower than children from a more group-oriented preschool program on tests of social skills."[5] A 1984 study conducted by the late Louise Miller at the University of Louisville found that by tenth grade male students who had gone to Montessori preschools scored higher on tests of creative thinking and academic achievement but female students scored lower.[6] Many of the studies, beginning with the Perry Preschool Study and the High/Scope Preschool Curriculum Study, have looked at children from economically disadvantaged backgrounds. It is not known whether the conclusions drawn from these studies apply to children from middle-class backgrounds.

A variety of studies show that children who have attended traditional or structured early childhood schools are generally more task-oriented and less aggressive with their peers. They also tend to do better on achievement and IQ tests. On the negative side, they show less independence and initiative, and their play is apt to be less imaginative. Children who have attended progressive or unstructured schools are usually seen as more independent and more apt to ask questions. They usually score higher on tests of problem solving and curiosity but lower on achievement and IQ tests.

Most early childhood schools in reality fall somewhere in between the extremes of structured and unstructured. Many combine some teacher-directed activities with ample opportunities for free play and interaction with peers. After reviewing relevant studies, Alison Clarke-Stewart, associate professor of education at the University of Chicago, has concluded in her book *Daycare* that the evidence points to "the benefits—for constructive activity, for intelligence, for later achievement, for positive motivation, persistence, and problem solving, and for social skills—of a preschool program that blends prescribed educational activities with opportunities for free choice, that has some structure, but also allows children to explore a rich environment of objects and peers on their own without teacher direction."[7] My own experience leads me to agree with her conclusion.

•• Goals of Early Childhood Schools

Sometimes you will find a school's goals explicitly stated in catalogs and other written material, but often you will have to ferret goals out for yourself by talking to the director and asking some probing questions. Good early childhood schools do not all look and feel exactly alike. Even among the same general types of schools, the atmosphere and the specific materials vary according to the individual personalities and philosophies of the teachers and directors. Some schools may put more emphasis on teaching children how to work together in a group, while others encourage children to spend the greater part of their day exploring materials independently. However, there are certain goals that many good early childhood schools do have in common. Based on my conversations with early childhood teachers and directors, on a careful study of the goals and criteria recommended by the National Association for the Education of Young Children,[8] and on my own observations in many different early childhood classrooms, I have come to the conclusion that a number of goals are shared by most good early childhood schools.

- • To promote the optimum physical, social, emotional, and intellectual growth of each child.
- • To provide an environment that is safe, warm, and nurturing, as well as stimulating.
- • To give children ready access to caring, intelligent adults throughout the day.
- • To furnish children with a variety of physical activities to enhance their physical skills and overall development.
- • To develop in each child a feeling of confidence and self-esteem.
- • To promote initiative and independence.
- • To help children learn respect for themselves and for others.
- • To stimulate a love of learning and a joy in the excitement of new experiences.
- • To foster children's awareness of others and to help them learn how to become part of a group, to share, and to take turns.
- • To help children develop a sense of responsibility for their own actions and for the well-being of others.
- • To encourage children's natural curiosity and interest in exploring their world.
- • To help children understand their environment.
- • To expose a child to a variety of new and interesting materials and experiences.
- • To give a child opportunities for imaginative play and for creative expression in music, art, movement, and dramatic activities.
- • To develop children's facility with language and their ability to communicate clearly and effectively both with classmates and with adults.

- • To expose children to a wide variety of children's literature by reading aloud and to thereby develop an ongoing interest in books and reading.
- • To help a child develop problem-solving abilities.
- • To give children a variety of experiences that will encourage the development of mathematical and scientific concepts.
- • To help a child develop a sense of competence through the mastery of age-appropriate physical, social, and intellectual skills using developmentally based materials and methods.
- • And last, but certainly not least, to try to create a partnership between home and school based on mutual respect and close communication.

This last goal, a sense of a partnership based on a feeling of being part of a close and caring community, is an important part of the early childhood school experience for parents and their children. Parents and children both learn from being part of an early childhood school. It is, after all, the early childhood teacher who gives parents, as well as children, their first school experience. And it is part of the responsibility of the early childhood teacher to teach parents—to teach them not only about new research in child development, about the ways young children master new skills, about how they acquire and process information, about their emotional and intellectual needs, but also something about the culture of school itself, about how to be a part of the community and to work effectively with the school for the benefit of their children.

When, how, and why our children begin school can have a profound impact on their feelings about school, on their later education, and even on their lives. We as parents must try to be sure that the decisions we make and the schools we choose are right for our children. We must choose our children's schools not because we believe certain schools will turn our three-year-olds into prodigies for us to exhibit as Wilderspin did his original superbabies over a hundred years ago, but rather because we believe that the schools we choose will help our children develop their true potential over time and in ways that are developmentally appropriate. As the authors of *Changed Lives,* John R. Berrueta-Clement, David P. Weikart, and others, have written, "A person's life is not transformed in some magical way by experience in a preschool program [early childhood school]. But a successful preschool experience can permanently alter the success/failure trajectory of a person's life in significant and positive ways."[9]

There are many good early childhood schools, but no one early childhood school is right for every child. Unless you happen to live in a fairly large city, you probably won't have the option of choosing from the many different types of early childhood schools we have just looked at. There may well be only one or two schools in your neighborhood. When you do not have a lot of choice, the quality of the school is more important than its expressed philosophy. If there are no schools near you that seem to meet the criteria for good early childhood schools, you may want to consider keeping your child at home or looking into some of the alternatives to early childhood schools discussed in chapter 4 such as parent cooperatives and "mommy and me" play groups.

In this next chapter, I will point out specific things you will want to look for in an early childhood school. And we will explore together ways to tell if an early childhood school is right for you and your child.

•• •• •• ••
F O U R
•• •• •• •• •• •• •• •• •• •• •• ••

A Parent's Dilemma: What to Look for, How to Choose

•• Location

Location is often the single most important factor in choosing an early childhood school. A neighborhood school is particularly important for very young children. Ideally a school should be within easy walking distance or a short car ride from home. In one mother's experience, "Being close to school makes a tremendous difference when you are trying to juggle your own schedule and get everyone out of the house in the morning. Our morning wasn't so rushed and there was time to let Ashley experiment with dressing herself and begin to develop a sense of independence. We were so close I didn't even have to worry about using a stroller. We could walk down the street together and chat with Ashley's friends and their mothers on the way to school." If there is no school within walking distance, be sure to inquire about the type of transportation required to get to the schools you are considering. Attending distant schools sometimes means a trip of various legs—perhaps two buses or a bus and a subway. This is harder on a family than just a bus or a subway by itself.

Distance may be more than just a matter of getting to and from school. It can affect after-school playdates as well. If most of the other children live in the neighborhood surrounding the school, it will not be as easy for your child to get together with those children after school. It may also be more difficult for your child and you to participate in after-school programs or play groups. It will be harder for you as a parent to spend time around the school helping out on trips or in the library. Physical

•• •• •• ••

distance from a school can increase the amount of time it takes for you to feel a part of the school and your child's life there.

If both parents in the family have a long commute to work or if you are a single working parent, you may want to consider looking at schools near your workplace rather than your home. More and more parents tell me they find it makes sense for them to send their children to a school close to their work so they can be available during the day in an emergency and also so they can spend time together on the commute in the morning and evening. The admissions director of a school in New York City reports that some parents commute happily with their children from as far away as Brooklyn, Jersey City, and Hoboken and drop their children off on the way to work in the morning.

If you have more than one child, you will probably prefer that they be in the same school. Otherwise, as one working parent of two young children said, "From the logistical point of view getting to school in the morning would be a nightmare." It is also helpful if other children in your neighborhood go to the school you choose for your child. For many parents, particularly working parents, carpooling can make a difference. It is also worth asking whether a school provides transportation. A few schools, usually those that comprise the elementary as well as the early childhood years, do provide transportation, and some private bus companies are equipped to take young children to and from school. Fees for private bus service vary greatly.

Travel and distance are relative, however. And some families seem to be able to travel comparatively long distances with little wear and tear on themselves or on their children. Other families fall apart at the mere thought of getting to a bus stop on time. The best school in the world will be unsuitable if you and your child arrive in a frantic rush and a terrible temper every morning. Before making any decisions, consider the dynamics of your own family—personalities, time, work schedules, freedom from other family obligations—to determine what makes sense for you and your child.

Remember, no rule applies to every family.

•• Educational Continuity

The next point to consider in deciding on a school is whether you want to send your child to an early childhood school or to an ongoing school (a school that goes through either elementary school or secondary school but includes an early childhood division). An ongoing school can give a sense of continuity. A three-year-old can look at an older child in the hallway and think, "This is where I'm going, this is what I'll be like some day." In some ongoing schools there is considerable interaction among the grades, and older children work with younger children either directly in the classroom or on special projects.

Parents sometimes feel a sense of relief when their child is admitted to an ongoing school, believing that their child's education is now settled and they will not have to worry about admissions again until college. However, this line of thought can backfire. When children are three or four, it is difficult, perhaps impossible, to know how they will develop and what their interests and talents will be. A school that seems perfect for a three-year-old may prove to be all wrong at thirteen. An administrator at one ongoing private school observed that over the years the bottom one-fourth of the senior class in her school had a disproportionate number of children who had entered as three-year-olds. Schools are increasingly aware of this potential problem, and in some ongoing private schools, in fact, many children are counseled out of a school they began in early childhood because they can not keep up with the work in the higher grades. Dr. James W. Wickenden, a former dean of admissions at Princeton who was cochairman of the admissions and scholarship committee of a school that recently phased out its early childhood program, has said, "It is difficult enough to judge academic competence and strength of character with people age 17. To do that at two and a half is asking the impossible."[1] Similar problems can occur in public schools that children attend from K through 12 if a child is placed in a gifted program at the kindergarten level, and there is not sufficient flexibility to allow the child to move back and forth between it and the regular program.

On the other hand, choosing to send your child to an early childhood school gives you the opportunity to rethink the question of education a few years later, after you have observed your child in an educational setting and have more information about the way your child is developing. At that time you can consider whether you want to send your children to a public or private elementary school without having to take them out of a private school where they have already begun to make friends.

In an early childhood school, the whole focus is on early childhood. The director's mind is on blocks and climbing equipment, not physics labs and basketball courts. The teachers are trained specifically in child development and the education of young children. The physical setting is specially planned to meet the needs of small children, and all the furniture and equipment are made to scale. The atmosphere is designed to be warm and nurturing and to make small children feel at home. The youngest students can have a sense that their early childhood school is their school, designed for them the way they are now, not the way they will be some day. I have seen young children become upset when older children in an ongoing school point at them and their friends in the halls and exclaim, "Aren't they cute!" A five-year-old in early childhood school can feel the pride of being looked up to by the younger children instead of being looked down on by older children.

Given the choice between an early childhood school and an ongoing school for a three-year-old, I have a predilection toward the early childhood school. However, there are no universal right or wrong answers here—only issues to be explored in relation to your own choices and preferences. If you decide on an ongoing school, you will want to make sure that the early childhood division is considered an important and integral part of the school. If, on the other hand, you decide on an early childhood school, you will want to be sure that the ongoing schools in which you might be interested later on anticipate openings for kindergarten and first grade.

•• Half Day? Full Day? Extended Day?

Some early childhood schools have part-time programs—a few hours several days a week. Others offer full-time programs— approximately the length of a regular school day five days a week. Still others offer extended-day programs from seven-thirty in the morning until seven-thirty at night. And some schools offer parents a choice between these options. Whether you choose a half-day, a full-day, or an extended-day program will depend not only on what is available in your community but also on the nature of your child and your own schedule. Some children thrive in a full-day program, while others are exhausted after a morning or afternoon with other children and need quiet time to themselves to relax and replenish their energy. If you are working full-time, you will need to take your child's energy level and personality into consideration as you decide between either a full or extended day at school, and a combination of school and home-based child care.

•• Teachers

Teachers are the key ingredients of a good early childhood school. Good teachers come in many different styles and personalities, but they all should be interested in young children and should clearly enjoy being with them. Early childhood teachers need to be perceptive and patient as well as intelligent. They need to be loving and warm, but they also must be able to set clear limits and be willing to enforce them. They should be trained in early childhood education. Head teachers should have a degree in early childhood education, and all teachers including assistants should have an understanding of the developmental patterns of young children. Your child's teacher should have a sense of what expectations and behavior are appropriate at which ages, and when different types of materials should be introduced. Some of the larger early childhood schools have brochures or catalogs listing the teachers and their training. If a school does not have a catalog, be sure to ask the person who shows you the school about the teachers' backgrounds and training.

The National Daycare Study undertaken for the federal government in the 1970s found that one of the most important factors in the effectiveness of an early childhood school or daycare program was the training of the teachers. Ellen Galinsky reported on the study in her recent book: "In programs in which the teacher caregivers had early childhood training, the children behaved more positively and were more cooperative as well as more involved in the program. These children also made gains on standardized tests of learning."[2] It is of course important that a teacher's training is relevant to his or her work with young children and that the training was not just a few courses taken for credit and then forgotten, but rather part of a lifelong interest in new research and communication with fellow teachers.

Another important issue is the rate of teacher turnover. Some turnover is to be expected in early childhood schools since many teachers are young, the pay is low, and a number of teachers leave the profession after a few years. However, in schools that have been in existence for a number of years, there should be a sense of continuity. In the larger early childhood school serving a hundred or more students, there should be a core of teachers who have been at the school for five years or more. In a smaller school with fifty or fewer students, look for continuity in leadership of the school, and perhaps one or two teachers who have been there for three to five years.

•• Administrative Leadership

Administrative leadership was identified as the most important factor in a school by a large group of directors who responded to a survey done by Childcare Information Exchange, a magazine for directors of early childhood schools and day-care centers.

The head of the school, often known as the director, is a key element in the quality of an early childhood school. He or she sets the tone of the school by screening and hiring teachers and providing for their ongoing training. The head also communicates the goals and philosophy of the school to both teachers and prospective parents. The head should be someone whose opinions you respect and with whom you feel comfortable talking.

•• Class Size

A third important factor in the quality of a school is class size. The National Daycare Study also found that the number of children in a class was an important factor in the overall quality of their experience, as well as in the gains they made in standardized tests. The NAEYC recommends in its 1987 accreditation criteria and procedures that groups for two-year-olds contain between eight and ten children and no more than twelve. For three-year-olds, groups should be between fourteen and eighteen children, with twenty the largest acceptable size. For four- and five-year-olds, groups may have as many as sixteen to eighteen, but should not exceed twenty. The NAEYC believes that the optimal child/teacher ratio for two-year-olds is one to four or one to five; for three-year-olds, one to seven or one to eight; for four- or five-year-olds, one to eight or one to nine.[3]

•• Physical Layout

An early childhood school should be safe, clean, and cheerful. Studies have shown that increasing the number of children in a given space also increases the level of aggressiveness. The NAEYC recommends a minimum of 35 square feet of indoor usable playroom floor space per child, and a minimum of 75 square feet of outdoor space per child.[4] The space should be arranged so that it is easy for children to move around the room from one activity to another and to work either individually or in groups.

•• Health and Safety

The most basic and fundamental issue in any early childhood school is the health and safety of the children it serves. An early childhood school should be licensed or accredited by an appropriate local or state agency. Licensing standards vary from state to state, but most states have codes concerning fire protection, sanitation, water quality, and childhood immunizations. In some states, early childhood schools must be accredited as well as licensed. Since 1985 the National Academy of Early Childhood Programs, under the auspices of the NAEYC, has offered voluntary accreditation for schools that meet national standards in curriculum, staff-child and staff-parent interaction, staff qualifications and development, administration, staffing, physical environment, health and safety, nutrition and food service, and self-evaluation. The decision on accreditation is made by a commission of early childhood experts. A few early childhood schools have chosen instead to be accredited by the National Association of Independent Schools (NAIS). Both organizations have vigorous standards, and as long as one or the other does the accreditation, you can trust the conclusion.

Small schools with less than sixty students may decide not to bother going through the rather lengthy accreditation process. This does not necessarily mean the school is not one of quality, but it does mean that you should check the credentials of the teachers and administrators carefully and make sure all state and local licensing requirements have been met. Call your local health department for a list of requirements and ask if the schools you are considering meet these standards. When you visit a school, check to see that children arrive and leave in a safe and properly supervised manner, and ask if the school requires a parent's written authorization before releasing a child to anyone else. Look for teachers at the door. Look also for crossing guards. If there are driveways near either play areas or walkways, what precautions are taken to protect the children? All outside doors should be locked or supervised by a responsible person to ensure that strangers cannot wander in. Outdoor play areas should be well supervised and protected from the intrusion of unauthorized people. A school should also have a plan for dealing with medical emergencies; its policy should be to request written permission from parents for emergency treatment in the event that the parents cannot be reached.

It is also important that the school's policy on attendance in the case of minor illnesses be in line with your own feelings. Are you the kind of parent who believes all children get colds? Or do you get upset at the thought of your child being in a room with a bunch of other children with runny noses and coughs?

You might also want to think about how protective you are. How do you feel about your child falling on the stairs or on playground equipment. Do you feel the occasional fall, cut, or scrape is just part of growing up, or are you the kind of parent who says, as a number of parents have said to me, "I don't want my children going up and down stairs by themselves. The thought of having them fall scares me." There are no right and wrong feelings about this. What is important is that you, as the parent, feel comfortable with the balance of freedom and supervision a school gives your child.

•• Philosophy

For most parents it is important to have a sense of shared values with others connected with the school. Spend some time identifying your priorities, and compare them to those of other parents you may know with children in the school. Are the same things important to you that seem to be important to the other parents? Do you seem to share priorities and values? Values can be as basic as promptness and attendance during a minor illness or as philosophical as the role of competition or the importance of community service. For example, a parent who is also a teacher was brought up to believe that an 8:30 arrival really meant 8:30—not 8:35. "If school starts at 8:30, I'm trained to be there at 8:30. If I take my child to school I want to know the other parents share this idea of all starting the class at the same time so that the children who are there first thing aren't interrupted by the children who arrive late every single day."

In terms of social philosophy, many schools make a point of playing down competition—even in games—by emphasizing a cooperative team approach to problem solving rather than individual accomplishment. If your family is naturally very competitive and likes to play to win, your child may have difficulty reconciling two such different goals. Young children are generally happier when they see a general consistency between home and school. More than a few parents have said to me, "We have a very relaxed life at home without a lot of structure so I think my child should go to a school with plenty of structure to balance what they have at home." My experience argues that this is a mistake and only ends up confusing young children. Children are far more likely to thrive when the amount of order and structure at school is consistent with the amount of order and structure in their homes.

•• Financial Considerations

For many parents financial considerations play a role in the selection of an early childhood school. Costs vary depending both on where you live and on whether you want an extended-day, a full-day, or a half-day program. Some programs charge by the week, some by the month or by the term. Others ask parents to sign a contract for the year. In January 1990 the United States General Accounting Office estimated the yearly cost of a quality program accredited by NAEYC at $4,200.[5] In some large cities—Boston and Minneapolis, for example—parents tell me they expect to pay between $5,000 and $6,000 a year for a full-time, quality early childhood school.

Early childhood schools run by religious groups sometimes have sliding fee scales depending on parental income. A few offer financial aid. Another option for some parents is a cooperative school. However, bear in mind that the reason cooperative schools are less expensive is that parents do a large percentage of the work themselves and all parents are expected to do their share. If you work full-time, a cooperative school may not be a realistic choice.

As a general rule it is not advisable to shop for bargains in early childhood schools. Quality education is expensive. While the most expensive school is not necessarily the best, schools with fees considerably below those of other schools in the same area may be cutting corners in ways that could be detrimental to your child's development and even safety.

•• Finding Early Childhood Schools

There are a variety of ways to find out about schools in your neighborhood. Since many early childhood schools are associated with churches, synagogues, YMCAs, or YMHAs, this is a good place to start your inquiries. Pediatricians are useful sources of information, and so are friends and colleagues with older children. To find out about public pre-K programs, call your local school district. Many communities have child-care resources and referral agencies (R&R) that provide information on early childhood schools. A number of large corporations also have R&R for employees. The National Association of Child Care Resource and Referral Agencies (see bibliography) can give you information on referral services in your community. Finally, if you need more names, check the yellow pages of your phone book under "Schools—Nursery Schools and Kindergarten."

Remember, however, that no matter how reliable your source or how enthusiastically he or she praises a school, that school still may not be right for your child. Always check things out for yourself with a visit to the school.

•• THE VISIT ••

Most early childhood schools encourage parents to schedule a visit without their child to tour the school, visit classrooms, and see children working and playing. Watch carefully how the teachers interact with the children. Do they look at children when they are talking to them? Do they get down on the floor with the children so they are at eye level some of the time? Do

A Parent's Dilemma •• 57

the teachers seem warm and friendly? Do they seem to like the children and be genuinely interested in them? Do they really listen to the children, or do they seem to be only half-listening—perhaps because they are busy doing something else? Most teachers, like parents, occasionally find themselves trying to do half a dozen things all at the same time and you should not fault them for this. However, there should also be times when each child feels he or she has the teacher's undivided attention. Are the children encouraged to express their ideas and feelings? Do the teachers encourage language development by asking children open-ended questions that cannot be answered simply yes or no? Are the teachers reasonably articulate? Do they speak grammatically and use language well? Do they seem to be talking down to the children? How are the children disciplined? Do the teachers guide and redirect the children? Do they criticize? How do they deal with a child who refuses guidance and suggestions? Ask yourself whether you are comfortable with the way problems that arise in the classroom are handled. Are rules clear and consistently enforced? Do expectations for children's behavior seem appropriate for the children's age?

How do the children interact with each other? Are they learning to share and cooperate? Do they seem to like each other? Are they quarreling and fighting? How do the teachers handle aggression? And once again, are you comfortable with the way they handle it?

Do you get a sense of close communication and sharing between teachers and parents? Do the teachers seem happy to see parents at the beginning and end of the day and to share anecdotes and new accomplishments? Are there regularly scheduled conferences, as well as informal exchanges?

During your visit to each school the most important thing you can do is to keep your eyes and ears open. Ask yourself the following questions while you are there and able to observe the environment for yourself rather than later when you are at home and struggling to remember your impressions:

Physical Space

•• Are the rooms clean and bright and reasonably spacious?
•• Are the walls freshly painted?
•• Is the equipment clean and in good repair?

•• Is there an outdoor play area?

•• Is the space well set up for the children?

Educational Materials

•• Are there books and pictures and age-appropriate materials and toys around?

•• Are the materials well organized and readily available to the children?

One astute grandmother described a visit to her granddaughter's school, which, at first glance, seemed to be a well-equipped nursery school complete with a pet rabbit. But on closer observation things were not quite right. The books and materials were on high shelves out of reach of the children, and the rabbit was locked in a small, dirty cage that was shoved in a corner. The children had no opportunity to pet the rabbit and interact with it, or to learn anything about animal behavior.

Activities

•• Do the children seem busily involved and happy? Is there sparkle and enthusiasm? Are the children smiling?

•• Are the activities adult or child oriented? Is the emphasis on product or process?

•• Does the children's artwork appear to be individualized? Do all the art projects look the same—is everyone making an identical pumpkin for Halloween? Of course, it is important not to jump to conclusions here without first finding out the intentions of the teacher. Five similar-looking snowmen could be part of an exercise in following directions rather than artistic expression.

Staff

•• Do the children appear to like the teachers and treat them with respect?

•• Do the teachers seem genuinely interested in the children and do they treat them with respect? Do they try to facilitate interaction between the children?

•• Do the director and teachers seem to be the sort of people you would be comfortable working with?

Philosophy

•• Does the school seem to try to fit the needs of each individual child, or is it your sense that it attempts to fit each child into the school?

•• How diverse is the student body? Are you comfortable with the degree of diversity?

•• Does the school appear to do what it says it will do in the brochure or other written material? This can be a tough question and may require reflection after the visit.

•• Do you understand the admissions process? Are you comfortable with it? The way in which a school handles its admissions can give you a sense of its priorities and often reflects its character.

•• Do you have the sense that you are really seeing the school as it is, or are you seeing just what the admissions office wants you to see?

•• Is the school open about its shortcomings as well as its virtues?

•• And, finally, does it feel right to you? Is this the kind of place to which you would be happy bringing your child every morning?

After you have asked yourself these questions, you may want to ask the school some of the following questions:

•• What is the background and level of experience of the faculty?
•• What is the rate of faculty turnover?
•• How diverse is the student body? The faculty?
•• When does the school year begin and end?
•• How long are vacations? Which religious holidays are observed?
•• Is the program full-day or half-day? What are the hours? Do they offer an extended-day option?
•• Describe a typical day.
•• How much time do children spend in group activities versus independent activities?
•• Are children grouped developmentally or chronologically?
•• How many openings are anticipated for your child's age group?
•• Are children accepted on a first-come, first-served basis, or is there a screening process?

•• Is there financial aid? On what basis is it awarded?

•• Are there age cutoffs for entrance? If so, what are they?

•• Will your child be one of the younger or one of the older children in the class?

•• To what extent does the school welcome children with learning problems? What kind of resources does it have to deal with them?

•• How is a child disciplined when he or she disobeys or acts out in the classroom?

•• How does the school handle separation? Is a parent permitted to stay in the classroom? For how long? (See chapter 6 for a discussion of separation issues.)

•• What are the opportunities and expectations for parent involvement? Are there any requirements? Does the school expect a greater time commitment than you can reasonably make? This can be a problem for working parents, particularly in schools run on a cooperative basis. Some schools have more appreciation than others of the needs of working parents, and acknowledge that they are not always available to come to the school during working hours.

•• What kinds of parent-teacher contacts are encouraged?

•• Is the school affiliated with any religious organization? What does this affiliation mean? Is there any required participation in religious services or instruction?

•• What are the expectations for students as they get older?

•• What schools do children go on to for kindergarten and first grade?

•• Is there bus service?

•• Does the school offer after-school or summer programs? If both parents are working, it may be important to find a school with interesting activities after school hours.

After your visit, sit down and quietly go over all your impressions. If you know other parents with children in the school, talk to them about their experience. Ask them what they feel the school's strengths and weaknesses are, and whether or not they would pick the same school for a second child. But remember that their children may be very different from yours and their experience may not necessarily be yours. Trust your own initial feelings and impressions. If you feel uncomfortable with a school, don't choose it for your child no matter how enthusiastic your friends may be about it. Also remember that in many communities there are a number of good early childhood schools, any one of which could give your child an excellent start. And there is never one school that is the only right one for your child.

•• Children with Special Needs

Many early childhood schools save a few places for children with special needs. If your child has special needs, it is important that you discuss them openly with the school you are interested in to make sure the school has the training and staff to give your child the help he or she needs. Public Law 94-142, the Education for All Handicapped Children Act, gives each state the responsibility for identifying, screening, evaluating, and providing appropriate educational services for all children with learning problems from kindergarten on up. Some school districts offer preschool programs under the federally funded Chapter I Program for low-income families. Your child could be eligible for a Chapter I preschool program even if you do not qualify as low-income if your local public school participates in the program. Parents should call either the board of education or the special education department in your school district for information about local programs and eligibility requirements. (See Bibliography for a list of helpful books on children with special needs.)

•• Alternatives to Early Childhood School

••PARENT-CHILD ACTIVITIES••

You may decide not to send your children to early childhood school because you cannot find a quality school near you or simply because you want to have your children at home with you. If you want to keep your two- or three-year-old at home, by all means do so. Your children are only going to be this age once, and you will never be able to change your mind and turn the clock back. If your children have space to play and explore, opportunities to be with other children, and caring adults to help them discover and define their world; if your children seem happy and fulfilled at home, and full of zest and joy of life; and if you yourself are content to have them at home, then relax and enjoy this time together. Your children will not grow up less intelligent or knowledgeable. They will learn from the conversations and experiences you have together, and they will grow up with the memories of the special time you have shared. Your children may initially have less experience in taking turns, following directions, relating to different adults, and getting along with children in a group, but there are alternative ways for you to introduce your children to group activities and help them learn social skills.

Alternatives to early childhood school include parent-run play groups, parent-child classes at the local Y or community center, and parent-child classes at gymnasiums and museums. Many of these classes are excellent and, provided you don't over-schedule your child, they can be a fine way for your child to get used to being with other children and doing things together in a group. Your child can gain experience in relating to other adults and begin to see adults as important sources of information and assistance. Perhaps most importantly, the classes give you and your child the chance to get out of the house and do something enjoyable together. Some classes run either on weekends or in the early evening to accommodate the needs of working parents. It doesn't really matter a great deal whether you and your child pick an art class, a music class, or a gym class. The important thing is that you both enjoy what you are doing and that your child has the opportunity to interact with other children and adults.

••PLAY GROUPS••

Another good alternative to early childhood school is a parent-run play group. Four or five neighborhood parents with children of roughly the same age get together once or twice a week for an hour or so. In some groups, the parents take turns having all the children play together in their house; in other groups the parents prefer to use a neutral space in a neighborhood house, church, or synagogue. If a neutral space is available, I recommend taking advantage of it. Two- and three-year-olds usually feel very possessive about their rooms and their toys and may see other children as unwelcome intruders. If you have to use one of your homes, pick a neutral space such as a dining room rather than your child's room, and keep a special set of toys that are brought out only for the play group. Most successful play groups have some well-planned short periods of structured activities that bring the children together in a group. Typically one parent takes responsibility for each session and plans group games, songs, or simple art projects for part of the play group. Such group activities are important because preschool-age children are just beginning to be able to play together. Much of their play is still what is known as *parallel play,* with two or more children playing by themselves without interacting with the children next to them. (For a more thorough discussion of the developmental abilities of children at different ages, see chapter 6.)

Parents often benefit from being a part of a play group as much as their children do. One mother who lives in a rural area said to me, "We started out with a few moms saying, 'Let's get together so the children can play and we can talk.' It was important for us to get together so we could talk to other mothers about our children and share ideas on how to cope with problems. It seemed to make us feel less isolated somehow." When parents move to a new community, becoming part of a play group is one of the best ways of making contact with other parents with young children.

•• Conclusion

The decision to send your children to early childhood school is a very personal one. There are no universal right or wrong answers. However, if you do decide you want to send your child to early childhood school, it is important that your needs and desires coincide with the school's. You will need to be familiar with the school's admissions procedures and understand how its decisions are made. In chapter 5, we will look at some of the factors schools consider in making admissions decisions, and we will explore your own role in getting your child into the early childhood school of your choice.

•• •• •• ••
F I V E
•• •• •• •• •• •• •• •• •• •• •• ••

Getting In: A Parent's Guide to Admissions

The September before my own son James turned two, I started thinking about sending him to early childhood school. All James's friends from our mother-child play group were going. I thought it would be good for James to have a place to go that was all his own where he could play and explore and make friends with children his own age. As an educator, I was familiar with most of the early childhood schools in the area. I chose three schools that I felt had provided a particularly fine early childhood experience for my former students and that were also reasonably near our home. I called a few friends who were teaching kindergarten and first grade in ongoing schools to confirm that my perceptions were still correct. Then I called the schools and made appointments to visit. My husband and I applied to all three, toured the schools, met the directors, and took our son for interviews. In each school the process differed slightly, but at all the schools we were impressed with the warm, friendly atmosphere and with the genuine interest expressed in us and in our son.

We visited the first school just before Halloween. My son became frightened by some life-size masks hanging on the wall and screamed for the first five minutes of the interview. At the next school, he insisted that I sit on the floor beside him while he drew pictures and built towers out of blocks. At the third school, he was asked what noise a duck makes and what happens to leaves in the fall. He refused to answer. Despite all my years of teaching, I knew—like all mothers—that my son was the cleverest and most precocious toddler to walk across the threshold of any early childhood school and, despite all my

•• •• •• ••

training in child development, I desperately wanted him to demonstrate his talents. Somehow I managed to keep silent and not suggest that he recite the nursery rhymes he said to himself before going to sleep at night, or count to ten as his grandfather had taught him to do, or even share the Spanish he had picked up from the baby-sitter. Despite his refusal to volunteer any of these unique talents and his insistence on behaving instead like an ordinary almost two-year-old, my son, like his friends from the play group, was admitted to all three schools.

Less than two years later the baby boom hit. The schools were overrun with two-year-olds, and there were not enough places in toddler programs for all of them. At a time when many secondary schools were having trouble filling their classrooms because of declining enrollment, neither the early childhood schools nor their admissions directors were prepared for the sudden onslaught of applicants. My son's school was forced to stop accepting applications for the next year on the first of October because it didn't have the staff to interview any more applicants. This situation continues today in certain areas. In some larger cities, the tight admissions situation has been accentuated by parents' applying to as many as ten early childhood schools out of fear that there will be no room for their child in any school. This has made things more difficult both for parents and for the schools, which often have little idea how many of their applications are serious. One admissions director at an early childhood school notes, "It isn't so much the number of applicants as the number of applications that has increased so dramatically."

The admissions picture for early childhood school can vary widely from year to year, and from school to school, even in the same general geographical area. Some schools may be actively seeking to fill empty spots, while others are bombarded with more applications than they can even begin to process. A school may have space for three-year-olds but not for toddlers, or vice versa. But unlike the lines outside a popular restaurant, the number of applicants does not necessarily equate with the quality of a school or its appropriateness for you and your child.

•• Publicly Financed Programs

Some public school districts have experimental pre-K programs, and as we discussed earlier, there are a number of publicly financed early childhood intervention programs. However, because most publicly funded programs try to determine physical, social, economic, and educational needs as criteria for selection, these programs are often limited to low-income families or children with special needs.[1]

Head Start, one of the best-known intervention programs for children between the ages of three and five, was established specifically for the benefit of low-income families. Space in Head Start is so limited, however, that educators estimate that it is currently available to less than 20 percent of the children eligible for it. Individual Head Start programs develop plans for recruiting and selecting children under HEW guidelines. Enrollment must reflect the racial and ethnic balance of disadvantaged families in the area. Children are assigned to programs based on an assessment of family situation, age, handicaps, developmental level, health, or learning problems. Ninety percent of the children in a Head Start program must come from families with incomes below the federal poverty guidelines. Ten percent of the children must be handicapped. Low-income handicapped children are given priority.

Preschool programs in public schools usually exist only as a result of initiatives by the local community school district. In some states funds are available on a competitive basis for experimental pre-K programs designed for three- and four-year-olds from low-income families. There are also grants for so-called umbrella programs—innovative pilot projects to meet special local needs. These needs might include a preschool program for gifted children, an after-school program, or a parents co-op. Pre-K programs may also be funded by an individual state legislator's discretionary funds. Other programs are funded through Chapter I, according to federal guidelines, for "low achieving children in low-income areas."

Two of the more successful publicly funded preschool programs have been Project Giant Step in New York City and Smart Start in Massachusetts. Eligibility for Project Giant Step is based on a combination of social and financial considerations, and approximately one out of five disadvantaged four-year-olds in the city participates in the program. Senator Edward Kennedy has called Smart Start his "top educational priority," and proponents of Smart Start hope to make preschool education available to every child whose family wants it, regardless of economic resources. According to Senator Kennedy, this is an "education program, a day-care program, a job program, a literacy program, a health-care program, a dropout program, and an anti-crime and drug abuse program.''[2] Elsewhere in Massachusetts, local school committees have authorized transition-to-kindergarten programs, which are partially funded by fees from parents. Scholarship assistance for families with financial need is available through the public schools of these communities. Before being admitted to transition programs, children are interviewed by the early childhood education coordinator to evaluate their readiness for the program. If children are deemed ready, admission is on a first-come, first-served basis. School districts in a number of states run summer programs to get children used to being in school and to introduce them to age-appropriate activities and skills. All children who will attend kindergarten in the district in September are usually eligible for the summer sessions. There are also a variety of special preschool programs for three- and four-year-olds who suffer severe developmental delays and for handicapped children referred by pediatricians. A number of states are experimenting with arrangements with private nursery schools and developmentally oriented day-care centers to allow more low-income children the benefit of early childhood school experiences. And one school district in Milwaukee has entered into contracts with private day-care centers to provide both child care and kindergarten to disadvantaged four- and five-year-olds.

Despite the recent increase in publicly financed preschool programs, there is still a lack of widely available public programs for children before kindergarten. However, if you think your child might be eligible for one of the publicly financed programs, contact your local board of education for information on programs in your district.

••Private Early Childhood Schools

Because most publicly funded programs are limited to low-income families, many families must seek alternatives in private schools. Private early childhood schools are often located in churches or synagogues. Some schools are part of national chains such as Kindercare or Children's World. Businesses sometimes run schools that combine early childhood school and daycare for their employees. These schools may accept neighborhood children on a space-available basis, and places are often eagerly sought. Several months before it opened there were already more than a hundred names on a waiting list for places in a school run by the developer of Heller Industrial Park in New Jersey. A few schools are affiliated with universities and are run as lab schools to test new educational theories and to train student teachers. Places here, again, are few and usually in great demand. Other early childhood schools are not separate schools at all, as we saw earlier, but divisions of ongoing schools. It is always a good idea to apply to more than one school. If the admissions situation seems to be particularly tight and you live in a large city, you might want to apply to as many as six.

If you are interested in a particular school, I recommend you call the admissions office and try to get a realistic idea of how many available spots the school actually has. Schools do not volunteer or publicly announce that information. One parent described this situation to me: "They were marching all these parents through the school and, if you were going on the basis of the tour, you would assume they were going to double the class of three-year-olds. It turned out that because they already had two sections of toddlers who would be going on to the three-year-old program, they had only eight openings: four for boys, and four for girls. They already knew they had some sibling applicants that they were going to have to take, and I remember sitting there thinking, 'This is pretty misleading for parents.'" Some programs that begin with infants and combine early childhood school and daycare as the children get older may be so small that they only take four infants a year. One teacher told me, "As soon as a mom gets pregnant she puts herself on a waiting list."

•• First-Come, First-Served

Many early childhood schools admit children on the basis of chronological age or date of application—a first-come, first-served approach. Dates for application vary greatly from one part of the country to another. In some towns you may be able to sign up during the September your child begins. A few schools are very flexible and accept applications throughout the year. Other popular schools stop accepting applications almost a year before a child would expect to begin. These schools are not trying to make things difficult for parents. They realize that they can give only a certain number of applications the kind of time and individual attention they deserve. The mother of a four-year-old recalls that when she began looking at programs in July, she was horrified to find that everything was full and her daughter had to be put on a waiting list. The next year she moved to another town only to discover that the available slots filled up by May. Another mother recounted her reaction to admissions deadlines: "This was my first child and I didn't know that you had to apply so far ahead of time. I called in February and found it was already too late. But we were lucky because the school called back three days later and said that they had a place for Nicholas." There are usually a few last-minute vacancies, but it is a good idea to plan ahead and apply ten to twelve months before your child is due to start.

••AGE CUTOFFS••

When you apply to a school, be sure to ask about age cutoffs. Some early childhood schools require that a child be three by June 1; others may accept children with September birthdays. Some schools insist that a child be toilet trained, others do not. In certain classes you will find that all the children have birthdays within a few months of each other, while other schools accommodate a wider age range within their groups. One mother expected that her third child would automatically follow her two older daughters to early childhood school, only to discover to her dismay that her last daughter missed the age cutoff by a month.

••Screening Applicants

Some schools, usually in large cities, do not accept children on a first-come, first-served basis. Instead, they try to make an assessment of both a child's readiness and the parents' compatibility with the school's particular program. These schools may use a variety of screening methods to make this assessment. The screening process usually includes an interview with both parents after they have had a tour of the school, and a subsequent meeting with the child. Schools interview parents because they are looking for a good match for their school. They are looking for parents who understand the school and will feel comfortable there. With very young children, unless the child has an obvious behavior problem or severe developmental deficit, the parent interview and questionnaire are often more important than the observation of the child. Some schools admit children solely on the basis of parent interviews and questionnaires without actually meeting the child. In general, in the admissions process for older children, more emphasis is placed on the child's own demonstrated abilities and talents, but at the early childhood level schools are every bit as interested in you as in your child.

••THE APPLICATION••

Schools usually ask parents to complete an application that contains questions about them and their child. The questions range from simple queries about allergies and medications to those that require more in-depth descriptions of your child's likes and dislikes, fears or anxieties, bedtime rituals, relationships with siblings, and responses to separation. It is often a good idea to look over your child's baby book before filling out an application or going to a parent interview. Many schools will want to know about the course of your pregnancy and whether your child was premature. They may ask questions about your child's developmental history: When did your daughter first crawl? Did she crawl forward or backward first? When did your son start to talk? What was his first word? His first phrase? Most schools will ask who cares for the child during the day and whether there are other adults such as grandparents, a housekeeper, or a nanny living in the household. Schools usually want to know whether a child has experienced any significant illnesses, traumatic experiences, or health problems. Some schools inquire whether there is any family history of learning problems. A school may also ask you to describe your child's personality, give examples of the ways he or she likes to spend time, and explain how anger or frustration is usually expressed at home and what kind of discipline you find most effective. Schools that don't ask these questions on the application may well ask them later during the parent interview. It is best to answer all questions simply and honestly without either putting your child down or trying to prove that he or she is a prodigy.

••LETTERS OF RECOMMENDATION••

Some schools may ask for the names of several people who know your family well. A few schools ask you to have one or two of these people write a letter. When a school asks for recommendations, it is important to remember that they want to find out as much as they can about you and your child, about your values and goals, and about how you function as a family. They are not interested in how many famous people you know. (See chapter 10 for some examples of effective letters.)

••THE PARENT INTERVIEW••

Parents are usually asked to meet either alone or in small groups with the head of the school or with the admissions director. The meeting may last anywhere from twenty minutes to an hour. Sometimes the child may be in the room playing while the parents talk. The head or the admissions director describes the school and explains its philosophy and goals. He or she may ask the parents specific questions about their child's interests, habits, likes, and dislikes. The parents, in turn, have an opportunity to ask questions about the school.

During the parent interview, schools are interested in:

1. Family dynamics. Do parents interact in a positive way with each other and with their child?
2. Whether the parents really seem to know their child. Are their expectations realistic?
3. How parents deal with separation issues. (See chapter 6 for a discussion of separation.)
4. How the parents react if their child misbehaves. Do they set limits? Are they firm as well as sympathetic, or do they throw up their hands and try to pretend it isn't happening?
5. The level of love and trust between parent and child. Does the child look to the parents for encouragement and guidance?
6. Whether the goals of parents and school are compatible. If there is a discrepancy in values, will the child be confused?
7. Whether the parents will trust and support the school.
8. Whether the parents and school will be able to pull together for the benefit of the child.

The interview process can be a shock to a parent. One mother remarked to me after an interview, "They ended up interviewing me most of the time. I felt like I was the candidate. They didn't spend much time observing my son; they didn't even seem to be trying to get a sense of him. The whole emphasis was on whether there was a good fit between the school and the kind of education we wanted for our son."

Try not to let yourself be intimidated by the process. Remember that most admissions directors are parents or grandparents. They have been in your shoes themselves. As one admissions director, whose own son was turned down for admission to six nursery schools and is now an honor student at an Ivy League college, said, "We have all been through this ourselves—we've seen it from the other side. We understand your apprehension and we realize how much you want the best for your child."

••THE CHILD'S INTERVIEW••

Many early childhood schools will also want to see your child either with or without you. This interview is not nearly as bad as it sounds. Schools are not looking for "the perfect child," nor have they been secretly commissioned to search out future Nobel Prize winners. The child's interview is a way for the school to get to know your child, to get a sense of your child's learning style and readiness for a particular program. A recent panel of admissions directors reassured its audience of anxious parents that they fully expected each child to act like a typical two-, three-, or four-year-old. A father reported to me, "The whole idea of going through an interview at that age [two] was appalling, but the fact is it was fun while Andrew was there and not at all anxiety producing."

Mitten Wainwright, the director of Park Avenue Christian Church Day School in New York and an early childhood educator for more than twenty years, says, "We don't worry about natural disasters like a young child throwing up, or wetting his pants, or refusing to come in the room because he thinks it's a doctor's office. What we're really interested in is not what happens but how the parent handles it. Do they get all upset at the child or do they take it in stride."

••WHAT TO TELL YOUR CHILD BEFORE
THE INTERVIEW ••

Parents often ask me what they should say to their child before the interview. Several longtime admissions directors have suggested that parents might tell their toddler, "You are going to meet a lady. She is called a teacher and she likes to play with children. I've met her and I think she's a very nice person. I want you to come and meet her too. She will share some toys with you and you'll have a chance to play with her, and she will show you some new ways to play with her toys. Mommy and Daddy will be there with you."

But before you say anything to your child, find out from each school exactly how your child's interview will be handled. Then tell your child in advance whether you will be in the room or not; whether there will be a tour of the school; and, perhaps most important from the child's point of view, whether there will be toys and a chance to play with other children. Again it is probably a good idea to take notes during your conversation with the school about these details since, as I mentioned earlier, the process is slightly different in each school. If you tell your daughter she will play in a classroom with other children and in that particular school the child goes off to another room alone with a teacher, with not a child or toy in sight; or if you tell your son not to worry, Mommy will be right there, and then he is whisked away at the door, you are setting the stage for problems. Misinformation can be very upsetting for a child.

••WHAT WILL HAPPEN AT THE INTERVIEW?••

One mother gave this description of her daughter's interview: "My daughter was invited to join a group of children in the class. There were a variety of play materials around the room. She moved among the group of children freely and played with the materials. The director talked to us and to her at the same time, but I had a very distinct feeling that she was assessing Sarah's readiness."

Another mother remembers that while she was talking to the admissions director, her son walked around the room. "Various materials had been set out and Charles was free to participate in whatever activity interested him: petting the rabbit, working on a puzzle, building with blocks. No one asked him to do anything, they just let him do what he pleased, but it was clear to me that they were watching what he was doing. As we were getting ready to leave, the teacher remarked, 'Oh isn't that wonderful how well he holds onto things.' So she was indeed looking at Charles's readiness.''

At another school, a parent recalls that the interview was conducted during the tour of the school and the admissions director seemed "to be more interested in Elizabeth's relationship with my husband and me than she was in her reactions to the things going on in the school. At the next school we visited, the interview was very structured. Elizabeth was one-on-one with a teacher doing a series of directed activities while we watched from another part of the room."

During most interviews for early childhood school, children are observed in small groups of five or six for thirty to forty minutes. They are given the opportunity to interact with each other and with two or three early childhood teachers, as well as with a variety of materials designed for young children. These materials may include simple puzzles, Play-Doh, Legos, blocks, paper and crayons, cars and trucks, dolls, cups and plates, and other play equipment from the housekeeping corner. At some point children are usually given a simple snack consisting of either fruit or cheese and crackers and juice. Teachers often use this time to get a sense of children's socialization skills as well as how adept they are at drinking from a cup and feeding themselves.

Teachers usually spend a few minutes talking to each child individually to get a sense of language development and how well the child expresses his or her ideas. Some schools structure interviews so that children are doing a series of directed activities alone with a teacher. These activities are often loosely based on Gesell's developmental schedules and may include such activities as building towers out of blocks, matching shapes, and naming objects. It is important for parents to remember that these activities are being used to help the school assess a child's developmental readiness and learning style, not the child's IQ (intelligence quotient). A child's developmental age (DA) is the age at which the child is functioning socially, emotionally, intellectually, and physically. Developmental age is a qualitative rather than a quantitative concept. It is not a numerical score but rather a series of observations on the way a child functions. Psychologists at the Gesell Institute stress that there are no right or wrong answers on a developmental assessment. Instead, a child's responses are that child's way of exploring, ordering, solving, creating, and predicting his or her world. Responses not only show something of what a child knows and understands but also reflect that child's self-concept and learning style. How accurate the assessment is depends on the experience and skill of the evaluator. You should never consider one developmental assessment a definitive statement on your child.

What Is Being Evaluated at the Early Childhood Level?

As the teachers watch the children interacting with each other and with the materials, they notice:

1. The children's response to each other.
2. Their response to the materials.
3. Their physical behavior and expressions.
4. Their language use, and whether their language is sufficient to communicate their needs.
5. Their approaches to problem solving.
6. Their motor control, both large and small.
7. Their tolerance for frustration.
8. Their ability both to focus on a task and to handle transitions between activities.
9. Their sense of confidence and security.
10. Their interest in exploring and interacting with the environment.

••TESTS••

Formal tests are seldom used to assess the readiness of normal children with no suspected deficits for early childhood programs prior to kindergarten. Many educators agree with Dr. Margaret M. Devine, former president of the World Organization for Early Childhood Education: "Children this age are essentially not testable" because they have difficulty understanding directions and do not take tests seriously. Tests are generally used only when problems or developmental gaps are suspected and to identify children who may need further evaluation and perhaps special help.

Tests are also occasionally used for admission to certain gifted and talented programs that begin before kindergarten. The most commonly used test for these programs is the Stanford-Binet, Fourth Edition, an IQ test which, unlike a readiness assessment, gives numerical scores and seeks to predict how well a child will actually perform in school. (See chapter 10 for a discussion of the Stanford-Binet and other commonly used IQ tests.) If IQ tests are used, they are generally used in conjunction with parent interviews and informal assessments of the child.

•• How Early Childhood Schools Decide

When schools make admissions decisions on other than a first-come, first-served basis, they usually give preference to the siblings of children already in the school and to the children of alumni/alumnae. If a school is affiliated with a church or synagogue, it will generally give preference to members of the congregation. Some ongoing schools give preference in their early childhood divisions to children they believe will remain through the elementary years.

It is important for parents to realize that early childhood schools are not looking for a class made up of child prodigies or academic superstars. Mary Solow, who has been involved in education for twenty-five years and is currently the director of Central Synagogue Nursery School, said to me, "We're not looking for the brightest and most beautiful. We are hoping that children will be relatively emotionally healthy and normal, and that their parents will be cooperative and supportive of our school. We care a lot about social kindness and decency and sharing. We know that not every child is going to be an A in physical and verbal development at age two or three. We're not looking for a class of geniuses. We make it clear from the beginning that we don't expect children to be able to say their ABCs or count to ten."

When they put together classes, early childhood schools first need to balance the ratio of girls and boys. Some like to have a mix of first, second, and third children as well as only children. Some look for a diversity of personality types and learning styles. Some look for children they feel will fit in comfortably both with the program and with other children in the class. Some try in a variety of ways, as we have seen, to assess children's developmental level and readiness for their program. Schools also look for the children they believe will benefit most from their program and who, by being part of a class, will in turn benefit the other children.

Most schools also look for parents they feel will be supportive of the school and be comfortable there, parents who seem to understand what the school stands for and who share its goals. They want parents who will be involved in school activities, will come to chapel in the morning if it is a church school, will help in the library and on trips, and will work with the teachers. Schools usually look for a certain amount of ethnic and economic diversity in the parent body, though this is generally not as great a factor at the early childhood level as later on.

••WHO MAKES THE DECISION?••

At the early childhood level, admissions decisions are usually made by the head of the school and, if the school is large enough to have one, the director of admissions.

••WAITING TO HEAR••

Several months or more may go by after you complete the application process before the school indicates whether or not your child has been accepted. One realistic father said to me, "I remember kind of sadly the anxiety a lot of people had when we were waiting to hear from schools. It reminded me too much of being a senior in high school waiting to hear from the colleges. Given the choices, at age two or three I don't think the stakes are that high—it's not like finding out if you're about to be drafted or something. Try to relax a little and have faith in your kids. They'll make out okay."

On the day my own daughter heard from her early childhood school, she and I were at a class at the Y. The two-year-olds were making tea and building castles. Their mothers were clustered by the puzzles. "I hate siblings," said one. "It's just not fair to the only child," said another. "I've been watching the mail every day, but nothing's come. And I don't even know whether that's good or bad," said a third. "You'll know by the envelope if she's been accepted," interjected the first mother. "Acceptances are always thick and businesslike. Rejections are thin and polite." The third mother sighed: "There's nothing to do but wait. It's like that stock market theory, the random walk selection; they put all the names up on the wall, close their eyes and throw darts. If they hit you, you're in, if not you're out."

On the way home that day, I reflected that not long before I had been on the other side of the admissions folder. As head of a junior school and a member of the admissions committee at a boys' school in New York, I had studied IQ scores and the results of screening tests that purportedly predicted future academic success as well as readiness for first grade. I had visited many different early childhood schools. I had watched children draw pictures and name objects and hop on one foot. I had listened to them tell their favorite stories. I had watched them at work and play in their classrooms, and I had read their early childhood school reports. I had met their parents and talked to their teachers. My colleagues and I had made our decisions and waited to see if they were right. The classes I helped put together were much like early childhood school classes. The children certainly weren't all geniuses, child prodigies, developmentally advanced, or always well behaved. The parents weren't all rich, or poor, or smart, or social, or talented; nor did they fit into any other simple category. The only common denominator I could find was that they all cared about their children's education enough to invest a considerable amount of time and money in it. They cared enough to get their children to school at eight-thirty every morning, to come to parents' nights and conferences, and to sit at miniature desks helping teachers make supplementary materials to use in the classroom. They were willing to work harder than average at being parents.

And what of the children themselves, the ones who were accepted—what would happen to them? According to the reports on their predecessors in the alumni notes, some would make it to the secondary school and college of their choice and others would not. Some would succeed in the eyes of the world or in their own secret dreams, and others would wish at fifty that they could start over again. All in all, they were probably very much like the children who ended up on the waiting list or the children who got the thin envelopes. Whether or not they ever got into the early childhood school of their choice, they would grow up and find jobs, get married, have children, and worry about where their own children were going to go to school.

When we got home, as I lifted my daughter out of her stroller

I noticed a thick envelope outside the front door. I breathed a sigh of relief.

••THE WAIT LIST••

The meaning of a wait list varies greatly from school to school. One school director told me, "I can't bear to send a rejection letter to the parents of a two-year-old, so we just put them all on the wait list even though we know we're never going to take them." Other schools feel it is fairer to put only those children on the wait list whom they plan to accept if there is an opening. If your child is put on a wait list and you are interested in the school, call the school, tell them how much you like the school, and try to get a realistic sense of what the chances are that a place might open up.

••If Your Child Does Not Get into the School You Want

No matter how smart and attractive your child is or what great parents you are, your child may well be turned down at several schools if you live in a large urban area with a fast-growing population of two- or three-year-olds. As Reveta Bowers, director of children's programs at the Center for Early Education in Los Angeles, said recently, "I tell parents that if your child doesn't get into this school, it does not necessarily reflect on your child. It does not mean that we found something lacking in your child. It does not mean that your child isn't smart and accomplished and well-rounded. It just means there are lots of smart and accomplished and well-rounded children and unfortunately we don't have the room to accommodate the large numbers that are seeking admission to our programs." Do not take a rejection letter from an early childhood school personally, and above all don't let it influence your feelings toward your child. Remember, your child is still his or her own wonderful, adorable, funny, and sometimes exasperating self, and your life together goes on with all its marvelous and awful moments still intact. Try to put the experience with the school behind you with the realization that no matter how much you thought you liked that school, it probably wasn't right for you and your child after all. Turn your attention to the schools where your child has been accepted. If you are still not sure which one would be the best choice, ask to visit again before making a decision. You may also want to spend some time reflecting on whether your child is ready for early childhood school or would benefit from waiting a year. In the next chapter we will look at the meaning of readiness and explore some of the ways readiness is assessed in young children.

•• •• •• ••
S I X
•• •• •• •• •• •• •• •• •• •• •• ••

Parents and Children:
Ready or Not

Children are ready for school when they have a basic sense of trust, a sense that no matter what happens they will be taken care of—they will be safe. Then they are able to separate from their parents and enter a relationship with other people in a new environment with new materials. If a child has trust, anything else can be taught.

ALEXANDRA ZIMMER,
DIRECTOR, THE MADISON
AVENUE PRESBYTERIAN DAY
SCHOOL, NEW YORK CITY

The idea that children should be "ready" for early childhood school is relatively new. The word *ready* comes from the Anglo-Saxon and originally pertained to riding, not school. Educators first began to apply the term readiness to children in the late 1920s and early 1930s as a result of studies by Dr. Arnold Gesell, founder of the Guidance Nursery at Yale. Gesell believed that each child passes through fixed developmental stages that are not necessarily related to the child's chronological age. Rather each child progresses through each stage at his or her own rate. Any attempt to train a child to sit, talk, or read before that child was developmentally ready was useless, and perhaps even harmful.

For many years the consensus among educators was that intelligence was based almost solely on a child's genetic inheritance, and hence was not greatly influenced by either environment or early childhood education. In the late 1930s, at the Iowa Child Welfare Research Station, Harold Skeels and other researchers challenged these assumptions on the fixed nature of

•• •• •• ••

intelligence in their work with mentally handicapped children. In the 1960s Benjamin Bloom at the University of Chicago found that intelligence could be significantly influenced by a child's environment and early education. The debate on the relative importance of genetics versus environment goes on, as yet unresolved. However, educators now consider that opportunities to explore, to learn new skills, to solve problems, to express oneself verbally, and to make one's likes and dislikes known with words are vitally important for all young children. Educators such as Jean Piaget and Jerome Bruner have described a child's development as a careful balance between genetic inheritance and environment—a balance that can ultimately be controlled by a child's own actions. Just as a child's biological time clock cannot and should not be rushed, we cannot alter the rate at which that child passes through the progressive developmental stages. However, most of us, parents and educators alike, now believe that a child's overall development can be enhanced by providing appropriate challenges when he or she is ready to respond to them. But which challenges are appropriate at which ages? And how do we know when an individual child is ready to respond to them?

In attempting to answer these questions, many educators maintain that there is no such thing as general readiness, only the readiness of a particular child for a particular early childhood school. Some argue that it is even a contradiction to speak of a child's readiness for a particular school since a good early childhood school should be flexible enough to meet the needs of each individual child. They stress that it is important to fit the school to the child rather than the child to the school. Other educators believe that, despite the flexibility of teachers and the child-centered nature of a school, there are nevertheless certain minimal social and verbal skills a child needs to be comfortable in an early childhood school and to benefit from all the social, emotional, and cognitive challenges.

As we look at the developmental factors that seem to indicate readiness for early childhood school, it is important to remember that no two children are alike and that each child will have his or her own timetable for reaching each developmental milestone. Birth order and family size can also influence a child's readiness for early childhood school. Some early childhood teachers find that the only child and the firstborn child may initially have a slightly harder time adjusting to school than other children. And Dr. Nina Lief, director of the Early Childhood Development Center of the Center for Comprehensive Health Practice, an affiliate of New York Medical College, observes that at school children from very large families often choose to play alone rather than interacting with the other children in a group, if older brothers and sisters tend to intrude on their play space at home. If your child does not seem to be ready according to the criteria I discuss, this does not necessarily mean that you should not send your child to early childhood school, but rather that you will want to choose the school very carefully. You will want to look for a particularly flexible school that is sensitive to the individual needs of each child. You may also want to look for one that mixes children of different ages together rather than one that groups children by chronological age.

As we think about our children's readiness for school, it is important to remember that research has shown that a child's developmental level bears no direct relation to that child's intelligence. A child can be of average intelligence and developmentally quite advanced. Conversely, a child can be highly intelligent and still lag behind peers in some areas of development. Researchers at the Gesell Institute have found, however, that most children do better in school if they are grouped by developmental age rather than by either chronological or intellectual age.

•• Sending Your Child to School at Two

A two-year-old is an explorer who loves to touch, taste, smell, and feel everything in sight. Many two-year-olds like water- and sand-play. They delight in filling pails with water or small stones. Both boys and girls like to play with dolls and stuffed animals and imitate daily activities such as taking a bath or going to bed. Many children this age are fascinated by books and enjoy carrying them around. They often want adults to read favorite stories over and over again. Most two-year-olds can walk and run easily. Some can also walk up and down stairs and kick a ball. Two-year-olds love naming things and can use simple three-word sentences. They are usually able to ask for the things they need, and some have a vocabulary of several hundred words. They can build a tower of six or seven blocks, string large beads, unscrew lids, manipulate Play-Doh, and paint and crayon. Many enjoy playing alongside other children in a style of play known as parallel play. Louise Bates Ames and her colleagues at the Gesell Institute say that the expression "terrible twos" is a misnomer since the average two-year-old is "a creature of considerable good will, quite willing and able to conform to the demands of those around him [her]."[1]

It is, rather, the two-and-a-half-year-old who is in a stage of disequilibrium. Ames finds that many two-and-a-half-year-olds are for a brief time "terrible and life is full of opposite extremes." Children this age can seem bossy and demanding. They often resent change and like to have familiar routines rigidly adhered to. While many begin to talk to other children, as well as to adults, most of their interactions with other children are negative. They aren't ready to share their possessions. There is usually a good deal of pushing and hitting when two-and-a-half-year-olds get together, and a lot of adult supervision is needed.[2]

Child-care experts agree that two-year-olds who are developing normally and have loving, supportive families do not need to be in school. Many are better off at home either with their parents or a qualified child-care provider. If you are able to be at home with your two-year-old, don't worry that he or she may be missing out on something by not being in school. Try to relax and let yourself enjoy being with your children and watching them grow. Talk to your children about the things you see and do together. Read to them. Be available to encourage their desire to explore and to help them make sense of their world. You will be giving your children all the stimulation they need. Remember that sending a child to school at two is often a response to the social and economic needs of parents rather than to the academic or developmental needs of the child.

There are, however, a few children this age who seem really hungry for new experiences. These are the children who may benefit from the opportunity to go to early childhood school. Early childhood educators often refer to the special programs they have developed for two-year-olds as "toddler programs." If you decide to send your two-year-old to school it is important that you choose one where the atmosphere is as much like home as possible—nurturing and secure, as well as stimulating. It should be a school where children are not expected to share or made to participate in group activities before they are ready. Lydia Spinelli, director of the Brick Church School in New York City, advises parents, "A toddler program mustn't be a watered-down version of a three-year-old program. . . . It is particularly important for teachers to adapt to a toddler rather than to expect him or her to adapt to them."

The environment in an early childhood school should be interesting and stimulating. It should not, however, be overly noisy or confusing with too many activities all going on at the same time. Beware of schools that promise to teach your toddler how to read and use flash cards and other inappropriate materials. Some studies have indicated that pressuring a child to learn skills such as reading before the child is ready can backfire and cause problems later on in school. Jane Healy, a learning specialist on the faculty at Cleveland State University, reports in her recent book, *Your Child's Growing Mind,* "It is possible to force skills by intensive instruction, but this may cause the child to use immature, inappropriate neural networks and distort the natural growth process."[3] (See chapters 3 and 4 for more information on selecting an appropriate school for your child).

While child development experts agree that for most children participation in a toddler program will probably make little difference in their long-term physical, emotional, and cognitive development, there are a few children for whom it could make a positive difference:

1. Children without ready access to other children or to an outdoor play space;
2. Children from two-career families who might otherwise spend the day at home alone with a housekeeper who may have little training in child development;
3. Children living in homes where English is not the primary language;
4. Children from economically or socially disadvantaged backgrounds;
5. Children from difficult home situations;
6. Children with special needs.

On the other hand, there are children who would benefit more from spending another year at home or in an informal play group run by their mothers, fathers, or a familiar caregiver. These are children who need gradually to get used to being with other children and adults. Some of these children are so closely bonded to their mothers and fathers that they consistently refuse to leave their laps in a new environment despite the enticements of friendly, reassuring adults and interesting toys. Other children are so scattered that they run constantly from one toy to the next without being able to concentrate even briefly on anything, often seeming to be unaware of the adults and children around them.

Andrew J. was one of the children I have seen for whom the transition from home to early childhood school was too abrupt. Andrew was the only child of older parents with well-established careers. He was a normal, bright, but somewhat reserved baby. His mother, a psychologist, gave up her practice to be at home with Andrew. The two were very close and spent much time alone together while his father was away on business trips. Just before Andrew's second birthday, his mother decided to return to her practice on a full-time basis. She was concerned about the lack of playmates in their neighborhood. She was also unable to find a suitable caregiver to provide the stimulation that she felt was important and that Andrew had grown accustomed to. Her solution was to enroll Andrew in a toddler program five mornings a week.

Although Andrew had had no trouble relating to the other children he occasionally saw on a one-to-one basis at home, he was overwhelmed at being in unfamiliar surroundings away from his mother, amidst a group of children he had never seen before. He reacted by becoming irritable and hard to please at home. At school he was fretful and disorganized. He clung to the teacher and demanded her undivided attention. He couldn't share with the other children and didn't know how to play with them. Fortunately, the school and his teacher were understanding and flexible. The teacher gave him individualized projects and arranged special play areas for him near her so he wouldn't be bothered by the other children. His mother changed her schedule so she could spend more time with Andrew after school. Slowly Andrew began to adjust to being in school and demanded less individual attention, but he continued to have trouble relating to other children and being part of a group. He is now five and is just beginning to relate to children in group situations. He likes children but still isn't sure how to play with them. For Andrew, separation from home and mother came too soon and too abruptly. He would have benefited from more exposure to other children in smaller doses in the familiar surroundings of home or in a parents' play group several hours a week before attending the toddler program.

Often it is the parent, not the child, who is really in need of a toddler program. And again there is nothing wrong with this. Parents should not feel guilty because they recognize that they need time off from their two-year-olds. As Louise Bates Ames and J. A. Chase said in their book *Don't Push Your Preschooler,* "It takes a super strong parent to keep up with one of these often adorable creatures twenty-four hours a day. . . . It is important to recognize your own personal tolerances, your limits of energy."[4] Parents need time to themselves to replenish their energy and to continue to grow as people. They also require time to pursue careers, and time to spend with other adults. Parents should be able to do this without worrying about how their children are being cared for in their absence. As we discussed earlier, many mothers and fathers find themselves living far away from the homes of their childhood, far from friends and relatives. Isolated in a strange city, they often need the support of being part of a community of other parents with young children. A toddler program in an early childhood school can offer this sense of support.

•• Sending Your Child to School at Three

Three-year-olds can walk up and down stairs, make fruit salad in a group, and tell you what they do and don't like. Three-year-olds can talk with other children rather than just at them. Many three-year-olds are also able to play with another child. They can express their wants and opinions verbally, and some have a vocabulary of over one thousand words. They love to be read to, and they love to ask questions. They can feed themselves and control their bladder and bowel. Their balance is good, and many can ride tricycles. They can also dress and undress themselves and even unbutton buttons. According to researchers at the Gesell Institute, three is an "age of delightful conformity, happy sharing, comfortable interpersonal relationships."[5] At three and a half, researchers again find many children in a state of disequilibrium. Many seem insecure and anxious. They may twitch and stutter, bite their nails, and suck their thumbs. Often there are daily battles over routines such as baths and bedtime. Many three-year-olds are at their worst around their parents and may project a much more positive image to their teachers or child-care givers. For both parents and children, this can be a good age to get out of the house. Early childhood teachers can also be a good source of support and advice for parents trying to cope with difficult behavior at home.

Three is the age many early childhood schools begin. Most three-year-olds are ready for a warm, nurturing, child-centered school. As we discussed in chapter 3, the teachers should be trained in child development and early childhood education. Schools should have plenty of interesting age-appropriate materials: blocks, paints, clay, sand and water tables, and dress-up clothes. There should also be ample outdoor space for running and climbing. Three-year-olds are curious about other children and adults, and they are ready to begin to have a sense of the classroom as a community. Most three-year-olds are able to manage physically, socially, and verbally at school. They can communicate their likes and dislikes. They can help make corn muffins or work on a collage with other children. They can follow rules, explore new materials, and begin to make friends and do things with other children in a group. Most children this age are ready to separate from their mother, father, or other primary caregiver. They are able to trust new adults, and they are secure enough to interact with them.

Readiness Predictors

Certain factors are often predictive of a three-year-old's readiness for a successful adjustment to early childhood school:

1. A sense of confidence and security.
2. Enough independence to begin doing things for themselves.
3. A desire to explore and to have new experiences outside the home.

4. The ability to separate from parents or other primary care-giver.
5. Sufficient verbal skills to communicate with other children and adults.
6. A beginning ability to relate to other children, to share, to take turns, and to be part of a group.
7. The ability to stay focused, and to sustain an activity briefly—not just to run around touching everything.
8. Physical development within a normal range for the child's chronological age.
9. The ability to deal with the physical demands of the environment—going up and down stairs, using the toilet.
10. The capability to use play materials in self-initiated and directed activities.

•• False Predictors

Parents sometimes focus on abilities and skills that actually have little bearing on readiness for early childhood school. To be ready for early childhood school, children do not have to know their shapes and colors, nor do they need to have the fine motor control to copy letters and shapes. On the other hand, your observation that your child seems precocious or likes to play with older children does not necessarily signal your child is ready.

Gretchen Lengyel, director of The Madison Playgroup and former president of the Parents League in New York City feels that "most three-year-olds are ready to go to school in the same way they are ready to go to the zoo—because they have the abilities to enjoy and benefit from both experiences."

The teachers and other educators I have spoken with agreed that the only children who should definitely not go to early childhood school at three are those who are (1) very scattered and unfocused, (2) are neurologically unable to control themselves, (3) have severe speech problems, or (4) come from seriously troubled homes. These children may need to be in a therapeutic setting where teachers have the special training and resources to help them. Parents should discuss appropriate local programs with their pediatrician, the head of the pediatric department at their local medical center, or the special education department in their school district. (See chapter 4 for more on children with special needs and also the Bibliography for a list of recommended books.)

•• Sending Your Child to School at Four

Four-year-olds love adventure and excitement. They often seem to be in perpetual motion. They are full of enthusiasm and questions about everything they encounter. They can skip, catch a beanbag, roller-skate, and ride a bicycle with training wheels. Many like to brag and exaggerate their exploits and accomplishments. They enjoy being with other children and can now play together in a group. They enjoy pretend play. They also like to make up rhyming games and tell silly jokes. Many children this age want to bring things to school to share with their friends or invite the friends over to play.

Four-year-olds are definitely ready for early childhood school. They are ready to share and make friends. They are ready to work together in a group with other children. They are ready for new experiences and new challenges. Four-year-olds are ready to experiment with different materials, to explore shapes and colors, to draw and to build, and to make collages. They are ready to learn how things work and to begin to discover and define their world. They seem more self-motivated and their attention span is getting longer. This is not to say that four-year-olds are ready for first grade or kindergarten. It does not mean that they should be sitting at desks filling in blanks in workbooks or memorizing addition and subtraction facts. It does mean that they are ready for the kinds of quality early childhood schools we discussed earlier.

In the past, access to publicly financed early childhood programs was generally limited to children with special needs. Children defined as needy have included children living in poverty, children with non-English-speaking parents, younger brothers and sisters of children with learning disabilities, and children who have been identified as having possible learning problems themselves.

Today, most educators feel that early childhood school is becoming an inalienable right for all our children, and they look forward to the day when funds will be made available to offer all four-year-olds the opportunity to go to early childhood school.

•• Understanding Separation: When Will Your Child Be Ready to Leave You?

When your children start early childhood school, you will wonder and frequently worry about how they will handle separation. Over the years parents have often questioned me about whether their children will be able to separate and, if they do, whether the separation could be harmful. A 1954 British study on maternal deprivation concluded that "lasting separation before age 2 is the only type of separation that can be shown to be deleterious in and of itself."[6] Subsequent research, as well as the personal experience of countless teachers and parents, indicates that short separations of the type involved in early childhood school are not harmful to children and do not have a negative effect on the natural bonds between parents and children.[7]

The late John Bowlby, at the Tavistock Clinic in London, did some of the classical studies on separation. He found that many children experience separation in three stages, though not always in the same order. In the first stage, the child actively protests the separation and does everything possible to prevent it from occurring. Some children do not protest immediately and may take several weeks to show their feelings. In the second stage of separation, children realize the failure of their protests and withdraw in despair, often showing little interest in other people or activities. The third stage consists of either a successful adjustment, in which the child becomes involved with the other children and in the classroom activities, or a lack of adjustment, in which the child becomes emotionally detached and avoids others, sometimes even the parents when they return at the end of the day.[8]

Psychologists have found that as painful as it may seem at the time, separation anxiety can actually serve a useful purpose by bringing the child and the teacher closer and making the teacher more aware of the child's needs. It is also important for parents to remember that, as early childhood development specialist Kathe Jervis points out, "the clinging and crying of very young children are healthy ways of expressing feelings and learning to cope."⁹

The age your children start school is a key factor in whether or not they will have difficulty separating from you. British psychologist Penelope Leach writes in her book *Your Baby and Child*, "There is nothing more devoted than a six month baby who has been allowed to attach himself to his mother—except that same baby three months later! . . . At around eight months he tries to keep you in sight every moment of his waking day; . . . [when this is impossible, the baby] will be uneasy, tearful or even panic-stricken."¹⁰ Some time between the ages of one and a half and two years, psychologists have found, children's growing awareness that they are really separate from their parents gives them an acute sense of their own smallness and vulnerability. Children at this age will often make desperate attempts to regain a sense of unity with their parents. Separation anxiety, characterized by constant demands and by clinging to parents and shadowing their every move, is an expression of a child's need to try to restore the lost sense of closeness and intimacy. Shortly after age two, however, many children begin to feel more comfortable with their sense of themselves as separate from their parents. This is also a time when many children are beginning to develop relationships outside their immediate families.

One of the reasons very young children have trouble separating from their mothers and fathers is that they believe that when their parents leave the room, they are gone forever. By age three, however, most children are able to retain a mental picture of their parents. They can hold onto this picture when their parents are out of sight and know that they will indeed come back. In his recent book *The Woman Who Works, the Parent Who Cares* (see Bibliography), Sirgay Sanger, M.D., founder and director of the Early Care Center in New York City, describes ways parents can help their children develop a mental picture. However, the age at which individual children are able to separate easily from their parents can vary dramatically, even between children in the same family. Teachers often find that children with exceptionally close ties to their mothers and fathers, and no real ties to other adults, find it harder to separate.

Some parents worry that separation will be a problem and are delighted to discover that it isn't an issue after all for their children. One father told me this story about his experience with his daughter: "We had a real fear that Amanda wouldn't want to go to school. She wasn't separating well. Every time we went out and left her with a baby-sitter, there would be a scene. But on the first day of school we were there and saw, to our astonishment, that our daughter was making friends with other children. It was a transformation; she really looked forward to going to school after that."

No matter how well you plan and think you have prepared your children, they may suddenly react in a totally uncharacteristic fashion when the moment comes to separate. In my own family, my son was always the one who approached both strangers and new experiences with a tentative wariness and cried in anguish when I left the room. However, to my surprise and delight, on the first day of school James trotted off quite happily with the teacher. My daughter, on the other hand, had always loved everything new and different; from the time she could crawl, she would go off on her own explorations. Everyone said Diana was just like her grandmother who, family legend has it, was always heading for California with her billy goat and wagon. But on the first day of school, my formerly fearless daughter suddenly and unexpectedly clung to me so tightly that it took both teachers to pry her loose. I can still see her outstretched arms and hear her heartrending cries as I left the room with the teacher assuring me that everything would be fine once I was out the door. I slunk out, feeling I had just abandoned my child. Ten minutes later I called from the phone booth on the corner and discovered to my relief that everything was indeed fine and Diana was happily building a castle out of blocks with two new friends.

As parents we are apt to think of separation as a one-time crisis. Once we have successfully weathered it, we tend to believe we will never have to worry about it again. But this is not always the case. Ellen Galinsky finds that children do "not separate once and for all" but rather that "separation is a gradual process of venturing out and returning for reassurance."[11] Separation problems are quite apt to reappear when you think they are a thing of the past. They often resurface after a school vacation, a bout with the flu or chicken pox, or even after a favorite teacher has been out sick. The prospect of going to a new school can also cause difficulties to reappear. Teachers notice that about the time children turn five and start talking about kindergarten, they sometimes show anxiety and need to be reassured that they don't have to leave their present school and all their friends that very day.

Suggestions for Dealing with Separation

1. Help your child become accustomed to being looked after by someone other than you—such as a grandparent, a friend, or a baby-sitter—before starting school.
2. Don't talk about all the exciting things you will be doing while your child is in school, such as taking the dog for a run or going to the playground with a younger sibling.
3. Include your child in planning what he or she will wear on the first day. Discuss whether your child wants to take a favorite toy to school safely tucked away in a backpack.
4. Talk to your child enthusiastically about the friends he or she will see at school and all the exciting new things they will do together. Remind your child of previous visits you made together to the school and discuss some of the things you found especially interesting.
5. Try to leave the house in a good frame of mind. Plan to get up early enough so you won't have to argue with your children about eating faster or letting them put their socks on themselves and so you are not frantically dashing around looking for your briefcase while the car pool is waiting.
6. Say good morning to the teacher and make sure the teacher knows your child has arrived and is helping your child get involved in some interesting activities.
7. Never try to sneak out of the room when your child isn't looking. Always say good-bye. If you don't your child won't trust you next time and consequently will be reluctant to let you out of sight.
8. When you decide it's time to leave, say good-bye and leave quickly. Don't linger for one last kiss and then another. You'll only make things worse.
9. Arrive promptly at pick-up time. Children may feel abandoned if they are still waiting after all their friends have been picked up.
10. Sometimes our children find it easier to separate from one parent than from the other. If this is the case with your child, let that parent be the one to take the child to school.

If your child has trouble separating from both parents, you might consider having a grandparent or a sitter take the child to school for a while.

Separation is easiest when children have experienced trust in their family environment. In building this trust, consistency and support are very important. We also need to try to help our children feel that it is all right to try new things and even to be wrong sometimes, to take chances and to make mistakes. Sometimes our expectations for our children are based on memories of our own childhood experiences and feelings. One mother whose child separated easily recalled that when she started school, she couldn't wait for her mother to leave. She didn't even want her to walk her to school. If parents believe school is going to be an exciting experience and that their children will be safe and happy, there is a very good chance that their children will feel the same way. Finally, try not to overreact if, despite having done all the right things, your child does cry at your departure. Remember, it is very likely your child will be perfectly fine once you are safely on your way.

•• When You Are Ready for Your Child to Be Ready

When you are ready for your child to be ready for school, your child probably will also be ready. A parent's readiness can be more important to a child's successful adjustment to early childhood school than the child's own level of readiness. Teachers in early childhood schools find it is often the parent and not the child who is not ready to separate. Some parents simply are not ready to let go. They still need to feel needed all the time. Some secretly fear that their child will indeed go running off down the hall at school with never a backward glance.

These feelings are very natural and should not be cause for concern. According to Dr. Robert A. Furman, assistant professor of child psychiatry at Case Western Reserve University in Cleveland, the parent feels both anxiety about the child's performance in a new environment and sadness at what appears to be the end of the first phase of childhood. Furman cautions parents that "until a mother has cried with the sadness of missing her child, she will not be able to help him [her] in dealing with any of his [her] feelings associated with missing her."[12]

Some schools hold informal group sessions for parents to help them deal with separation. A number of working parents have told me that they feel the separation experience at school is harder on them than on parents who are at home with their children. As an attorney explained, "All of us who work feel so vulnerable because we're not there with our children. As soon as I left the room I heard my daughter screaming, 'Mommy! Mommy! Mommy!' I was shaking; it was the hardest thing I had ever been through." Some working mothers tell me that they feel the experience of separation can be particularly difficult for parents with high-powered careers who are used to controlling their world. They may tend to see their child going off to school as their losing control for the first time. Even though they are used to leaving their children with baby-sitters, some feel school is different because, as one mother said to me, "We hire the baby-sitters to look after our children and make them feel good. And if things don't work out we can always find someone else. At school we're no longer in control over how our children will be judged or even who will judge them."

If you have such concerns about separating from your children, it would be helpful to talk with parents of slightly older children who have been through the process and can offer reassurance based on experience. At the same time, try to hide your concerns from your children; be careful not to inadvertently communicate your uneasiness either in words, by telling children over and over again how much you are going to miss them, or through body language, by lingering too long over good-byes. If children sense their parents are anxious about a new experience such as going to school, they may also become anxious and carry this anxiety with them.

Many parents do not worry about the short separation from their children that school brings. If you are one of these parents, you should realize that this, too, is a very natural reaction and not feel guilty. Many devoted parents see their children's time in early childhood school as a brief respite from the constant emotional and physical demands of child raising. They see it as an opportunity to begin to get their own careers back on track, a time to think about going back to graduate school, to finish a dissertation or the novel that was started before the baby was born—or even to read the newspaper before the news is two weeks old. One mother told me that when her fourth child started school, a friend caught her skipping down the road.

•• Compatibility Between Parents and School

Perhaps the most important factor of all in the successful adjustment of children to an early childhood school is the children's intuitive sense of a fundamental compatibility between their parents and their school, a sense of shared values and goals, and the knowledge that both parents and school are working together for the children's best interests. As one early childhood educator said, "If adults don't trust the program, the child won't trust it and be able to make friends and take advantage of all that is going on."

•• Conclusion

Most children are ready for early childhood school at three. Some are ready before three. They have the ability to cope successfully with the social, emotional, and intellectual challenges of being part of a group. They can enjoy interacting with other children and adults and with a variety of interesting materials in a new environment outside their home. They are ready for a school where the teachers are trained in early childhood education, where the activities are individualized enough to meet their needs in a stimulating but noncompetitive environment, and where the curriculum is based on the development of the whole child. Most children are ready for early childhood school because their parents have loved them and helped to make their lives comfortable, happy, and secure. As a result, they have the confidence and trust to relish the challenge of new experiences.

Some children will go to early childhood school whose parents have not been able to give them this sense of confidence and security. And some of these children will find the love and trust and confidence at school that other children have found at home. Children will go to early childhood school for a variety of social and economic reasons that have little to do with their competencies or the developmental milestones they have passed. If the school is sufficiently flexible, and the teachers and parents are caring and patient, these children, too, will adjust in time.

The age at which your child should begin an early childhood school is a question that cannot be answered by either parents or educators alone. The answer will not come from standardized tests, questionnaires, or formal studies. It will come from a knowledge of the nature of available early childhood schools and of the needs and nature of your individual child. Going to early childhood school won't make your child a future valedictorian or a Westinghouse finalist. It doesn't guarantee an Ivy League education or the presidency of IBM. But it may give your child a taste for the excitement of learning and the joy of discovery.

Early childhood school should be process-oriented, not product-oriented. And the process is childhood. Our children can be taught many skills: they can learn to count and to recite the alphabet; they can be taught to identify shapes and colors and to read and write their names. But their childhood must not be hurried in the process. As parents and as educators, we need to remember that our children have many years to write their names and to study calculus, but very few to build castles out of blocks or to see dragons in the clouds.

•• •• •• ••

PART II

Your Child in Elementary School

•• •• •• •• •• •• •• •• •• •• ••

•• •• •• ••
S E V E N
•• •• •• •• •• •• •• •• •• •• •• ••

Starting Your Child in Elementary School

A feeling of family . . . that's the concept. Family. The school must embrace, encourage, believe in and support the child the way a loving family does, a family to be sure with high standards. And as one family is different from another, each school should be allowed its differences.

RONALD BAZARINI, *BOYS: A SCHOOLMASTER'S JOURNAL*

Elementary school, the next step on the educational ladder, plays "a key role in the developmental transitional rites of passage from home to the outside world,"[1] according to educational expert Allan Shedlin, executive director of the Elementary School Center, a nonprofit national study and resource center. For some children elementary school is their first introduction to the world outside of home and family. For all children, it is an important milestone that confers on them both status and responsibility. Children spend more of their lives in elementary school than in any other educational setting—up to twice as long as high school, college, or graduate school. It follows then that elementary school may have the greatest impact on their lives. Even as adults, many of us still have the friends we made in elementary school and remember our teachers—more vividly than we remember our college professors. It is in these school years that our children can be turned on both to a specific subject and also, with the right teacher and the right curriculum, to the excitement of learning. They can also be turned off by the wrong teacher and the wrong curriculum.

Elementary school used to start with first grade and end at either sixth or eighth grade. Today most schools begin with

•• •• •• ••

either a full- or half-day kindergarten, but the highest grade varies from school to school. Some schools stop after fourth or fifth grade, and the older students go on to intermediate, middle, or junior high schools. Elementary schools may be separate schools located in their own building and presided over by their own principal or head of school, or they may be a division in an ongoing or comprehensive twelve- or thirteen-year school. Elementary schools are sometimes called grammar schools, or grade schools, and if they happen to be part of an ongoing school, they may be referred to as lower schools. There are approximately 61,500 public and 24,400 private elementary schools. About 12.4 percent of elementary school children attend private schools. More than 55.4 percent of the private school children are enrolled in Catholic schools, about 28.7 percent go to religious schools of other denominations, and approximately 15.4 percent attend nonsectarian private schools.[2]

•• Parental Choice

For many years parents had little choice about where their children went to elementary school. Children were expected to attend the local elementary school in their district and, with the exception of the relatively few children who went to religious or private school, most of them did just that—and many still do. However, over the last thirty years the tradition of the neighborhood public school has been breaking down in some parts of the country, as parents have become concerned about the ability of their local schools to deal successfully with the societal changes and challenges we discussed in chapter 1. *A Nation at Risk*, published in 1983 by the National Commission on Excellence in Education, states: "The educational foundations of our society are presently being eroded by a rising tide of mediocrity that threatens our very future as a nation. . . ."[3] Parents worry about a variety of educational issues confronting our schools today from the consolidation of school districts to lagging test scores. They are troubled also about the failure of many schools to teach the basics, and they wonder about the effects of teacher strikes, school board battles, and tax cuts on their children's education. Beginning in the 1960s, some districts founded alternative schools to provide options to the traditional elementary school. These new schools were sometimes called free schools. Some literally had no walls, and students gathered in learning centers rather than classrooms. Other districts created magnet academies that had special teaching styles or stressed certain subjects such as science, mathematics, or music and art.

By 1986, 68 percent of American parents favored increased parental choice concerning their children's education. Former secretary of education Lauro F. Cavazos called parental choice "the cornerstone to restructuring elementary and secondary education."[4] Ten states (at this writing) and many local school districts allow parents to decide which school their children will attend. Model programs exist in District 4 in East Harlem, New York City, and in Cambridge, Massachusetts. Children have been able to attend any of the fifteen elementary schools in District 4 since 1974. In Cambridge a system of controlled choice has been in effect for the past eleven years. Parents are counseled by parent volunteers at a school information center before designating their first three choices. The district then assigns students to schools, taking into account both the parents' choices and the district's commitment to ensuring a representational racial mix. Educators in both cities have found that involving parents in choosing a school has led to a variety of positive changes, ranging from more parental involvement in children's schools to higher test scores for the children. In District 4 the percentage of children in grades three through nine reading at or above grade level went from 16.4 percent in 1973 to 65.4 percent in 1987. In 1973 the district ranked thirty-second out of thirty-two districts in citywide reading tests; in 1989–90 it ranked nineteenth out of thirty-two districts. Educators in both districts also report that they are losing fewer students to private and parochial schools.

Other school districts and states are experimenting with a variety of programs. Colorado permits choice within a home district; Washington has open enrollment based on educators' approval. In Minnesota a child may attend any school in the state if there is space and the transfer doesn't lead to increased segregation. Iowa, Nebraska, Arkansas, Idaho, Utah, and Ohio have similar open-enrollment plans. Wisconsin has been experimenting with vouchers for low-income students to enable them to attend nonsectarian private, as well as public, schools and Oregon is considering a similar plan. This policy, however, is currently facing court challenges in Wisconsin. Some choice plans include free transportation for all students; others provide it only for families with incomes below the poverty level.

••SUPPORT••

Proponents believe that choice will lead to the general improvement of all schools, because when parents have the power to choose, schools in turn are compelled to be more responsive to the needs of their students in order to maintain enrollment. Many other communities have experienced positive results similar to those noted in District 4 and Cambridge.[5]

So far, though, in most communities only a small number of students have actually elected to leave their neighborhood schools; in Iowa less than one-third of 1 percent, in Nebraska less than one-fifth of 1 percent, and in Minnesota less than one-half of 1 percent elected to transfer out of their home district.[6] Educators point out, however, that the goal of any program permitting choice is not to persuade all students to leave their neighborhood schools. In fact, it is not even necessary that large numbers of students actually transfer to schools outside their districts for choice to be effective. The very possibility of choice changes the parents' role from passive observers to active participants in their children's education. Whether parents elect to stay with the neighborhood school or move to a new school, they are making a commitment to that school and to their children's success. This kind of parental involvement and commitment helps children to have a successful educational experience in any school.

••OPPOSITION••

Choice has opponents as well as advocates. Some educators and political leaders argue that choice will result in inequality and elitism and will polarize schools by reinforcing both their weaknesses and their strengths. These educators believe choice will increase the tendency to divert money and other important resources away from the very schools most in need of them. They also fear choice will lure away the most able students, thereby creating a new kind of discrimination based on academic success and social class. Some cite St. Louis as an example of what can happen to inner-city neighborhood schools. In the St. Louis plan, minority students from inner-city schools are given the opportunity to attend elementary school in sixteen largely white suburban districts. The inner-city district has itself established a variety of magnet schools intended to draw nonminority students into the city from the suburbs. Achievement scores have risen for the black students who transferred to the suburban schools; however, some educators and parents have expressed concern that the remaining inner-city neighborhood schools have lost funding and many quality teachers to the magnet academies.

Opponents to choice also fear discrimination against poor families and recent immigrants, who may not be well informed about their options and thus unable to take advantage of them. And some parents have voiced concern that when children transfer out of a local district, their parents lose a degree of control over their children's education because they do not elect the school board that helps determine educational policy in the new district.

Clearly, choice is not a one-sided issue.

Advocates of choice respond to criticisms by noting that no one school or educational program is right for every child. Moreover, wealthy parents have always been able to choose which schools their children attend by either moving to a neighborhood with more effective schools or sending their children to private school. Choice gives middle- and low-income families similar options about where their children will go to school. Both advocates and opponents have compelling arguments to support their position.

Joe Nathan, at the University of Minnesota's Humphrey Institute of Public Affairs, concludes after summarizing the research on choice that successful choice plans have the following elements in common: they include teachers in planning and implementation, they have effective outreach programs for parents, they counsel parents about available options, they have admissions procedures that encourage a mix of students of different abilities and backgrounds.[7] For choice to work, it is, of course, essential that parents understand their options. But they also need to know what makes a school effective and how to find one for their children. Choice is not a panacea for all the problems schools face today. But it does empower parents to have a voice in their children's education. Whether you live in an area that permits choice in public education, whether you are comparing public and private schools, or whether you are scrutinizing your district's one school, ultimately, you are the one who must demand quality. You must know what is expected of your children by your schools. And you must help set the tone and the attitude your children have toward the value of education.[8]

••EFFECTIVE SCHOOLS••

"How will I find a good school? How will I know a good school if I see one?" These are questions parents frequently ask me. And as I listen I realize that it has not always been easy for parents to find answers. As parents of young children today, it is easy to feel a sense of frustration and helplessness on reading or hearing yet another account of the deplorable state of American education or a review of the many ways our schools are failing to meet the needs of our children. But, as we all know, bad news makes better copy than good news. And the bad news is only part of the story. It is unfortunately true that there are schools that do reflect ineffective leadership, incompetent teachers, uninterested, absentee students, apathetic parents, dilapidated buildings, and a mindless, repetitive curriculum. But it is equally true that there are good schools with strong leadership, dedicated teachers, well-kept buildings, a challenging curriculum, involved parents, and, last but not least, students who are filled with curiosity and are eager to learn. And these schools are flourishing.

••Ten Common Denominators of Effective Schools

Good schools cannot be typecast; they are large and small, in big cities and in rural areas, in areas of affluence and in poor communities. Some have open classrooms and multiaged class groups; others have self-contained classrooms and a more traditional format. However, despite all the apparent diversity, evaluators have identified ten common denominators of effective schools: (1) effective leadership, (2) a professional and committed staff, (3) quality teaching, (4) ongoing staff development, (5) a strong curriculum, (6) a sense of shared goals and expectations, (7) a positive school atmosphere, (8) an ongoing process of self-evaluation, (9) good communication both within the school and with parents, (10) and the support and involvement of both parents and community.[9] In many good schools, children are also encouraged to take responsibility for their learning and to share in some of the decision making. I have found these or similar common denominators in effective schools no matter how diverse they may seem at first.

1. Leadership:

Effective principals or school heads are strong leaders with high but realistic expectations for their students and staff. Effective principals are not tucked away in administrative offices devoting their days to paperwork. They are not anonymous voices on an intercom. They are highly visible around the school. Strong principals know what's going on in their schools: they visit classrooms and talk to parents and teachers; they know their students by name and congratulate them on their accomplishments. Effective principals have authority but they are not authoritarian. They know when to step back and let talented teachers teach without a lot of bureaucratic interference. They have the confidence to empower their teachers and to give them a role in decision making.

2. Staff:

In an effective school there is the sense that everyone cares about the school and that they are working together as a team. The janitor cares that the halls are clean and the teachers care that the children learn. The teachers are dedicated as well as qualified. They are excited about teaching and they want to help children share in the excitement of learning. No matter how effective they are, good teachers are always looking for ways to improve. Good teachers see themselves as leaders and innovators. They feel empowered and supported.

3. Instruction:

There may be many different types of instruction in an effective school. Good instruction is lively and creative, yet thoughtful and carefully attuned to the interests and abilities of the students. It is flexible and individualized enough to challenge gifted students without frustrating those who learn at a slower pace.

4. Staff development:

Good teachers are continually looking for new and more effective ways to teach. They go to workshops and take courses and visit other teachers' classes. They also help train new teachers and run in-house workshops. One teacher who was nearing retirement told me excitedly about the previous summer vacation she had spent studying children's literature on a grant at Oxford so she could share new ideas with her students.

5. Curriculum:

A good curriculum is well planned and diverse. It is also both challenging and age-appropriate. It is not confined by school walls but knows how to take advantage of community resources. Children learn not only basic skills but also how to solve problems, do research, and test hypotheses. They learn how to ask questions and where to find answers. Workbooks are kept to a minimum and children spend their time reading literature instead of answering multiple-choice questions. A good curriculum is never static but always flexible enough to be open to the changing needs of students and the interests and talents of teachers.

6. Goals and expectations:

In effective schools goals and expectations are well-defined and shared by everyone involved in the school. Academic excellence is clearly valued and students are intended to work hard. Students know that they are expected to succeed and that their school believes they will. Standards are high but realistic, and individual differences in learning rate and style are understood and appreciated. Rules are clear and consistently enforced. And students know that courtesy and respect are expected in interpersonal relationships.

7. School atmosphere:

When you walk into an effective classroom or school, you can almost feel it in the air. There is a sense of excitement and joy. The children are active and involved with what is going on in the classroom. They are not daydreaming, passing notes to each other, reading comic books under their desks, or acting out. The teachers are not apathetically filling out forms and checking answers in an answer book; they seem animated and interested, and responsive to the children's needs. There is the sense that both the students and their teachers are engaged in important work. Sally Reed, the editor of a 1986 issue of *Instructor* magazine on "Good Schools," had this to say about the atmosphere she found in effective schools: "In a good school, kids' successes are very visible—evident in their art, their writing, their behavior, their esprit de corps."[10]

8. Self-evaluation:
Good schools do not rest on their laurels. They continually question both what they are doing and how they are doing it. They know where their students are academically and are aware of their individual strengths and weaknesses. Good schools are open to new ideas and always searching for ways to do things more effectively.

9. Communication:
Good schools foster communication. Teachers share ideas and problems informally over coffee as well as formally in faculty meetings. Some schools I know have monthly lower school potluck dinner meetings at different teachers' homes. After dinner the teachers sit around talking about goals, sharing ideas, and brainstorming. In effective schools teachers are also available to students and parents on a regular basis and encourage them to share information and concerns.

10. Parent and community involvement:
Good schools recognize that parents are partners, not adversaries. Administrators and teachers seek to involve parents in meaningful ways in their children's education. Parents, in turn, willingly volunteer their time and talents in the library, in the classroom, and at book fairs and benefits. Good schools are also in tune with their communities. They use community resources to enrich their students' educational experiences, and many involve students in the older elementary grades in community service projects.

Effective schools are not all cut from the same cloth. As I have said before, they may look and sound very different. Some are public, others are private or religious. Some are large, others are small. They can be traditional or nontraditional, coed or single sex. Their very difference is one of the things that makes them unique. But each has a clear sense of mission and an understanding of how to fulfill that mission. And all share to a greater or lesser degree the common denominators we have just examined. In the next chapters, we will examine some of the educational options you may want to consider. We will also discuss key factors in finding the right fit in a school for your child and suggest specific questions to ask when you visit.

E I G H T

Educational Options

Basic schooling must do three things. It must (1) give the young an introduction to the world of learning; (2) give them all the skills of learning; and (3) give them the incentives and the stimulation to continue learning without end after schooling is ended.

MORTIMER J. ADLER, *PAIDEIA PROBLEMS AND POSSIBILITIES*

Henry James, Sr., the nineteenth-century philosopher, traveled across Europe with his family in search of the perfect school for his five talented children. Most of our own parents had neither the time, the money, nor the inclination to follow this approach. Many of us merely walked down the street to the neighborhood public school. If we came from a family with strong religious traditions, we might have gone to a religious school. If our parents went to private school, they might have sent us to their old school or, if they lived in a different part of the country, to the one that seemed most like it (or unlike it) in atmosphere and philosophy. Our parents assumed that we were getting the kind of education we would need for the future. Starting school today is neither so simple in one sense nor so restricted in another. There is a new consumer awareness among parents, many of whom try to define what they want in a school and then "shop around," looking at different kinds of schools and comparing them in terms of their own goals.

Almost all of us today have some degree of choice about the schools we entrust with our children's education. We make choices by the decisions we choose to make and by those we choose not to make. Regardless of whether or not we elect to

•• •• •• ••

send our children to the neighborhood school, we are making a choice about their education, and that choice should be an informed one. Although you personally may not have all the options discussed in this chapter when you plan your child's education, it is important for you to understand the options you do have and to consider them carefully in terms of both your own child's personality and talents and your needs as a family.

•• Public School

Approximately 90 percent of American children go to public elementary schools. Many families feel it is part of their duty as citizens to keep their children in public school and support the system. Public schools are financed by local, state, and federal taxes. Every state has a state department of education under the direction of a chief state school officer. Local school districts handle the day-to-day operation of public schools, but the ultimate authority rests with the states. There are about 15,400 public-school districts in the United States. They range greatly in size: some districts encompass an entire city, while others serve only a small town. Each school district has either a board of education or a school board that is responsible for general educational policy: finances, hiring teachers, approving curriculum decisions, and overseeing the maintenance of buildings and grounds. School board members may be elected by the people who live in the district or appointed by the local government. Most districts also have a superintendent who is appointed by the board to see that its policies are carried out. The superintendent and the school board are responsible for hiring principals to direct the day-to-day operations of each individual school.

All public schools have provisions for children with special needs. Federal law mandates that all children be given a free public education appropriate to their educational needs. The Education of All Handicapped Children Act of 1975 and the Rehabilitation Act of 1973, Section 504, ensure that each child covered under these acts receives an individualized education program (IEP). The child must be reevaluated and a new IEP issued every three years. Parents must be involved in all decision making.

There are no equivalent federal laws mandating services for gifted children, though the government does provide federal funds, and approximately half the states require schools to serve gifted children. Some districts have special classes for gifted children, some have pull-out programs in which children are taken out of regular classes for enrichment activities and special instruction, and some try to individualize their curriculum sufficiently to challenge gifted children within a regular classroom.

Public schools vary from district to district. In addition to the traditional neighborhood school, your public-school system may include magnet schools, specialty schools, alternative schools, and open schools. These schools, which operate within the public-school system, may focus on particular subjects such as mathematics, science, foreign languages, or the arts, or they may offer nontraditional teaching styles. Some public schools have special programs to bring writers and artists into the school to work directly with students. Extracurricular activities vary greatly from school to school, and many are funded by local PTAs. Some schools have instrumental instruction, choral groups, ballet, art, drama, gymnastics, swimming, tennis, and a variety of athletic teams, while others offer only the minimum state requirements.

Class size and student/teacher ratios also vary depending on state and local funding and the priorities of local school boards. Differences are apparent in neighborhood districts in the same state; in New Jersey, for example, one district in an affluent area reports a student/teacher ratio of eighteen to one while another in a disadvantaged area has a ratio of twenty-seven to one. These disparities can make a significant difference in terms of time and attention for individual children. See chapter 9 for more information on class size and local funding.

Another major difference between schools may be student attendance rates. Attendance rates give a good indication of both student interest in learning and also the value the parents in your community place on education.

Achievement test scores also reflect school differences. However, the correlation is usually not as direct as parents may assume. Consistently low test scores are cause for concern, but high test scores may mean that teachers are spending valuable class time drilling students on test taking or structuring their curriculum around test questions. There is more to getting a good education than taking tests, and it is unwise to make school decisions solely on the basis of test scores. The tests themselves have been criticized for their reliance on multiple-choice questions and their relative inability to assess either the depth of student knowledge or creative thinking and problem solving. Test scores for local districts are published annually in community papers, and in 1992, the National Assessment of Educational Progress (NAEP) plans to make public a report on a comparison of state-by-state student achievement.

Many school districts are currently working to make public schools more responsive to community needs and to help them function more effectively. Proposals have been made to remove much of the decision making from government agencies and give it instead directly to principals, teachers, and parents. In Chicago parents have a majority vote on local school councils. These councils develop educational goals, review textbooks, and approve local school budgets. They have the authority to fire principals who do not meet the specific goals outlined in their contracts. The Chicago reforms, however, are currently facing challenges in court. Meanwhile, parents are also becoming active in decision making in Seattle where they may serve on school-based management teams. Similar reforms are under consideration in Texas, Ohio, and Kentucky as parents tackle school issues from discipline and safety to testing and ability tracking.

While parental involvement in decision making is not guaranteed to cure all the problems schools face, it is a good place for you as a parent to begin. Parents who exercise judicious choice and stay closely involved in their children's schools can often find ways not only to give their children a quality education but also to give them many of the advantages of a private/independent school education within the public school system.

Your neighborhood public school does more than educate children. It may also serve as the locus of the neighborhood—bringing parents and children together with other members of the community. The school may lend its gymnasium or auditorium to community groups for meetings and special events or its playing fields (if it is a suburban or country school) to local sports teams. The school is also where everyone goes to vote. The community, in turn, provides resources for the school: the police officer who comes to discuss safety, the senior citizens who volunteer in the classrooms, the local businesses that invite student groups to visit, and the school board members who approve the budget.

More than 70 percent of the entering freshmen at Ivy League colleges come from public school. The key to a good education in either a public or nonpublic school is a good principal, qualified, dedicated teachers, an active parents' association, and the other common denominators of effective schools discussed in chapter 7.

•• Nonpublic Schools

••RELIGIOUS OR PAROCHIAL SCHOOL••

There are many religious or parochial schools in the United States. Some are affiliated with a specific church or synagogue. Others, such as Roman Catholic and Anglican-order schools, as well as some of the Jewish schools, are fiscally independent and thus are considered independent schools.

The largest group of religious schools in this country is run by the Roman Catholic church. In the Catholic parochial school system, the bishop appoints a superintendent to oversee parish schools, which are financed by a combination of parish subsidies, student tuition, and school fund-raising. Classes are taught by both religious and lay teachers. In the last twenty years, the proportion of religious versus lay teachers has shifted dramatically. In many schools religious teachers now make up less than 50 percent and in some schools less than 20 percent of the faculty. Approximately 2.5 million children, or about 5.6 percent of the school-age population, attend Catholic elementary and secondary schools. Enrollment has declined in recent years, and many elementary schools have closed or merged with schools in neighboring parishes. However, enrollment in Catholic early childhood schools has doubled in the past five years. A proposal is currently under consideration to establish a national Catholic parents organization to include Catholic schools in public policy debates on school choice. Discussions are underway concerning plans to start financial endowments to partially fund individual schools.

There are also Episcopal, Lutheran, Presbyterian, Baptist, and Seventh-Day Adventist schools. The Religious Society of Friends, also known as Quakers, runs schools around the country. Quaker schools stress the importance of educating the whole child, respect for individual differences, social commitment, and volunteer service. Many parents, regardless of their religious affiliation, find the Quaker educational philosophy very appealing.

Some synagogues run Jewish day schools. Orthodox day schools are known as *yeshivoth*. In an orthodox Jewish day school children often have a ten- or eleven-hour school day, with Judaic studies until three o'clock in the afternoon, and general studies afterwards. Jeffrey S. Gurock, professor of Jewish history at Yeshiva University, notes that day schools have traditionally reflected the belief that "a major part of being Orthodox was studied seclusion from the ways of America."[1] Today, however, many schools successfully combine religious education with academic excellence in secular subjects.

A number of states have seen a recent increase in fundamentalist and evangelical Christian church schools. Unlike the more established religious schools, some of these schools are not regulated by state or national organizations, and a few may fail to meet minimum educational standards. However, the majority belong to either the American Association of Christian Schools or the Association of Christian Schools International and comply on a voluntary basis with local and state standards. The private school office of the Department of Education estimates that noncomplying schools account for less than 10 percent of enrollment.[2]

Parents choose to send their children to religious schools for a variety of reasons. A number of families have strong religious beliefs and traditions, which they hope to reinforce by sending their children to religious schools. Studies have indicated that attending a religious school can make a difference in adult beliefs but generally only among those children who also come from a strongly religious family. Some families consider religious schools because they like both the smaller classes often found in these schools and the emphasis on educating the whole child. Other parents feel religious schools are more likely to be interested in children's total development, not just their academic progress. Some of the personal feelings and experiences of parents are backed up by studies such as the one conducted by the National Assessment of Educational Progress in Princeton, New Jersey, showing that students in Catholic schools are less likely to drop out of high school than students in public school, and that they also tend to score better on standardized tests in reading and mathematics.[3]

Families who are not affiliated with a particular religion may choose to send their children to religious schools for a variety of reasons. Some parents tell me they like the sense of discipline and the emphasis on morals and values; others say they feel that a particular religious school offers a better education than local public or nonsectarian private schools. One family with whom I talked was unexpectedly transferred to a small city in Indiana and needed a school for their young daughter. The father had gone to a private school, the mother to Catholic schools, but after some research they discovered that the most intellectually exciting school in their neighborhood was the Torah school. They enrolled their daughter, and she developed a passion for learning that delighted her parents. Some families without a strong religious identification may choose a religious school for financial reasons. Diocesan and order-related religious schools are often able to charge lower tuitions than nonsectarian schools because they receive support from a parent religious group and are not solely dependent on tuition income.

Not all families with strong religious beliefs send their children to religious schools. Some parents may decide instead to send their children to public or nonsectarian private/independent schools and give them their religious instruction after school. A parent who had made this decision explained to me that she felt that "a child's religious identity may sharpen more in an atmosphere where they have to compare their beliefs to other people's instead of being part of a religious community."

The fact that a school is located in a church or a synagogue does not necessarily mean it has a strong religious emphasis or that administrative decisions are influenced by the religious organization. Schools that have a sectarian affiliation are apt to stress the religious practices of that denomination. Other schools may be nonsectarian and have an ecumenical approach. Such schools often welcome a diverse population from many different religious backgrounds. Some private/independent schools, on the other hand, while not technically religious schools in that they are fiscally independent, may nevertheless have a religious affiliation, and you may discover that chapel attendance or the memorization of Bible verses is part of the program. As one parent said to me, "I'm Jewish, my wife is Catholic. We were delighted to find a [private/independent] school where there was great respect for different religious traditions. It was not technically a religious school and yet religion wasn't banished from the environment. There was a spiritual feeling, yet it wasn't denominational."

••PRIVATE SCHOOL/INDEPENDENT SCHOOL••

A *private school* is generally defined as "any non-public educational, pre-collegiate institution operating in accordance with the laws of the state in which it is located. Such schools may be denominational or nonsectarian, privately owned or not-for-profit, discriminatory or nondiscriminatory."[4] Some private schools are also independent schools. An *independent school,* as defined by NAIS, is a nonpublic school that fulfills the following criteria:

1. It is fiscally independent of tax or church funding.
2. It is governed by a self-perpetuating board of trustees, directors, or advisers.
3. It has a stated policy of nondiscrimination in admission and employment.
4. It is recognized by the Internal Revenue Service as a not-for-profit organization.
5. It is approved by a recognized evaluative process, such as the one provided by the six regional accrediting bodies and certain independent school associations.[5]

There are approximately 24,400 private schools in the United States. Some of these private schools are also independent schools. Many of the independent schools are members of the National Association of Independent Schools (NAIS), a nonprofit, tax-exempt voluntary membership organization that serves as an advocate for independent precollegiate education. Parents often mistakenly assume that private and independent schools are the same and tend to use the terms interchangeably. However, while all independent schools are private in the sense that they are not publicly controlled or financed, not all private schools are independent. A private school, in contrast to an independent school, may be set up by an individual or a group of individuals as a for-profit enterprise.

This distinction between private school and independent school is important because in some parts of the country private schools are largely unregulated. Anyone may be permitted to set up a private school regardless of his or her professional qualifications or the merits of the proposed curriculum. As of 1984, Idaho, Kansas, Michigan, North Carolina, South Dakota, and Tennessee had mandatory accreditation and eleven additional states had voluntary accreditation. Today a minimum of thirty states have at least one private school organization that accredits member schools. Some states have eight or ten such organizations. However, not all these organizations are recognized by state education boards. Standards vary from state to state and so does terminology—some states use the term "approval" and some use the term "accreditation." Dr. Charles J. O'Malley, former executive assistant to the secretary for private education, U.S. Department of Education in Washington, reports, "Our office has worked with other private and public school associations encouraging state and private school leaders to develop a process wherein private school associations accredit their member schools, working in concert with state and regional agencies. Florida, Virginia and Texas have already done so and other states are currently considering moving in this direction."

NAIS member schools have all been accredited by a regional association authorized by the state regulatory educational authority to grand accreditation. To be accredited, schools must go through a formal self-evaluation, which may take six months or more, and an examination by a committee of educators, who review the self-evaluation, observe classes, and interview administrators, faculty, parents, trustees, and students. The committee prepares a report for the Commission on Accreditation with its recommendation for or against accreditation. The report also gives suggestions on ways a school can improve its effectiveness. If accreditation is granted, a shorter follow-up examination occurs five years later and a complete reexamination after ten years. If a school ceases to live up to the required standards, it loses its accreditation.

Most schools list their accreditation in their catalogs or other literature. If a school does not mention accreditation or approval, ask the admissions director or school head. You can also write to NAIS for a list of accredited schools in your area. If a private school has not been accredited or approved by a recognized state or regional organization, you must check it out very carefully. First examine the credentials of the teachers—these are often listed in the literature. If they are not, ask about them. Ask to see a copy of the curriculum and call the local board of education to make sure that the curriculum covers the material mandated by your state. You should also call your local board of health to be sure that the school has been licensed by the state, has insurance, and is in compliance with basic health and safety rules.

Because private/independent schools are not under direct state control, administrators frequently have more freedom in choosing faculty, making curriculum decisions, and selecting textbooks. Curricula are often more flexible than in public schools, and teachers may have more freedom to shape curricula to student interests and needs. There are no district-mandated textbooks, and teachers may play an active role in choosing the books they use in class. It is also easier to dismiss ineffective teachers because most private/independent school teachers do not belong to a union and do not have tenure, as do public school teachers. This is also true for ineffective principals or school heads. In a private/independent school, if the head is not performing satisfactorily, he or she may be dismissed by the board of trustees and a new head installed. Ineffective teachers can be dismissed directly by the head of the school.

Classes are often, though not always, smaller in private/independent schools. The student/teacher ratio averages around ten to one in the elementary grades. This does not necessarily mean that your child will be in a class with only ten other children; more likely there will be two or more teachers working with a class of between sixteen and twenty-four children. Smaller classes and/or more teachers often translate into more individualized attention for all children. Like good public schools, good private/independent schools offer an assortment of extracurricular activities such as music, art, drama, dance, and a variety of individual and team sports.

The ways in which parents perceive private/independent schools and their impact on children's education varies widely in different parts of the country. In some communities parents vie to get their children into private/independent schools; in other communities parents don't consider them. One parent from the Midwest explained, when I asked her about private/independent school options, "Here the children in the private schools are the ones with the problems, the ones who for some reason weren't able to make it in public school."

Private/independent schools are not training grounds for an elite American aristocracy. While the degree of diversity varies from school to school, most students come from a wide variety of social, economic, and ethnic backgrounds. And the majority of private/independent school parents were themselves educated in the public-school system, as were many of the teachers and administrators. In fact, the new president of NAIS, Peter D. Relic, was formerly superintendent of the Charlotte-Mecklenburg, North Carolina, public schools. Some independent schools actually had their beginnings as alternative public schools. Other private/independent schools have entered into partnerships with neighboring public schools to share resources and ideas.

Unlike those private schools that serve the interests of a specific religious or ethnic group, private/independent schools do not discriminate on the basis of race, color, national, or ethnic origin. Many actively seek diversity and may well be more diverse than some public schools. In some cities there are organizations that recruit students of diverse ethnic backgrounds into the private/independent school system. The oldest national recruiting organization is ABC (A Better Chance), founded in 1963 and located in Boston. ABC recruits eighth, ninth, and a few seventh graders for private/independent boarding and day schools. ABC has regional offices in New York City and Oakland, California, and part-time recruiting staffs in Atlanta, Detroit, Los Angeles, and Cincinnati. Organizations that concentrate on younger children include the Independent School Alliance for Minority Affairs in Los Angeles, Early Steps in New York City (which recruits for kindergarten and first grade), and Prep for Prep, also in New York, which tries to identify intellectually gifted and motivated fifth and sixth graders (see Appendix). Prep for Prep has been instrumental in the establishment of similar programs such as Buffalo Prep in Buffalo, New York, and The Stepping Stone Foundation in Boston. NAIS maintains a toll-free minority hotline for parents and grandparents who want guidance on private/independent school options (see Appendix).

·· Large School? Medium-sized School? Small School?

Schools can range in size from less than a hundred students to more than a thousand. Many elementary schools have between three hundred and six hundred students. Large schools (one thousand or more students) have a number of different classes at each grade level. Parents sometimes have a say about the class where their child will be placed and hence which teacher he or she will have. Large schools tend to have large facilities and more extensive resources. They are more apt to have state-of-the-art science labs and computer rooms. In the upper grades, large schools may offer more electives and a wider variety of sports and other extracurricular activities. Because of their size, they usually draw on a wider population group and hence may be more diverse ethnically, socially, and economically. A confident, outgoing child may well thrive in a large school. He or she may relish the sense of choice and stimulation, and the opportunity to interact with a larger and more diverse group of children. On the other hand, a child who needs a lot of discipline and structure may have trouble in a large classroom. A quiet, shy child can feel lost in a large school. The individual attention and nurturing environment of a small school (under three hundred students) may be just what a shy child needs to foster specific talents and give that child a sense of self.

Small schools may have only one teacher per grade. Sometimes classes are smaller and there may be more opportunities for individualized attention. This is more apt to be the case with small private/independent or religious schools than with public schools. On the other hand, small private schools generally offer fewer elective courses, a narrower selection of extracurricular activities and sports, and less in the way of special resources such as music teachers, coaches, librarians, learning specialists, and school psychologists. In public schools these services are usually provided by a district staff to all schools in the district, regardless of size.

For some children a medium-size school (three hundred to one thousand students) that combines some of the options of a large school and some of the warmth of a small school may be just the answer. There is no right or wrong, no good or bad in terms of school size. There is merely the right fit for you and your child.

•• Elementary School or Ongoing School?

Elementary schools include just the elementary grades. Children leave elementary school and go on to an intermediate school, a junior high, or high school depending on whether the elementary school ends after fourth, sixth, or eighth grade. An ongoing or comprehensive school continues through high school. Many of the same arguments that we discussed in relation to early childhood school versus ongoing school apply to the decision between elementary school and ongoing school. (See chapter 4.)

One additional factor you may want to research is the ease with which children are able to move between public and nonpublic schools at different grade levels in your school system. In some communities, if you decide to send your child to a public elementary school for the first six years, but want to send him or her to a private/independent school at the junior high school level, there may not be any spaces unless the school in question plans to expand enrollment at this grade level. This is not a problem, however, if the schools begin in junior high.

•• Traditional or Nontraditional?

Traditional education tends to stress basic skills. The curriculum is usually clearly defined with quite specific academic objectives. The focus is likely to be on reading, writing, arithmetic, spelling, geography, history, and grammar. Organizational skills, study habits, and homework also are stressed. The day has a predictable pattern of lessons and activities. Children are usually expected to study material and read books that have historically been considered important parts of Western culture. Recently, however, many schools have started to incorporate multicultural education into their curricula. (See chapter 9.) Classrooms in traditional schools tend to be quieter, and children are more apt to sit at desks. There is often an emphasis on courtesy, politeness, and respect for teachers. Teachers tend to be addressed formally. Sometimes there is a school uniform or dress code.

Nontraditional education is often based on the educational theories of John Dewey and the tradition of progressive education (see chapter 2). Nontraditional schools usually appear freer and more informal. Classrooms seem busier, noisier, and often messier. Teachers are sometimes called by their first names and, within reason, children wear what they want to school. Classes may be ungraded and children of different ages grouped together in the same room. Some classrooms are organized around activity centers. Students tend to wander around the room working on individual projects or in groups with other students. Learning is more often done through direct contact with people, places, and things than through textbooks. Curricula may be quite flexible, with teachers planning around the interests and concerns of the children. Sometimes an interdisciplinary approach is used that combines various fields into one theme instead of dividing material into separate subjects.

As a general rule, children with good self-motivation and an internal sense of organization tend to do well in nontraditional classrooms, while children who need more structure and external sources of motivation are more apt to thrive in more traditional settings. However, it is important to keep in mind that the concepts of traditional and nontraditional education are not hard-and-fast. There are many points of crossover, even within the same school, and most good schools combine elements from both traditions. A school that calls itself traditional may in fact be more innovative than one that calls itself nontraditional.

Don't be misled, then, by labels. The same words may mean different things to different people. To some people "traditional" conjures up visions of regimented rows of formally dressed children saying "yes ma'am" and "no sir." To others it may mean appreciation for standards of excellence and a respect for the feelings of others. To some people "nontraditional" is synonymous with mayhem and illiteracy. To others it means the encouragement to develop as an individual and to pursue one's talents in a warm, supportive environment. Look behind the label. If the school calls itself traditional or nontraditional in the brochure, find out what it means by the term. And above all, go and look, then judge for yourself whether it seems right for your child.

•• Competitive or Noncompetitive?

At the early childhood level, virtually all educators agree, overt competition is counterproductive and may result in early burn-out or in a serious loss of self-esteem. For children in elementary school, intense, stressful competition is still not viewed positively. Individual children, however, react very differently to varying levels of competition, and there are no hard-and-fast rules. Research by Carol Gilligan, a professor of education at Harvard who initiated the Dodge Study of girls and young women at Emma Willard School, has indicated that girls tend to work better in an environment that focuses on cooperative learning, while boys prefer competitive activities. Nonetheless individual boys and girls vary greatly here. Highly competitive schools don't guarantee later academic success. A child can receive an excellent education in a noncompetitive environment. In fact, some of the most visibly successful adults went to rather low-key schools from which they came out feeling personally successful and good about themselves. Bear in mind that the kind of competition one child finds stimulating can seem over-whelming to another equally talented youngster. It is important that you understand your child and choose an environment in which your child will have more opportunity for success.

•• Coed School or Single-Sex School?

From the early childhood level up to kindergarten, virtually all schools are coeducational. Even schools that are single-sex later on tend to have coed early childhood programs. Most public elementary schools became coeducational in the late 1800s, but many religious schools and private/independent schools are single-sex. Educators are divided over the relative advantages and disadvantages of coed versus single-sex schools.

Educators who favor coeducation argue that schools should reflect the fact that males and females coexist in society. Children, they reason, need to learn to be comfortable working and playing with people of either sex, and the day-to-day interplay between boys and girls in the classroom helps children achieve this goal. While advocates acknowledge that sexual stereotypes can exist in a coed environment, they believe that if a school is aware of the potential for a problem, teacher intervention and school philosophy can diminish any negative impact. When you visit coed schools, check to be sure that sexual stereotypes are not being reinforced inadvertently in the classroom, with all the boys clustered around the computers and the girls in the book corner. Also make sure there is a good balance of boys and girls. Children experience distress when they are in the distinct minority in a class. It is not a good idea to let your child be completely outnumbered by the other sex. Both sexes should also be represented among the teachers. Some research on incidents of sexism in classrooms has indicated that they are more apt to originate with teachers than with students.

Not all educators believe that a coed classroom is the best environment for elementary age children. They point out that boys and girls tend to separate naturally by kindergarten or first grade, and thus a coed school may not be a more natural environment and may actually reinforce sexual stereotypes—with the science room and computer clubs becoming the boys' territory while the literary magazine and the library area become the girls' turf. In a single-sex school, they argue, all avenues are open for both boys and girls without artificial sexual boundaries. In coed schools girls may defer to boys, letting them automatically be captain of the team or not challenging them as readily in class, thus diminishing their own leadership experience. Boys, on the other hand, may be restricted from developing their interests and talents by stereotypes of what is and isn't okay for them to do. One teacher, who has taught in both coed and single-sex schools, explained his position to me this way: "Boys are still not really supposed to show their softer characteristics, yet they have them. A boy can be his real self more easily with other boys. He can even cry at the end of a game if there aren't any girls around. In a world that needs to break down macho images, I'm not sure a coed school is the way to go."

A few parents, on the other hand, tell me that they find more emphasis on sports and the competition more intense in a single-sex school. This, they feel, can be a negative for a child who wants to participate in sports but lacks the athletic skills to make a team because he or she is competing against everyone in the grade.

Most of the research on single-sex and coed education has been conducted on the college or secondary school level, where researchers have found that "male students got more attention than female students and had more intellectual exchanges with teachers."[6] Catherine Krupnick, a researcher at Harvard, has found that when women participate in class discussions they are "interrupted far more frequently than men."[7] Ironically, studies have also indicated that teachers often believed they were paying more attention to the women in their classes when in fact video replays clearly showed they were favoring the men.[8] Reviewing these studies, Anne Chapman, academic dean at Western Reserve Academy in Ohio and cochair of the Council for Women in Independent Schools/Gender Committee, notes, "Teachers often expect boys to do more work independently, ask them higher-order questions, and criticize them more for misbehavior. . . . Girls are more often shown how to do something or have it done for them, and teachers' questions to girls are less frequent and less probing. . . . More pressure is put on boys but . . . more attention is also paid to them by teachers."[9] Valerie Lee, assistant professor of education at the University of Michigan, has found that these issues are particularly apparent in chemistry classes, where boys are more apt to dominate discussions and teachers in turn overtly pay more attention to boys.[10]

Does this research mean that given a choice you shouldn't consider a coeducational school for your child? Not necessarily. While I personally believe that many children, particularly girls, benefit from being in a single-sex school during the elementary years, I also realize that you cannot isolate a child from sexism, even in a single-sex school. But you can help your child not to be harmed by it. Be aware that your child can have some of the negative experiences in class that Chapman describes. You can defuse much of the negative impact of sexual stereotyping in a school through your own awareness and willingness to discuss the issues with your children, as well as by serving as a positive role model. Bear in mind too that the overall quality of an elementary school can be as important as its gender composition.

•• Bilingual School?

Bilingual education has been the subject of intense debate for a number of years—sometimes pitting those who advocate native language instruction against other groups in favor of a constitutional amendment making English the official language. Bilingual schools in this country date back to the 1840s. They began originally in New York and Cincinnati in response to the needs of recent immigrants. The new bilingual schools enabled children to study basic subjects partially in their native language and partially in English until they gained sufficient fluency in English. In 1968 the Bilingual Education Act assured federal aid for bilingual education. By 1974, in response to the needs of increasing numbers of Hispanic and Asian immigrants, the Supreme Court ruled that public schools should provide special programs for students with a limited background in English. The government currently budgets approximately $121 million in federal funds for bilingual education. Programs known as transitional bilingual education are available in about seventy different languages. Approximately 60 percent of the students currently participating in the programs are Spanish speaking.

Some educators believe that bilingual programs help non-English-speaking students to both retain their cultural heritage and attain an education; others feel they tend to further segregate minority students from mainstream American life and consign them to second-class citizenship. The U.S. Department of Education recently completed a study on the effects of three commonly used bilingual education programs on Spanish-speaking students in elementary school. The first program sought to immerse children in English, the second gradually shifted into English over a four-year period, and the third spent six years on the transition. Researchers found that all three programs were effective in educating Spanish-speaking students with limited backgrounds in English and that they were all helpful in enabling the students to keep pace with their English-speaking peers.[11]

Bilingual education outside of publicly mandated programs is often available only in large cities. Students are frequently the children of foreign diplomats or of families living in this country on temporary business assignments. Some English-speaking parents hoping to give their children the advantage of learning another language at an early age also seek out bilingual schools. M. Gerard Roubichou, the president of the Lycée Français in New York, argues the importance of bilingual education, saying, "Our school . . . must prepare the children to become citizens of the world, by motivating them to discover, early in life, that the divisions caused by language and culture are not natural.

When one knows that the world comprises different visions, one cannot but respect others."[12]

It is difficult for a child to become truly bilingual unless there is regular reinforcement of the second language at home. Parents who want their children to become bilingual and who don't already speak a second language will want to see that their children have frequent access to the language through newspapers, magazines, tapes, movies, and radio programs, and perhaps even consider studying the language themselves. Even if the parents happen to be bilingual or trilingual, not all children can handle learning two languages simultaneously. Teachers often find that young children who are bilingual experience language delays of six months or more. They may shift back and forth unintentionally between languages and have difficulty establishing a dominant language. Even children who successfully master two or more languages sometimes test lower on the verbal sections of standardized tests in the early years of elementary school than peers of equal ability. A study of bilingual children in Quebec found their language skills less developed at the age of three than nonbilingual children. However, by second grade this difference had disappeared.[13] Children who are experiencing difficulties in either expressive or receptive language skills may find their difficulties compounded by trying to master a second language. Time devoted to learning two languages in school may also mean that there is less time available for reading, writing, and math instruction. For able students the enrichment of a second language may more than make up for any time lost, but for children who are having difficulty in mastering the basics of reading or math, this is definitely a factor to consider. The choice of a bilingual school should not be made without carefully considering all the factors involved for you and your child. And though there are frequently trade-offs to be considered in the decision, in families where there are strong personal reasons for fluency in two or more languages, the trade-offs may well be worthwhile. (See Appendix for relevant organizations and resources).

•• Financial Considerations

The United States spent $24.7 billion of taxpayers' money on education in 1990, and appropriated $27.4 billion for spending in fiscal year 1991. Nonetheless, America spends less on elementary education than thirteen other industrial nations—Sweden, Austria, Switzerland, Norway, Belgium, Denmark, Japan, Canada, West Germany, France, the Netherlands, Great Britain, and Italy.[14]

Gone are the days when Socrates sat under a tree with the youth of Athens at his feet discussing philosophy without the benefit of libraries, computers, science labs, and audiovisuals. Learning itself has become more complex. We need teachers with the wisdom of Socrates and the technical skills of Leonardo da Vinci, but we also need modern equipment to give our children the education they need to understand our world. We need decent salaries to attract and retain effective teachers, and we need libraries and laboratories, microscopes and telescopes, musical instruments, audiovisual materials, acoustical sound auditoriums, gymnasiums, and computer rooms.

There are many reasons why quality education is expensive, beyond the cost of physical plants and equipment. Teacher salaries are rising dramatically, and while salaries are still low in terms of education and training, they are considerably higher than they once were. There is, moreover, steady pressure to continue these increases in order to attract and keep talented men and women in the world of teaching. Most teachers now also have benefit packages similar to those of other professionals, including health and life insurance as well as pensions.

Government regulations for the health and safety of students also increase costs. Expensive alterations are sometimes necessary to comply with stricter fire and health regulations. One school was told it had to replace all its elevators before school would be allowed to open. Asbestos identification and abatement procedures have taken an immense toll on some school budgets. As life becomes increasingly complex and more families break apart, schools find they need more specialists. Many schools now have social workers, psychologists, reading specialists, educational testers, and even psychiatrists on staff, in addition to the school nurse we remember from our own school days.

In 1990–91 our public schools spent a national average of $5,208 per pupil. There were, however, considerable differences among the states, with Utah spending the least per pupil ($2,767) and New York the most ($8,680).[15] There are also significant disparities among districts within the same state. Disparities in expenditures exist largely because local property taxes have traditionally been the main source of funding for public schools. Many parents and educators see the property tax as perpetuating educational inequities. Property values in poor school districts are lower and hence generate less in tax revenues than in wealthier districts. A district's relative wealth is determined by the value of taxable property, not by the income of residents. Rich districts can finance large school budgets with relatively low taxes, while poor districts, with fewer taxable assets, must set higher rates to meet even minimum educational standards. Some states also base funding on attendance rather than enrollment rates, so districts with high truancy rates may also lose income.

In 1973 United States Supreme Court ruled that "equal access to education is not a fundamental right under the Constitution and that federal courts are thus not obliged to remedy disparities in financing of school districts." Relief for the schools from disparities in funding must come at the state and local level. In June 1990, the New Jersey Supreme Court ordered the state to equalize spending between poor urban districts and wealthy suburban districts. There have been court challenges to school-financing systems in at least ten other states, including California, Texas, Minnesota, Connecticut, Oregon, and Alaska. Another factor in the school finance controversy is related to the recent "graying" of many communities. Across the country senior citizens and parents of school-aged children argue over school budgets as they try to reach a consensus on educational spending. Many districts have been forced to go on austerity budgets in communities where most families no longer have children in public school.

Money does not necessarily lead to educational excellence. In fact, some studies, such as the Coleman report in 1966, have found little correlation between student achievement and school spending. However, differences in state and local expenditures have led to discrepancies in class size, teacher/student ratios, and curriculum quality within states. In one New Jersey school district, which spent $7,015 per pupil, 93 percent of the students passed state tests, while in a neighboring district that spent half as much, only 23 percent passed the same tests. School budgets are one of many factors that can affect school quality, which in turn can have a significant influence on your child's education. And you, in turn, can have an impact on your school budget. As a concerned parent, you should become knowledgeable about your local school budget. Attend community board meetings and take an active stand to win community support for budgets that provide the resources for a quality education.

••TUITION••

Tuition is not an issue you need to think about if you elect to send your child to your local public school. However, if you choose a public school in another district, tuition may well be a factor you need to consider. Many public schools charge tuition to students from out of the district. In some districts the charge is nominal; other districts use a formula to compute the tuition, which can, in some cases, be nearly as high as private school tuition.

Nonpublic schools are not supported by federal, state, or municipal taxes, and receive their funds from private sources. There are, as we previously discussed, two types of nonpublic schools: private and private/independent. Private schools may be funded by churches or synagogues or other organizations. Tuition in private parochial schools is generally lower than in nonsectarian private schools due to support from the religious organization. Private schools may also be run by one or more individuals on a for-profit basis. Private/independent schools, however, as nonprofit institutions rely solely on tuition, endowment interest, and voluntary contributions from parents, grandparents, alumnae/alumni, and friends of the school.

Catholic elementary schools spent an average of $1,476 per pupil in 1988–89. The average tuition in a Catholic elementary school for grades one to eight was $924. NAIS private/independent day schools spent an average of $6,150 per pupil in 1989–90. Tuition in independent schools has risen an average of 8 percent a year since 1983–84. For 1991–92 NAIS cited the following median tuitions: first grade, $6,000; sixth grade, $6,885; ninth grade, $8,275. However, tuitions will vary considerably from one region of the country to another and between suburban and urban schools. A number of schools in large cities have cited the following tuition scale as more representative of the schools in their area for 1991–92: first grade, $10,000; sixth grade, $11,000; ninth grade, $12,000. Occasionally if the tuition at one school seems higher than at a neighboring school, it may reflect a difference in accounting practices rather than actual cost and the school may be including things such as lunch and snacks that other schools are listing under additional expenses. Always ask what expenses are included in the tuition. Schools do not generally make refunds for a child's absence or withdrawal. However, many offer tuition refund insurance plans. Be sure to inquire about possible options.

••PAYMENT OPTIONS••

A few schools have graduated fee schedules that are related to parental income. Some schools offer reduced tuition to faculty children. Others offer merit, no-need scholarships to attract students with special talents. Merit scholarships are rare at the elementary school level and may be used by schools that are not fully enrolled. NAIS discourages member schools from using merit scholarships.

You should talk directly to a school about your payment options. Some schools have tuition management plans that allow parents to pay tuition in installments. A few schools have developed brochures explaining to parents different ways to help finance their child's education. Some schools are members of organizations that will help parents plan and budget payments. Two such organizations are headquartered in Boston: The Education Resources Institute (TERI) and Knight Tuition Payment Plan. Be sure to inquire whether a school is a member of a tuition-planning organization.

Loans are another alternative. Some elementary schools offer loans as an alternative to need-based financial aid. Most loan programs require schools to be participants in the program and generally do not deal directly with parents. Ask the director of admissions or the business manager whether the school participates in a loan program and what the repayment terms are. Some programs charge parents application fees and require that they establish "creditworthiness." A few loan programs, including Knight's Extended Repayment Plan and The Tuition Plan in Concord, New Hampshire, will work directly with parents. Eligibility for loans is based on a review of past and present credit history and an analysis of your debt versus income ratio. The Tuition Plan requires, in addition, that a parent be employed full-time and have a minimum income of $30,000. Most loans are short-term, repayable over a period of one year to four years. Loans should not be taken out without careful consideration of the potential for incurring additional debt each year. However, they can be a good alternative for a family expecting a much larger income in a few years.

••FINANCIAL AID••

No one should make a decision on a school for a child solely on the basis of expense. Almost all parochial and private/independent schools have some need-based financial aid. Approximately 20 percent of private/independent school students receive aid and, according to one regional association, "one does not have to be a pauper to qualify." Fifty-nine percent of Catholic elementary schools offer financial aid. The amount of available aid varies widely from school to school; and a few of the larger ongoing schools may have financial aid budgets of more than $500,000. Financial aid is usually awarded according to predetermined financial aid tables.

Many factors come into play in determining financial aid: parents' ages, the number of years left before retirement, the number of siblings in school or college, and other individual financial obligations or medical problems. Generally, current income is weighed more heavily than assets. Parents are asked to fill out financial aid forms (FAF) and provide copies of recent tax returns. Many schools use the Schools and Scholarship Service (SSS) in Princeton to process their financial aid forms. In this case, parents send their forms directly to SSS, which in turn reports back to the schools. Some schools ask for the first two pages of IRS Form 1040; others want to review all tax returns and W2 forms. Parents must apply for financial aid on a yearly basis.

Some schools are more flexible than others in their financial aid policies. Many heads of schools have access to discretionary funds that may be used to supplement scholarship aid or to tide a family over during unexpected hard times. As one school administrator said, "If a child comes along with a special talent, I'll knock down a barrier or two if need be to get the money to pay that child's way." Once a child is attending a school, many school heads will go to extraordinary lengths to ensure that the child is able to continue. Some schools have financial aid supplements that pay additional fees allowing children to participate in extracurricular activities sponsored by the school.

It is important for you to be straightforward with a school

about your level of financial need. In general, do not worry that the need will prejudice your child's chances for admission to a private/independent school. Schools try to make admissions decisions independently of financial need. You should, however, ask in advance whether this is in fact the case at a particular school. While some schools don't have the financial resources to have truly need-blind admissions, most schools make it a point to have some scholarship funds available. Schools do not identify the students who are on scholarship, and no one will know that your child is on scholarship unless you say so. For a checklist of questions to ask on financial aid, see chapter 9, "Finding the Right Fit."

••Additional Costs••

Many schools, both public and nonpublic, assess fees for lunch, snacks, gym uniforms, supplies and books, music, physical education, carpentry, and photography. These can range from several hundred dollars to more than $1,500. When you look at a school be sure to ask about additional fees. One private/ independent school listed the following additional annual fees, which I found representative of other schools in the area: lunch and snacks, $1,025; supplies and books, $230; physical education, $230; carpentry, $135. When you look at a school be sure to ask about additional fees.

Additional child care is another expense to consider. Parents are expected to be closely involved in their child's life at school. Being involved means attending evening meetings and parent-teacher conferences. It also means going to soccer games and track meets, class plays and concerts, science fairs and book fairs, class trips, sports days, bake sales, and auctions. If you have a younger child at home, your child-care costs may rise dramatically.

••School Uniforms••

Some schools require children to wear school uniforms. Prices are generally reasonable, but it is seldom necessary to buy uniforms new, as many schools have outlets where parents can buy them secondhand. Some schools provide free uniforms to needy students. Parents generally agree that it costs far less to dress a child in a school uniform than in the latest designer jeans.

••TRANSPORTATION••

While many school choice plans provide free transportation, some do not. Be sure to ask. Some districts also provide free public transportation for parochial and other private-school children if they live a predetermined distance (this varies) from school. In urban areas, children who live the required distance from school are eligible for free bus passes. Private bus service to and from school in some areas may cost $1,500 or more a year.

••VOLUNTARY CONTRIBUTIONS••

Neither state and local education budgets nor tuition income cover the total cost of a child's education. Some private/independent schools estimate that tuition covers only three-fourths of the actual cost. Parent volunteers in both public and nonpublic schools raise hundreds of thousands of dollars through a variety of fund-raising events such as fairs, auctions, dances, and benefit performances to pay for librarians, music and art teachers, computers, and science equipment. Many after-school programs, extracurricular activities, and enrichment programs are also funded by parent contributions.

Many schools solicit annual contributions from parents, grandparents, alumni/alumnae, and friends of the school. These contributions are often referred to as "annual giving." Revenue from annual giving may be used to buy special equipment not included in the school budget and additional books and periodicals for the library. In private/independent schools, annual giving is also used to augment faculty salaries, offer seminars and enrichment programs to faculty, and provide financial aid. Annual giving is technically voluntary, but some schools have close to 100 percent parent participation. Gifts may range from $25 to over $10,000, with an average gift in some schools running around $1,000. Schools make a special effort to let parents know that all gifts, no matter how small, are greatly appreciated. Schools often put out an annual report listing names of contributors.

In public schools, new buildings and other long-range capital improvements are usually funded by special bond issues; in nonpublic schools they are funded by capital campaigns. It is always a good idea to find out whether the school you are interested in is about to undertake a capital campaign, either to increase endowment or to expand its physical plant. Capital campaign goals can easily reach millions of dollars. During a campaign it is customary for parent volunteers to personally solicit other parents for gifts and pledges, and it is part of the volunteer's job to make it difficult for other parents to refuse.

••ADDITIONAL CONSIDERATIONS••

Schools generally make a big effort to play down economic differences between students, but comparisons between houses and personal possessions still are often part of the hidden curriculum of elementary schools. In some communities, you may also find what one school administrator described to me as "a kind of cultural keeping up with the Joneses." Children's reactions to going to public school in a wealthy suburban district or to being on scholarship at a private/independent school depend very much on their parents' reactions. How well you and your child deal with economic differences will depend on your values and on how these values are reflected in your daily life and in your conversations with your children. Sometimes it can seem that every child is taking ballet lessons, skating lessons, piano lessons, violin lessons, cello lessons, French lessons, chess lessons, or art lessons. If your children sense that you feel envious and insecure around other parents, they may also feel envious and insecure. If, on the other hand, you truly believe that you are giving your children a valuable gift by giving them the best education you can find, then economic differences probably won't matter as much.

One final point you should consider is the school's financial health. Given the general economic uncertainty and school-age population changes, financial stability could be an issue. In some areas public schools have experienced severe budget cuts— teachers have been laid off and enrichment programs canceled. A few private ongoing schools and high schools have closed or merged as a result of increasing costs and declining enrollments, and some have found themselves forced to find innovative ways of raising additional money quickly in order to stay open. Sometimes parents have had little advance warning of financial difficulties. If your child has been accepted in a school and you have any doubts about its financial stability, ask to see an audited financial statement.

•• Private School Now or Later?

Many parents who intend to send their child to private/independent school for part of their education ask whether they should spend their money on a five-year-old or save the money so they can send that child to a private secondary school or college later on? Diane Irish, head of the lower school at The Chapin School in New York City, expressed the feelings of many of her colleagues:

That is not an easy question. Much depends on the nature of the child, and much depends on the environment of the school. One must ask what sort of enrichment can the school offer my child in terms of intellect, citizenship, and self-esteem. One must further ask, "Is the school equipped to deal with developmental differences or learning style differences?" In the early years a young child may benefit most from the individualized approach and the focus on self-esteem often found in independent schools. As the child increases in maturity and motivation, she may benefit from the ability of the independent school to be responsive to special interests and talents. Guidance personnel is also a strong commitment of an independent school's resources. Much depends on the size and quality of the public schools in a particular community. In the large school the older child may be able to negotiate and pull from it what is best from the typically larger public school. Size and quality of public schools are obviously going to vary from community to community. In a poor, rural community in Vermont, there is an extraordinarily fine high school which won an award in 1988 for being one of the ten top high schools in the country. The classes are small; the faculty is intelligent, energetic and innovative in their approach to learning. Their computer/history teacher was chosen as an alternate for the recent tragic space shot and spent weeks doing special training for the job. He is now a new state legislator, and the school hires a substitute for the six weeks he is away at the capital in the winter. You can imagine the lessons the students learn from this dynamic young man in terms of relevancy and firsthand experience.

As parents consider this question in terms of their own plans, it is important to remember that a private-school education is not automatically the best education for your child. Current statistics indicate that 80 percent of families with incomes of $50,000 and above elect to send their children to public school.[16] In many communities the public schools may offer a comparable or better education. However, if you believe that the education offered by the private/independent or parochial schools in your community is superior, and you feel that your child will benefit from the greater individual attention provided by these schools, my recommendation is that you make this choice now while your child is young and not yet in command of his or her destiny. Later, by the age of thirteen or fourteen, if your children have caught on to the joy of learning, if they have mastered basic skills and begun to learn how to learn, they will be more able to take hold of the future and learn on their own, independent of their educational setting.

Finally, whether you choose a public, a religious, or a private/ independent school for your child, it is important that the school be a good fit. In the next chapter, I review important educational issues such as curriculum and class size, show you how to look at a school, and give you a checklist of key questions to help you determine whether or not a school is right for you and your child.

•• •• •• ••
N I N E
•• •• •• •• •• •• •• •• •• •• •• ••

Finding the Right Fit

Most of us spend a lifetime learning to let our intellect bully our intuition. After we have brought our most reasoned analysis to bear on narrowing the list of schools best suited to our child, we must let our guts guide us. As parents we really do know which school is likely to be best. So after visiting a school, if our intuition tells us to flee, we should flee—with nary a second thought.

ALLAN SHEDLIN, JR.,
EXECUTIVE DIRECTOR OF THE
ELEMENTARY SCHOOL CENTER,
NATIONAL ADVOCACY
RESEARCH AND RESOURCE
CENTER

Before you even begin looking at elementary schools, you must have a sense of what you are looking for so you can fairly and accurately judge the schools you visit in terms of your own needs. You know you want an effective school and you know the general, philosophical common denominators of effective schools. Your community, however, may have a number of good schools, and your task is to find the ones that will be most effective for your own child. What do you do? My first suggestion to parents is that you take some time to consider what your child is really like. What does your child enjoy doing? What kinds of things seem to excite your child and arouse intellectual curiosity? What seems frustrating? Does your child appear to thrive in a structured or unstructured environment? Is your child quiet or rambunctious? Does your child prefer to work on projects independently or with other children? Have you noticed

•• •• •• ••

any special interests or abilities? Does your child seem self-confident, appropriately independent, and at ease with others, or do you sense that your son's or daughter's ego needs a boost?

Next I would ask you to consider your philosophy and values. What are your own goals? What are your goals for your children? How important is academic excellence to you? How important are athletics and extracurricular activities? Try to define what it is you really want for your child. Curriculum, teaching, class size, and student discipline are all issues you will want to consider carefully in your search for the right fit in a school for your child.

•• Curriculum

Do you want a curriculum that stresses basic skills or teaching children how to think? Or a combination of both? Do you prefer a curriculum that focuses on the classics of traditional Western culture or one that includes multicultural traditions and feminist thought? Or, again, a combination? It is not within the scope of this book to outline a grade-by-grade elementary school curriculum. Instead I have elected to describe recent research to give you a sense of what you should look for in an effective curriculum, and also to raise questions you may want to ask.

All schools should have a clearly written curriculum with well-defined goals and objectives for each grade. There should also be a sense of progression and continuity from grade to grade. France and a number of other countries have a standardized, national elementary school curriculum, but the United States does not. Curriculum varies from state to state, between districts within the same state, and sometimes even between schools in the same district. Six states mandate minimum course content, and nineteen states establish learning objectives for locally developed curricula. Sixteen other states have curriculum guides and sample curricula.[1] For years there has been an ongoing debate among educators about what children should be learning in elementary school, and a number of parents and educators have raised the issue of national standards. In August 1990 the first steps were taken toward setting national standards in mathematics for students in grades four, eight, and twelve. If this venture is successful, other disciplines may follow suit.

••Kindergarten Curriculum••

Studies have shown that despite modern sociological and technological changes, our children's rate of physical, mental, and emotional development has not really changed. On the surface, our children may appear more sophisticated, but they are not really more mature or more intelligent than we were at similar ages.[2] Children in kindergarten learn, as they always have, through hands-on exploration and discovery. They learn through the opportunities to make choices, to express their thoughts and feelings, to describe activities and events. They learn math concepts by comparing and measuring, by manipulating concrete materials, by building with blocks and cooking. They do not learn by marking answers in workbooks. Children learn about science by working with plants and animals, by conducting simple experiments, by going on field trips to farms, markets, zoos, aquariums, and bird sanctuaries, and by walking through fields and forests and along streambeds and on beaches. Children prepare for reading and writing by imaginative play, by telling their own stories and listening to the stories of others, by acting out the plays they make up, and by hearing teachers read poetry and tales of mystery and adventure. Most children do not learn by sitting quietly filling in blanks or being asked to master formal reading and math skills.

All good kindergarten curricula are rooted in children's own experiences. They make use of the many traditional open-ended materials developed by Montessori and Froebel, and they expose children to "real books"—the classics of children's literature as well as contemporary works. They encourage children to work both independently and cooperatively with other children. They draw on children's natural curiosity and seek to give them a feeling for the excitement of learning.

••First Grade and Beyond••

Ruth B. Love, former superintendent of the Chicago public schools, defined the mission of elementary schools as teaching children "how to learn, rather than merely prescribing what to learn."[3] Her point becomes increasingly relevant every year as the information explosion causes factual information in textbooks to be dated by the time the textbooks are published.

As our society grows increasingly aware of its multiethnic and multiracial roots, many educators and politicians have sought to incorporate this awareness into our children's school curricula. A national debate is currently taking place over multicultural studies versus the traditional curriculum focus on Western civilization. Supporters of multicultural studies cite a need for "sharing a common heritage in the general society and simultaneously dealing with each other's diverse subcultures."[4] They argue, like Bill Honig, state superintendent of public instruction in California, that "history has not included enough examples of the variety of groups that make up this country."[5] In California new textbooks approved by the state school board include information on African kingdoms and accounts of historical events told from a Native American perspective. In New York State a committee of scholars and educators recently proposed a "curriculum of inclusion" that has become highly controversial; some educators criticize the changes as insignificant, while others cite concerns about subjecting an academic discipline to the politics of pressure groups. School districts in a number of cities, including Washington, Indianapolis, Pittsburgh, Milwaukee, and Atlanta, are also in the process of instituting a multicultural curriculum. Many will follow a plan initiated in Portland, Oregon, where scholars were commissioned to write essays on the contributions of American and African blacks in six different fields. These contributions were then incorporated in the curriculum. Future essays are planned on the contributions of Asians, Native Americans, Hispanics, and Pacific Islanders.

One effect of the current debate on multicultural studies has been a revived focus on social studies and a concerted effort among leading educators to improve the curriculum in general to make it more interesting and relevant to children.

••READING••

Many parents see reading as the single most important part of their child's elementary school curriculum. And rightly so— learning to read ranks along with your child's first words and steps as an important developmental milestone. The introduction to *Becoming a Nation of Readers,* compiled by the Commission on Reading, finds that reading "is a cornerstone for a child's success in school and, indeed, throughout life."[6] *Reading* is defined in the report as "the process of constructing meaning from written texts."[7] It goes on to compare reading to the performance of a symphony orchestra:

First, like the performance of a symphony, reading is a holistic art. In other words, while reading can be analyzed into subskills such as discriminating letters and identifying words, performing the subskills one at a time does not constitute reading. Reading can be said to take place only when the parts are put together in a smooth integrated performance. Second, success in reading comes from practice over long periods of time, like skill in playing musical instruments. . . . Third, as with a musical score there may be more than one interpretation of a text. The interpretation depends upon the background of the reader, the purpose for reading, and the context in which reading occurs.[8]

Traditionally, beginning reading programs have been divided into those that stress the decoding process of phonics and those that emphasize whole-word recognition and meaning. There are many variations on and combinations of both approaches. Despite years of debate, there is no conclusive proof that one method is clearly more effective than the other for all children. With both methods, some children have learned to read easily and others have had difficulty. Children with keen auditory discrimination often respond to the sounding and blending of phonics. Other children with strong visual recall may respond better to sight words. The U.S. Department of Education concluded in its 1986 report, *What Works: Research About Teaching and Learning,* that "children get a better start in reading if they are taught phonics."[9] According to *Becoming a Nation of Readers,* in programs where phonics is stressed, children have a decided advantage in tests of word identification, but they "also do better on tests of sentence and story comprehension, particularly in the early grades."[10] The report acknowledges, however, that some reading programs try to "teach too many letter-sound relationships and phonics instruction drags out over too many years."[11] Reading is not just decoding unfamiliar words, it is also knowing the meaning of words, understanding how they are used in the context of a story, and being able to draw inferences and see subtleties. As the report emphasizes, "Each encounter with a reading selection should serve the dual purpose of advancing children's skill at word identification and helping them to understand that reading is a process not simply of word recognition, but one of bringing ideas to mind."[12]

More than 90 percent of elementary school teachers use basal readers in the first few grades. *Basal reading programs* are packages of teaching materials including reading readiness workbooks, graded anthologies with a controlled vocabulary, teacher's manuals, and supplementary materials such as word cards, audio tapes, and filmstrips. They are generally developed by groups of authors working with educational publishing companies. Traditionally, basals have presented reading as a series of discrete skills of increasing complexity rather than as an integral part of a child's language development. They have generally emphasized meaning rather than decoding. However, all major reading programs today include phonics. Basal readers have been criticized over the years for their limited, rather bland vocabulary as well as for the insipid nature of many of their stories. Publishers have responded by seeking to make basals more interesting and relevant to children's lives, and also by trying to integrate reading into the total language arts program. Despite the recent improvements in basals, a reading curriculum should be heavily supplemented with independent reading and trade books. And teachers also need to be encouraged to incorporate their own ideas and materials into the curriculum. Some teachers start children with basals but then move on to children's literature by second grade with supplementary work sheets to reinforce specific skills. Seventy percent of schools have trade books or real children's literature as an integral part of their reading curriculum.

Many teachers are increasingly enthusiastic about the Language Experience (LE) approach to reading. LE draws on all the language experiences children bring with them when they start school. Children learn to read initially by making experience charts and by narrating their own stories and real-life adventures to the teacher. The teacher writes the stories down and reads them with the children. Because the words and thoughts in the stories are their own, children seem to recognize them more readily and also find it easier to make the connection between sound and symbol. Later on as language skills are introduced, children learn to write and read their own stories.

Children are also encouraged to learn from each other by discussing and sharing their stories with the group.

Whole language, also known as emergent literacy, is currently the favorite approach of many educators and is being used in an increasing number of classrooms across the country. Originally developed in New Zealand, it is a holistic approach to reading and writing that seeks to unify language skills: reading, writing, thinking, speaking, and listening in a developmentally based program.

Whole language, like LE, builds on the knowledge and skills children bring with them when they enter school. There, children are encouraged to interact both with other children and with teachers in classrooms designed to promote the exploration of language through a wide range of age-appropriate activities. Reading and writing are taught simultaneously. Children learn to play with language, to tell stories, to draw pictures, and to write about them, first by scribbling and then by using invented spelling. Children discuss their drawings and "read" picture books and other books with familiar stories. Reading aloud both with and to children is an essential part of the whole language approach. Children are exposed to good children's literature on a daily basis. They read books together with the teacher and learn to predict what will happen in a story, to draw inferences, to think about character development, and to understand cause and effect.

Whole language is supported by a variety of professional organizations including the International Reading Association (IRA), the Association for Supervision and Curriculum Development, and the National Association for the Education of Young Children.

Individualized Reading (IR) is another approach currently in favor. IR emphasizes meaning and content. Children choose their own books from selections of children's literature available in the library or classroom. They read independently and advance at their own pace. Teachers often meet one-on-one with students to discuss both the selection of books and the books themselves. Many schools use IR to supplement other approaches.

Programmed learning presents children with written material and questions, usually on a computer screen. After mastering a skill or concept, they move on to a more difficult level, working at their own speed. "Writing to Read" is a computer-based, multimedia early childhood literacy program for children in kindergarten and first grade. Developed by John Henry Martin, a former principal and superintendent and marketed by IBM, the program is currently used in seven thousand school districts. Mississippi is planning "Writing to Read" labs for every elementary school.

Other less common approaches you may encounter include linguistics and SRA. Linguistics begins with the alphabetic code and emphasizes oral reading. One method, the Initial Teaching Alphabet (ITA), which was popular in the 1960s and 1970s, uses forty-four characters that represent the sounds of English more accurately than our alphabet. After learning to read and write with ITA, children move back to the conventional alphabet. Some children handle the transfer easily, others experience varying degrees of difficulty. Today ITA is sometimes used as an alternative approach for children who are having difficulty understanding sound-symbol relationships.

SRA, a form of programmed learning without the computer, uses a series of graded reading kits devised by Science Research Associates. Children progress through colored cards as they master skills. SRA was initially used as an enrichment activity for children who had mastered the basic skills on which the rest of their class was working. Today these students would be given independent reading, and SRA is more apt to be used as an alternative remedial method. Reading Recovery is another remedial method developed by a researcher from New Zealand. It is currently being used in school districts in twenty-two states with first graders who are having difficulty with beginning reading. The Ohio Department of Education is doing a longitudinal study to determine its effectiveness.

Jeanne Chall, professor of education at Harvard, reviewed the most frequently used reading programs in her classic book, *Learning to Read: The Great Debate*.[13] She concluded that while no one program is best for all children, in the beginning many children, particularly average or slow learners, benefit from a decoding approach, and that many teachers and children need some structured materials at first. Chall's research indicates, however, that the most important factor for success in reading is not the method used but the teacher's skill and the atmosphere the teacher creates in the classroom. Studies have shown that children are more apt to learn to make connections and deepen their understanding of written material not by answering questions in workbooks but by writing and group discussion. Good teachers also realize that no two children learn in precisely the same manner, and that teachers must be flexible and concern themselves more with understanding a child's learning style than with rigid adherence to any one method.

By the end of third grade, most of the fundamentals of reading will have been covered, but skills continue to be taught through fourth grade. Most children have mastered the decoding process and are able to pronounce most words whether or not they know their meanings. During third grade, if not before, children usually begin reading to gain information in other subject areas. It is important for teachers to provide linkages between the information children find in books and the information they encounter in daily life. If children are reading about ships or airplanes, they will benefit from a trip to look at a real ship or airplane. Third grade is often a good time for parents to invest in an encyclopedia or take out a subscription to a children's magazine. Children learn to skim passages for main ideas and relevant pieces of information. This is the time when children are expected to begin reading critically—exploring subtleties, looking for character development, making predictions about what will happen next in a story, and drawing inferences about what the author is really saying. A good reading curriculum will ask children to discuss, analyze, and write about the books they are reading.

A good reading program will appreciate that children learn at different rates and in different ways. It will also take into account what reading teachers have always known, namely, that reading ability usually does not develop evenly in children but comes instead in sudden bursts after periods of seemingly little progress. A good reading program will not expect all third graders to understand and enjoy the same book. It will encourage choice both for children and teachers. If a teacher likes a book, there is a far greater chance that the students will enjoy it also. A good reading program will have a resource room and specialists available to encourage and help children who are having difficulty.

The U.S. Department of Education report *Becoming a Nation of Readers* finds that reading achievement is directly related to the amount of reading children do both in school and outside school.[14] As you evaluate reading programs, it is important to keep in mind that no matter how good the reading curriculum is at school, few children will become real readers unless books and visits to the library are an integral part of their life at home. Of more concern than which method is used to teach reading in school are statistics showing that half of our children read less than ten pages a day. Children are more apt to become good readers when their families show them by their actions as well as their words that they believe in the importance of reading. Daily reading of real books both at school and at home is an important part of all good reading curricula, and the goal should be not just to teach children how to read but to inspire them to want to read.

••WRITING••

Educators find a direct correlation between learning to read and early writing. IBM recently announced a writing program to complement "Reading to Write." "Writing to Write," designed to be used with children up to second grade, is currently being tested in thirty-one sites around the country. After children have written a story on the computer, a computer-based voice synthesizer reads the story back and children analyze their writing.

Children should be encouraged to write regularly from kindergarten on. A good curriculum gives children the opportunity to express their thoughts on paper or computer without worrying, at least in the early years, about the mechanics of writing and spelling. It encourages children to write every day; to write about the pictures they draw, about trips they take, about their feelings and experiences; to keep journals and to write letters, poetry, and plays, as well as stories. It teaches children to think like writers, to plan, to incorporate feedback from peers, and to revise and edit. It gives children opportunities to share their writing with other students by reading what they have written and by putting together collections of stories and poems.

••MATH••

Mathematics comes from a Greek word meaning "inclined to learn." It is more than memorizing number facts, filling in answers, or plugging numbers into the right formula. Mathematics is a way of looking at the world in three-dimensional terms.

It is a language with its own highly developed symbol system. It involves analysis, measurement, statistics, estimation, prediction and probability, logic, and problem solving. It entails reading and interpreting charts and graphs, discovering patterns, understanding abstract concepts, and seeing the relationships between objects.

A recent poll indicated that math is most children's favorite subject in elementary school, but by high school interest falters and confidence in math skills drops, particularly among girls.[15] Harold W. Stevenson, professor of psychology at the University of Michigan, has found that by first grade U.S. students are already behind their Japanese peers in math, and the disparity increases between first and fifth grade.[16] Other studies have shown that the gap is greater in problem-solving abilities than in computational skills.

President Bush has pledged that by the year 2000, U.S. students will be first in the world in mathematics achievement.[17] The National Academy of Sciences has called for significant changes in the teaching of math in elementary school and beyond—changes that include focusing more on problem solving and less on computational skills in the early years. The academy's suggestion that children be encouraged to use calculators has been implemented in the recent revisions of the SATs. The new guidelines also encourage children to work collaboratively in groups on problem-solving strategies, and recommend that schools have math specialists on their faculties rather than leaving the teaching and planning of curriculum in the hands of nonspecialists.

The National Council of Teachers of Mathematics (NCTM) is also calling for changes, proposing that:

•• Classrooms be viewed as mathematical communities instead of disparate groups of individual learners.
•• Students learn to rely on mathematical evidence and logic instead of answer books or teachers.
•• Children be encouraged to develop mathematical reasoning.
•• Teachers emphasize invention, conjecturing, and problem solving rather than rote memorization and "mechanistic answer finding."

•• Teachers emphasize the real-world application of mathematical concepts.[18]

The goal of a math curriculum, most educators agree, should be to teach children to think mathematically rather than to memorize facts and procedures they may not understand. Working with objects that they can look at and hold helps children understand concepts as they move gradually from concrete to abstract reasoning. A good math curriculum will continue to use the manipulative materials introduced in kindergarten such as blocks, chips, and Cuisenaire rods. It will provide children with opportunities for hands-on experience in measuring and designing models to scale. A good math curriculum encourages children to discover patterns and make conjectures. It teaches children to estimate and develop problem-solving strategies. Its goal is to help children become mathematically literate.

•• SCIENCE ••

The American Association for the Advancement of Science has proposed a shift in emphasis from learning facts that may be quickly outdated to understanding underlying scientific concepts. A good science curriculum teaches children to find information, to make and test hypotheses, to set up and implement experiments, to record data, and to report findings. It teaches children the scientific method by giving them opportunities to "do science," to participate in hands-on laboratory experiments. As the U.S. Department of Education report *What Works* puts it, "Reading about scientific principles or having a teacher explain them is frequently not enough. Cause and effect are not always obvious. . . . Experiments help children actually see how the natural world works."[19] Ideally a good science program should be led by teachers who understand both scientific concepts and the learning styles of children. Teachers who do not have scientific training should be encouraged to attend workshops to increase their own understanding of the concepts they are teaching. Sister Mary Lauretta, a teacher cited in a recent history of the Westinghouse Talent Search, said of her own preparation, "I had to do extra work, too. I had to learn how to use a microscope. . . . I had to learn more about grains, so I worked with people in the brewing industry where grains are used.''[20]

••SOCIAL STUDIES••

Social studies, in most elementary school curricula, includes history and geography, civics, current events, and introductory sociology. It may also include economics, anthropology, and consumer and environmental education. A successful social studies curriculum is often more dependent on the initiative and creativity of individual teachers than many other subjects. Columbia University's American history textbook project has recently reviewed textbooks in current use and found that many were merely catalogs of facts that transmitted little of the excitement, adventure, and romance of real history. Films also can be a mixed blessing. When films and other audiovisuals are used to add a sense of realism and immediacy to a curriculum, they can be an asset, but their overuse or substitution for a thoughtful lesson plan can have a negative impact on learning.

Students should be taught to interpret, analyze, and challenge. They should know how to read and interpret maps and graphs. They need to learn research skills and how to make critical judgments. The Columbia project recommends that schools make more use of primary sources and literature relevant to the period. One teacher who followed this approach in a unit on the Victorians had her third graders keep a journal pretending they were Victorian children. Before starting the journal the children read stories about Victorian children, visited museums to see portraits of Victorians, and researched all aspects of Victorian life from what they ate for breakfast to the kinds of illnesses they had. In another class, fourth graders designed and built castles and battering rams to illustrate medieval siege warfare. For both classes social studies became the stories of real people, places, and things. Educators see hands-on activities such as building models, going on field trips to museums and historic sites, writing journals and skits, and discussing ideas in class as key both to understanding history and to making it come alive for children.

••LANGUAGES••

Only 5 percent of American children study a foreign language in elementary school, and only the District of Columbia requires a foreign language course in high school. However, this statistic may soon change; academic and popular interest in language proficiency is growing as the world shrinks and we spend more of our lives working in an international environment. Ninety-three schools are currently experimenting with voluntary immersion programs. The goal of these programs is to make children bilingual. One of the earliest experiments with an immersion program in a public school was in Culver City, California, in 1971. Children in kindergarten and first grade were taught initially in Spanish; English was gradually introduced in second grade, and by sixth grade 40 percent of the curriculum was in English and 60 percent in Spanish.[21] PS 87 in New York City is one of the schools offering a Dual Immersion Language Program. The classroom has an equal number of English- and Spanish-speaking children, and instruction alternates between the two languages.

There are also less intensive foreign language programs available in a number of schools. One program, FLEX (Foreign Language Experience), does not strive for mastery of the language but seeks instead to introduce children to a new language in a low-key way and to the culture of the people who speak it. It is usually taught by the classroom teacher, who is not necessarily proficient in the language. There are twenty- to thirty-minute sessions once or twice a week. Children are not usually taught to read or write the language. Another approach, FLES (Foreign Language in Elementary School), gives children a more in-depth introduction that includes reading and writing as well as fluency in the spoken language. Classes are usually taught by a special language teacher and may include up to five hours of instruction a week.[22] (See also "Bilingual Schools," chapter 8.)

••COMPUTER SCIENCE••

The goal here should be for your children to feel comfortable with computers and begin to see them as an integral part of their lives. They should be able to write simple programs and to draw, calculate, write, retrieve, and store information on a computer. Computers should not be used merely as electronic flash cards to drill children in basic skills but rather as a way to encourage invention and the mastery of complex skills. Herbert Kohl, author and educator, believes that we "have to be creative and perhaps even wild in our use of computers in the classroom. We must use them for what they are: complicated storage retrieval and choice machines, rather than linear textbooks or flashcards."[23]

Computers are as vital to our children's education as the abacus and slate were to an earlier generation. They help children record and organize scientific data. They are research tools, and they are also a means to encourage critical thinking. Many children find writing on a computer easier and more fun than writing with a pencil and paper. This is particularly true for poor spellers and for children who have difficulty with the mechanical process of writing. For all children there is a special excitement in reading their own words on the screen in front of them.

As you evaluate a school's computer curriculum, these are some of the questions you will want to ask yourself: Do computers seem to be an integral part of the curriculum? Are children encouraged to see computers as resources to use in a variety of ways, or do they use them only during computer period? Are the computers in the classroom, or are they tucked away in a special computer room? Are there enough computers for children to have easy access to them? Are the children being taught word processing and simple programming, or do they only use the computers for drill or games? And finally, do the teachers appear to be knowledgeable about computers and comfortable working with them?

••LIBRARY••

The library should be an important part of every child's life at school. Some schools have full-time librarians, others share part-time librarians or rely on parent volunteers. Classes are usually taken to the library once a week to take books out and listen to the librarian read stories. By fifth grade, children should know how to use the card catalog and do simple research. Parents can help their children feel comfortable using the library by seeing that they have library cards and go regularly to the local public library. It is important to talk to children about the books they select. And parents can also help by making a point of seeing that books are returned to the library on time.

••THE ARTS••

The arts are a vanishing part of the curriculum in many school systems across the country. They are usually first to be mentioned in cost-cutting recommendations because many school boards see the arts as frills rather than an essential part of a good elementary school curriculum. This is ironic at a time when research indicates the important role they play in children's development and even in their motivation for learning.[24] There are, however, some fine programs. One is the Artists-in-Schools Program sponsored by the National Endowment for the Arts, which brings poets, dancers, musicians, painters, and other artists into the schools to work directly with students and teachers.

••PHYSICAL EDUCATION••

A good physical education program includes learning through movement. It gives children an awareness of their bodies and how they function. It provides activities to develop balance, flexibility, and coordination. Physical education should develop physical fitness and help children learn the skills necessary to participate in sports as they get older. A good physical education program seeks to involve all children, not just those born to be athletes. A few minutes spent watching a physical education class will give you a good indication of the quality of the program. If only the most athletic children are participating and all the others are clustered on the side talking, you know it is not a well-thought-out program.

••EVALUATING YOUR SCHOOL'S CURRICULUM••

Many curricula look good on paper. To find out how good an individual curriculum actually is and how or even whether the stated goals are met, you will have to be prepared to ask questions. While there is no one right answer to all questions on curriculum, and while even the experts don't always agree, you should expect thoughtful responses that indicate an understanding of the underlying educational issues and research as well as school policy. It is also important that the school's responses coincide with your own educational philosophy and expectations for your child.

1. Ask about continuity between grades. A school may have a curriculum coordinator or plan meetings between teachers in different grades and different divisions to ensure continuity.

2. What percentage of the students met the goals?

3. How do parents determine whether their child is meeting the goals?

4. How often is the curriculum reviewed? When was the last review? What is the review process? Many schools review curriculum annually. Some schools hold informal weekly meetings to review what they are doing and why, and to discuss new theories and materials. Dr. Stephen Clem, director of academic services for NAIS, recommends a total curriculum review every five to seven years. He cautions that this should not be a "let's fix what's broken approach" but rather a thoughtful review that "reflects an understanding that what happens in one classroom affects the entire school."

5. What support services are available for those who need additional help in reading or math? Answers will vary. Some schools have resource rooms with specialists available during the day. In other schools teachers may come in early or stay after school to offer help. Still other schools suggest outside tutoring at the parents' expense.

6. How flexible are the goals for student achievement? How do they take into account individual differences? Is everyone intended to be on page 31 of the math textbook on the same day, or are children encouraged to work at their own rate? Responses will vary greatly here between schools. While some flexibility is always desirable, occasionally a curriculum is so flexible that children and parents are uncertain of expectations. It is again important that you believe the degree of flexibility is right for you and your child.

7. Is work in one subject integrated with work in another subject? Children studying westward expansion in social studies could be reading books on the period such as *Caddie Woodlawn* and *The Little House on the Prairie*.

8. Look for teacher-made materials and hands-on manipulative materials such as Cuisenaire rods, tangrams, and geoboards in math and laboratory experiments in science.

9. Who chooses the textbooks and what role does the teacher play in the selection? Are the textbooks reviewed and updated on a regular basis?

10. Ask whether direct experiences such as class trips and museum visits play a role in the curriculum.

11. How much flexibility is given to individual teachers to modify the curriculum to fit the needs and interests of their students? Again answers will vary here, but research indicates that teachers who take an active role in shaping the courses they teach are generally more interested and effective teachers.

Copies of curricula are usually available to parents on request from the school or by writing to the state board of education. Questions should be addressed either to the principal or the deputy superintendent (if your district has one). In a private school either the head or the head of the lower school is your best source of information. Some private schools enclose an outline of their curriculum with their catalog.

After you review the official curriculum, you will want to consider the hidden curriculum. Every school has its own hidden curriculum consisting of the things children learn through their everyday interchanges with teachers and peers—things that are not necessarily part of the intended curriculum. Children learn many things by watching the adults around them, including how much the school values academic excellence and student achievement, fair play and sexual equality, friendship, trust, and community spirit or whether it is just paying lip service to these ideals. Keep your eyes and ears open. Be aware of both verbal clues and body language when you visit a school. This is the best way to pick up on the subtle nuances of a hidden curriculum.

•• Teaching

The quality of the teaching is the single most important factor in the quality of a school. The intelligence, interest, educational background, and training of the teachers your children encounter will have the greatest effect on the quality of their education.

You will find considerable differences between school systems in the educational backgrounds and training requirements for teachers. Public-school teachers must be certified in the state in which they teach. Thirty-nine states currently require teachers to pass a standardized test before being certified to teach, but there is no uniformity in the areas tested and in what constitutes a passing score. Thirty-eight states have minimum course requirements in general education, and twenty-one states require a basic skills or college admissions test before candidates start teacher education. Fifteen states evaluate classroom performance before certification, and thirty-nine states require teachers to renew their certification.[25] There are no certification requirements for teaching in a private/independent school. Most schools, however, require a B.A. degree in the liberal arts plus courses in education and child development. A few schools require an M.A. in the subject being taught.

Research has begun on initiating reforms in teacher education that will make it more intellectually rigorous. National teacher examinations were first introduced in 1990 and are currently being revised and updated. In a report entitled "Tomorrow's Teachers," the Holmes Group, a consortium of institutions of higher education, recommended that all teachers have a liberal arts degree plus course work in child development and education and teaching internships. Degrees and courses do not, of course, guarantee good teachers, but they do help to ensure that prospective teachers have mastered basic skills and the fundamentals of child development and acquired some teaching skills.

"How can you tell if a teacher is good?" is a question parents frequently ask. It is relatively easy to spot poor or ineffective teachers during even a brief classroom visit. Their classrooms are either rigidly controlled or disorganized and chaotic. The children look bored and restless. The lessons are poorly planned and appear perfunctory and uninspiring. The teachers themselves seem unprepared and uninterested in both their teaching and their students.

Really great teachers, on the other hand—the ones we remember as having made a difference in our lives—have more than credentials and competency. They have a love for their subject matter and an intuitive ability to understand children and inspire them to share the excitement and complexity of learning. You can sometimes but not always spot really great teachers by watching the expression on the children's faces and listening for the subtle vibrations in a classroom that tell you something important and exciting is going on.

Most teachers fall somewhere in between these extremes. Like most of us they have their strengths and weaknesses, and it is important that you feel comfortable with the balance and sense that you can respect the teacher's ability and judgment. If you have an opportunity to observe a class, note the interactions between the teacher and the children, and try to get a sense of the classroom dynamics:

1. Does the teacher appear to enjoy teaching? He or she should seem enthusiastic about the subject matter and have a good understanding of it. The lesson should appear well planned but flexible.
2. Who is doing most of the talking? The teacher? The children? A combination? Research shows that children learn more effectively when they are active participants rather than passive observers. The teacher should be good at listening as well as at explaining.
3. A good teacher seems interested in all the students, not just one or two superstars.
4. In a coed class it is important that the teacher has similar expectations for girls and boys, and gives equal encouragement.
5. Note whether the teacher speaks clearly and grammatically and whether he or she uses a varied and interesting vocabulary.
6. Do the children seem to like and respect the teacher?
7. Observe whether the children appear actively involved in learning.
8. Can you see your child flourishing in this class?

If you aren't able to visit a classroom, try to talk to parents whose opinion you respect about the teachers their children have had. Ask them what they see as the teacher's particular strengths and weaknesses. Ask them whether they would want a second child to have the same teacher. Try to talk to some of the children in the teacher's class. Do they seem excited and involved with the things they are learning and doing at school? Ask them what they like best about school. Ask them what they would change if they were in charge for a day. But don't expect every parent and every child to be equally enthusiastic. Not every teacher is equally effective with every child. Even the best teachers will have the occasional dissatisfied parent or disgruntled student. And remember that no matter how good a teacher is, you can't always be certain that the chemistry will be right between your child and that teacher for optimal learning.

•• Class Size

Class size is determined by guidelines established by local school boards. Financial considerations often play an important role in a community's decisions. Research indicates that children in smaller classes are at a decided advantage, particularly in the first few grades. For five-year-olds NAEYC recommends a group not larger than twenty, with one adult for every ten children. For six- to eight-year-olds they recommend that groups not exceed twenty-four, with one adult for every twelve children.[26] Project Star, a study conducted by the Tennessee Department of Education in collaboration with Tennessee State University, looked at the achievement of children in grades K through three in small (thirteen to seventeen) and regular (twenty-two to twenty-five) classes. Students in the smaller classes performed at a significantly higher level on standardized reading and math tests, with low-income children showing the greatest benefit. If a school puts children in separate ability groups for subjects such as reading and math and science, the overall size of the class may be less important than the size of the actual teaching groups.

You will want to ask schools about current class size, but you will also want to ask what their policy is on overflow. Do they create another class or do they send in a paraprofessional? Are parents asked to help? How many additional children do they need to create another class? What effect does a large class have on computer use, field trips and lab time in science? You will also want to find out the school's policy on attrition. If a class shrinks, will it be kept as a separate class or will it be amalgamated into another class. If children are grouped for reading and math, ask about the size of these groups.

Classes are usually, but not always, smaller in private/independent schools, and occasionally you may run into a class that is too small. Very small classes of less than twelve children can become cliquish and inbred, thereby limiting a child's choice of friends and even inhibiting social development.

•• Student Discipline

Discipline is an issue of mutual concern to parents and schools. Students reflect in school the values they learn at home. When you visit a school, student behavior is one of the first things you will notice. Are the children attentive and respectful or disruptive and rude? Is professional help available for disturbed children? How are other children affected by disruptions? Does the teacher have quiet but firm control of the class? Is the teacher able to concentrate on teaching or does he or she spend most of the time disciplining students? Do you sense a consistency of expectations about student behavior throughout the school? Does the principal or head of school exert a sense of leadership?

•• Additional Issues

Tracking or ability grouping is another issue currently being debated by educators and school officials. Advocates of tracking believe it enables each student to progress at his or her optimal level. Quick students, they argue, are not held back waiting for others to catch on, and slower students are not put under undue pressure to keep up. Opponents, on the other hand, believe that tracking stigmatizes some children, leading to both lower academic expectations and a reduced sense of self-esteem. While the facts aren't all in, some of the research seems to indicate that while high-achieving students may benefit from tracking, less-able students appear to suffer. Some educators feel that tracking in the early grades may be particularly apt to result in self-fulfilling prophecies. One solution to the problem of tracking that a number of schools are exploring is an increased emphasis on cooperative learning. These schools encourage children of differing abilities to work together in small groups to solve problems. Many schools that do track only do so in math and reading; other subjects, such as science, writing, and social studies, are taught in mixed-ability groups.

Some schools believe it is part of their mission to teach moral values; other schools believe their job is to teach academic subjects and that a child's moral education is best left to parents. What are your views here? Do you feel the development of moral values is the responsibility of the parents, the school, or a combination of both? This issue has led some parents and schools into court; each may have different and equally strong opinions, and it is important that you be in agreement here with the school you select. Some schools encourage children to participate in volunteer work and community service. Is this important to you?

On a related though less crucial issue, how important are good manners to you? Do you feel that it is important for children to say please and thank you and to learn to look a person in the eye when they shake hands? Do you feel the teaching of good manners is the responsibility of the school, the parents, or once again a combination of both? Think also about the kind of atmosphere you feel comfortable in. Do you want a school to seem warm and cozy, or do you prefer a more formal environment? Do you like the idea of bringing your child into the classroom in the morning and having an impromptu chat with the teacher, or would you prefer just to drop your child off at the door? Do you feel more comfortable with teachers sitting at desks, or do you prefer to see them sitting on the floor with the children? These are not necessarily mutually exclusive, but some schools offer more opportunities for informal exchanges than others. How do you feel about school uniforms? Are you a formal or an informal person? Do you like being addressed as Dr., Ms., Miss, Mrs., Mr., or by your first name? Do you want to invite teachers to your house for dinner? Do you want a teacher to call you at home or the office with news about your child's progress? Would you rather wait for an official, scheduled conference? Remember, though, the perception of atmosphere can be very individual. I know two parents who recently visited the same school. The first saw it as stiff and cold; the second felt it was warm and inviting. The first remembered only a spelling lesson with children sitting in a row with a teacher asking questions and hands going up. The second remembered only recess with children tumbling around laughing and joking.

And finally, remember that location can still be an important factor in selecting an elementary school, although one not quite as crucial as with an early childhood school. The issues, however, are often the same. A neighborhood school can help an elementary school–age child have a sense of continuity between home and school. It is easier to play with classmates after school and to be involved in after-school extracurricular activities. The very act of walking to school alone can be a big boost to a child's ego. However, location should no longer be a single deciding factor, and some children seem to be able to handle a fairly long commute with relative equanimity.

•• Researching Your Community Schools

Bear in mind, as you begin your research, that the so-called hot schools, the ones all parents in a certain community seem to want in a particular year, come and go like fads in skis and tennis sneakers. Remember, too, that no one school has all the smartest children or all the best athletes. In the real world there is no such thing as a ''best school'' or even a school that is right for all children. Children are individuals. Their temperaments and abilities are different. Their needs are different. With elementary schools, as with early childhood schools, no one school can be best for every child. Neither is there only one school that is right for your child. There may well be many schools where you and your child can flourish.

If your child is already in an early childhood school, the director of that school should be your first and most reliable source of information about elementary schools. He or she will have seen how a variety of children have fared over the years at different schools. Your priest, minister, or rabbi may also have helpful suggestions, particularly if he or she has known you and your family well over the years. If your child has been in play groups or taken classes at a local Y or community center, ask the director of the program about elementary schools. Pediatricians can be a good source of information if they have practiced in your community for a number of years. But remember two things when you ask a pediatrician for advice. First, pediatricians are more apt to be consulted when a child is having problems at school than when things are going smoothly, and this can influence their perspective on a school. Second, some pediatricians may be affiliated with individual schools in the role of school doctor. This can also make their opinions less objective.

Many parents say they find real estate agents to be knowledgeable and helpful about schools. Bear in mind, however, that a real estate agent's commission may influence his or her advice. Other parents have reported that their companies provided good advice. Often when companies relocate employees, they assist in finding schools for the children. Friends and colleagues can also be a good source of information. So can the people you socialize with, your tennis partners, your running companions, and the parents of children you meet in the playground. Ask them where their children go to school and whether or not they recommend that school. Just remember you may have to take some of this "park bench gossip" with a grain of salt.

Talk to other parents who have children in the schools you think you may be interested in. Seek out a few parents whose children are just starting out and several other parents whose children have been at the school for a few years. It is best to talk to more than one or two parents, because a child with social, emotional, or academic problems could be having a difficult time in what may be a very effective school for many other children. On the other hand, a child could be such an overachiever that he or she is having a good experience in a mediocre school. Talk to some of the older students in an ongoing school or comprehensive school. Find out what they like about the school. What are their criticisms? If you don't know anyone with children at the school, ask the admissions officer to give you the names of some parents who would be willing to talk to you, but remember that the parents will probably be strong supporters of the school and will offer few criticisms.

All schools—public, private, independent,and religious—are listed in your phone book. Public elementary schools are usually listed by district under city government offices such as the department of education. For more information on public school options, call your local board of education. Some public school districts have special information centers where parents can go to find out about the different schools in the district or township. Religious schools, private schools, and private/independent schools are listed alphabetically under "School" in the yellow pages and by name in the white pages of your telephone directory. For more information about Catholic or Jewish schools, call the local archdiocese or board of Jewish education respectively. The Religious Society of Friends is located in Philadelphia and the address is in the Appendix. For information on schools run by other denominations, consult your church or other denominational headquarters. In large communities, Y's sometimes sponsor school fairs or group information centers to inform parents about public and nonpublic schools in the area.

There are different approaches to researching private/independent schools. In some communities, parents associations serve as repositories of information. In New York City, for example, the Parents League of New York has done extensive research on private/independent schools and compiled, in cooperation with the Independent Schools Admissions Association of Greater New York, a very helpful directory of approximately 130 schools. The Parents League also runs a school advisory service with parent volunteers as consultants. (See Appendix.) Ask other parents whether there is a similar organization in your community. There are also national directories of private/independent schools that can be found in your local library. *Private Independent Schools: The Bunting and Lyon Blue Book,* and *The Handbook of Private Schools,* Porter Sargent Publishers, Inc., are two of the better-known directories. Additional information on directories is listed in the Bibliography. Some parents also find the advice of educational counselors helpful. Their advice is expensive, however (placement fees usually range from $500 to $2,000), and it is often an unnecessary expense for most elementary school parents. You should also keep in mind that educational counselors are not regulated by state or federal law, and in most states anyone can set up shop and call him or herself an educational counselor regardless of qualifications. If you believe that special circumstances make you need such individualized counseling, contact the Independent Educational Counselors Association in Forestdale, Massachusetts (see Appendix), for a list of qualified, responsible counselors in your area.

After making this general survey, you can put together a list of schools you think you would like to know more about. The length of your list will depend on where you live: in a small community it might only have two schools; if you live in a very large community, it might initially have as many as eight or ten. Call each school and ask for a catalog and any other material such as newsletters, calendars, and literary magazines the schools are willing to send. Most private/independent schools and many public schools have a variety of written materials that are compiled by the school itself or by parent groups and that contain useful information. Read them carefully before you make an appointment to visit. Are they thoughtfully presented and well written? A poorly written catalog implies lower academic standards; even if it has been written by a hired consultant, the school has, after all, given this person a green light to speak for the school.

On the surface, schools may sound very much alike, but if you read carefully, you will note both clear and subtle differences. In some brochures, quotes from faculty members or the head of school can reveal the atmosphere of the school and the educational background and interests of the speaker. See what the literature stresses, and what it fails to mention. Does it give you a clear sense of the school's mission? Does the school emphasize those areas you feel are important to your child's education? Does the school's philosophy seem to match yours?

Parents sometimes ask why they should do all this research before they have even seen the schools. My answer is that school visits take far more time than reading a catalog. It is a waste of both your time and the school's time to spend most of the morning visiting a school without first knowing something about it. If you know you have no interest in sending your child to a particular school, you need not visit it.

•• Visiting Schools

If, after doing all your homework, you like the sound of a school and feel it might be right for you and your child, the next step is to make an appointment to visit it. Most schools, both public and nonpublic, welcome visits by interested parents. Whenever possible both parents should visit a school together in order to compare impressions afterwards. A single parent might want to ask about bringing a grandparent or a close family friend. The procedures for visiting vary somewhat from school to school: some schools hold very formal structured tours and large group-information sessions, and there is little chance for parents to linger and poke around the classrooms or ask questions of students or teachers; other schools have a more relaxed approach and welcome parents' interest and inquiries. No school permits parents to wander in and out of classrooms at will, because that would be too disruptive for the students. However, if you keep your eyes open and have a bit of persistence, you can usually find out everything you need to know. As one veteran admissions director observed, "Any school conveys its character if you look into the eyes of the children and listen to the words of the teacher."

You often get a feel for a school the minute you walk in the door. Some schools just seem to feel right. Something about the school makes you feel at home. Keep your eyes and ears open. Listen to the children, listen to the teacher. Watch how the children react to the teacher and to each other. How large are the classes? Do the teachers and children seem comfortable with the number of children in the room? Observe how the children move about the building. Do they go from one activity to another lined up as classes, or do they go off informally in small groups? Look at the children's work on the walls. How much variety do you see? Are all the compositions similar, or do you note individual approaches to an assignment? Is some of the work unfinished, or does it all seem to be intended for display? Listen to what the teacher says and how he or she says it. When you look at a classroom, try to imagine how it would feel to be a student in that classroom. Visualize your child as a student in the classroom, doing the things they are doing, interacting with the teacher and the other students.

How do you feel about the principal or head of school? The philosophy, leadership style, and personal authority of the principal/head is a key element of any school. This is the person who sets the tone and style for the school, establishes and communicates school policies, maintains discipline, attracts and keeps talented teachers, and determines which personal and academic qualities to emphasize. He or she evaluates and assigns teachers, allocates funds, and plans and oversees school schedules and routines.

The principal/head gives a sense of continuity to a school—by being there on the first day of school and following your child's progress from year to year throughout elementary school. It is important that the principal/head is a person you trust and whose judgment you respect. He or she should also be someone with whom you feel comfortable talking. The principal/head is the person you will talk to if you want to transfer to another school or if you have difficulty with a teacher. You will also want his or her support and advice when your child is ready to move on to the next level of schooling. If your child should encounter any academic or other problems, the principal/head will be involved in finding solutions. In some of the larger twelve-year schools with fairly autonomous divisions, the head of the junior or lower school will be in charge of your child's early school experience, so the personality of the head of the entire school is not quite as important. In fact, you may not even meet the head of the school in the admissions process. The personality of the principal/head may also be less important in schools with a strong sense of tradition and a very low rate of teacher turnover. If a brief meeting with the principal/head is not part of the regular school admissions process, call and ask for an appointment. In the unlikely event that you can't get an appointment, talk to parents with children who are already in the school and get a sense of how they feel about the head of school and the direction in which the school seems to be moving.

As you tour a school and peer into classrooms, try to get a sense of how the philosophy stated in the school's brochure is translated into the day-to-day activities. Look at the textbooks the children are using. Do they seem to be well written and age-appropriate? Are there real books in the classroom, or only workbooks? Is there a school library, and do children visit it regularly on their own or in groups? Are the children using computers and other audiovisual aids as learning tools or games? How is the school's stated philosophy reflected in the books and educational resources you see being used in the classrooms and in the teaching styles and interactions between children and teachers? In the lower grades, are there hands-on manipulative materials such as blocks and Cuisenaire rods for math? Are there science projects around the room? Does there seem to be space and equipment for children to do experiments?

•• A Checklist of Questions to Ask the School

Many of these questions will be familiar, for they are similar to the ones you asked about early childhood school. Some of the answers will be different, however. You may also want to refer back to questions listed in the sections on curriculum and teaching.

Public and Private/Independent Schools

•• What is the size of a typical class and what is the maximum number permitted?

•• Does the school have a full- or half-day kindergarten?

•• What is the educational background and training of the faculty?

•• What is the rate of teacher turnover?

•• How diverse is the student body? How diverse is the faculty?

•• To whom do parents go if there is a problem?

•• What types of specialists are available?

•• Describe a typical day. There is no one correct response here, but there should be a variety of classes and a balance of physical activity and academic work.

•• What is the relationship between time spent on individual versus group activities?

•• How does the school handle individual differences?

•• Does the school track children and group them by ability and, if so, on what basis is this done, and are decisions discussed with parents?

•• What are the educational goals for children in kindergarten, first grade, etc.? How do they compare with state requirements?

•• How does the school assess children's progress? Are there set minimum standards for promotion to the next grade level?

•• Which junior high, secondary schools, or colleges do students go on to when they graduate? Do students who live in large cities regularly attend competitive, specialized high schools and academically rigorous private secondary schools?

•• What kind of extracurricular activities are offered?

•• Does the school have athletic teams, and at what grade level do they begin?

- • Is there a dress code or uniform?
- • What are the admissions procedures (if you are applying to a school out of your district or to a private/independent school)?
- • Are there age cutoffs? Ask whether your child will be one of the older or younger ones in his or her class.
- • What are the opportunities and expectations for parent involvement?
- • What kinds of parent-teacher contact are expected or encouraged?
- • What kind of accommodations are made for two-career families who can't come to daytime conferences or meetings?
- • Are there after-school or summer programs available?

Public Schools

- • If enrollment expands beyond twenty-five students, will another teacher be hired? If not, will aides be hired or will parents be asked to help out in the classroom?
- • If enrollment expands and no new teachers are hired, will children be moved to another school?
- • If enrollment shrinks, what kind of cutbacks would occur?
- • How are teachers assigned?
- • If there are teacher cutbacks, who is dismissed first, the last hired or the least competent?
- • What role do parents play in the decision-making process on issues such as curriculum and school policy?

Private/Independent Schools

- • How many openings are anticipated at your child's grade level?
- • Do they have a waiting list for admission at your child's grade level?
- • Is there a bus service and, if so, what does it cost?
- • Does the school have any religious affiliation and, if so, what does this mean?
- • How much is the tuition?
- • What type of tuition payment plans are available? Tuition management plans? Loans?
- • What are the additional expenses? Lunch? Books? Extracurricular activities?

•• What scholarship assistance is available, and how is eligibility determined?

•• Approximately what percentage of students are on scholarship?

Some of these questions will be answered either in general discussion groups or by the person giving the tour. If you are applying for a selective school, you will have to balance your need to know against the possibility of antagonizing the admissions officer with too many questions. You may decide to wait until your child has been accepted and then go back for another visit to ask the remainder of your questions.

•• Postvisit Assessment

Discuss your impressions after a school visit with a spouse or friend. List the things you liked or didn't like about the school while it is all fresh in your mind so you can go back over this later when you are ready to make a decision. If you neglect this step, you will find the schools all disappear into a hazy blur in your mind and you can't remember whether school B was the one with the gerbils or the one with the new gym and whether school X had the music teacher who demonstrated how children use Orff instruments or the principal who talked about test scores. With the latter, it is important to remember that, while test scores are important, they are only part of the picture. What your child is actually doing and learning on a day-to-day basis in the classroom is, in the long run, more important. For more on this subject, see the discussion on curriculum.

•• Making a Decision

An educator and parent of six said to me, "You choose a school in the same way you choose your friends or the place where you live—a natural affinity—because it feels right. Because you like it for what it is, not for what you would like to make it, or for what other parents say about it." Don't choose a school because it is said to be difficult to get into, you think it will help your child get into another school later on, or you think that once your child gets into the school you will be able to change it into something else.

Despite all your research and hard work, it is important to realize that sometimes the final decision on the school for your child may not be entirely in your hands. You may live in a community with one public school. Or you may live in a community where there are many applicants for only a few private/independent schools and the admissions process is very competitive. Depending on demographics, some years may be tighter for admission to certain schools than others. Schools may be forced to refuse admission to children they would love to take if they had the space. Try to understand that, disappointing as it may be at the time, not getting into a school is no reflection on you or your child.

In the next chapter we will discuss competitive admissions from the school's point of view. We will look at the various ways schools put together their classes and how they determine which candidates will be a good fit. I will guide you through the various steps of the admissions process so that you will be able to give the school an accurate picture of yourself and your child. Remember that while there are never any guarantees, the more you and a school know about each other, the better the chance the fit will be right.

•• •• •• ••
T E N

•• •• •• •• •• •• •• •• •• •• •• ••

Getting Your Child into the Elementary School of Your Choice

I sit around feeling the kicks in my belly and I think do I want this kid to be subjected to all this pressure? But do I go back to my school for the alumnae lunch? You bet!

—A MOTHER EXPECTING HER
FIRST CHILD

If you are fortunate enough to live in a community with an excellent neighborhood school and admissions is not an issue that concerns you, you can skip this chapter. If, on the other hand, you live in a community where the neighborhood public school is not a viable choice, where good schools, both public and nonpublic, have more applicants than they can accept, then read on.

•• Issues in Public-School Admissions

Unless you are applying for a specialized program, there are no admissions tests for public school. If the school you want your child to attend is the neighborhood public school for which you are legally zoned, your child must be accepted by law. Age cutoffs for kindergarten vary, but the trend is toward raising the entrance age. "Nineteen states now require a child to be five on or before September 1st to enter kindergarten."[1] Requirements for registration vary from state to state but usually include a birth certificate, a certificate of immunization, and proof of legal residence. Some states may also include eye, ear, and dental screening requirements. A few parents have told me they were asked to produce a copy of their mortgage to prove they were legal residents. Some states, such as California, allow parents to

•• •• •• ••

send their children to school in the district where they work. When parents are divorced or separated and a child spends time regularly with both parents, the child can generally attend school in either district. To find out local requirements, call your nearest public school or board of education. In a small town you might first try the town hall for information.

If you think another school within your district would provide a better educational experience than your neighborhood school, ask the principal of your original school about an intradistrict transfer. In most districts these are fairly easy to obtain. For a school outside your district, you will need an interdistrict transfer, which is usually obtained from the person in charge of interdistrict transfers at the district or township headquarters. Most districts permit transfers for particular needs, including after-school child care, the need for special academic programs or services, health needs, and transportation. Problems with social adjustment and academic incompatibility are also sometimes considered valid reasons. Before you put in a request for a transfer, ask to look at the list of reasons your district has found acceptable in the past. It is often a good idea to back up your request with letters from psychologists, doctors, or educational experts who support your decision to transfer. If your request is denied, you have the right to appeal, and if that fails as a last resort to go directly to a member of the school board or the superintendent. Know, however, that superintendents tend to support the decisions of their principals.

A larger district may have open-enrollment schools available on a first-come, first-served basis to any child in the district. In those communities that do have open-enrollment schools or choice plans, admissions decisions are made in a variety of ways when there are more applicants than spaces in a particular school. Some operate on a first-come, first-served basis; others use various types of lotteries; some give preference to siblings of students who are already at the school; many make special efforts to maintain ethnic and racial balance. A few schools ask parents to fill out questionnaires about their philosophy of education and to explain why they feel the school is right for their child.

The competition to get into a popular public school can be as stiff as for any private/independent school. Some parents choose the school first, then look for a house to buy in that school district. Some schools with particularly fine reputations for educational excellence may have more than four times as many applications as they can accept. In some schools parents line up at six o'clock in the morning in October to preregister for classes the following September. In addition to standing in line, parents back up their applications with letters of recommendation from influential family friends and parents of children in the school, as well as reports from the early childhood schools and day-care centers their children have attended. The success of this approach varies with the school, but it certainly can't hurt and it may be helpful in certain cases if the letters are from people who know you and your child well. Some parents have resorted to using the addresses of friends or relatives who live within the district to try to beat the system and get their child into the school they want. Others have told me stories about getting employees to slip their name into the lottery or to put it at the top of a list. Both methods can backfire. Parents have been sent to court in California for falsifying their legal address, and children are taught a lesson in dishonesty every time they fill in a phony address on a school form.

Until all public schools provide an equivalent education, the best strategy is to do your homework early. Find out what your options are. (See the section in chapter 9, "Researching Your Community Schools.") Call the schools, find out when they have open visiting days or tours of the school, and arrange a visit as soon as possible. Ask if any special tests, interviews, or recommenations are required. Find out about application dates and preregistration. Talk to the parents of older children to find out how the system works in your district. Be the first, not the last, in line on preregistration day. Educators and parents agree that choice works best for those who are both prepared and knowledgeable.

•• Issues in Private School/Independent School Admissions

The competitiveness of private/independent schools admissions depends on where you live, on the quality of the public schools, on the number of good private/independent schools, on the percentage of parents in your community who want a private-school education for their children, and the number of families with children your children's age. In some communities schools may have more than three hundred applications for twenty places in their kindergarten class, while in other communities schools plan to accept twenty-five out of twenty-five applicants. If you are interested in a particular school, find out how many places are available at your child's grade level. Schools that accept most of their children into early childhood divisions may have room for some new students in kindergarten or first grade. If a school begins with kindergarten, there may still be a few openings for first grade. Families move away and many schools increase class size as the children get older. Ask the admissions office when the school begins accepting applications and whether there are age cutoffs for kindergarten and first grade. Many private/independent schools have the same age cutoffs as the local public schools; however, the trend in many areas is toward a June cutoff for boys and a July or August cutoff for girls. Also ask if there are any special requirements for admissions: some Montessori elementary schools, for example, require a child to have attended a Montessori early childhood school.

As we discussed earlier regarding early childhood schools, many private/independent schools give preference in their admissions process to special groups. Schools with religious affiliations generally, but not always, give preference to children of members of that church or synagogue, and sometimes also to members of the denomination. Many schools give preference to siblings of children already in the school, and if the school has been around for a while, to children of alumni/alumnae. In some cases, acceptance is almost automatic for siblings, in others it is not. Hence, it is never a good idea to assume a younger child will be accepted, particularly if the school is popular or your second child is less developmentally advanced than the first. One mother assumed that her younger child would join her older daughter at school, despite the fact that she and her pediatrician had noticed some developmental lags. She never looked at another school. After the interview, she was told by the director of admissions that the school just wasn't suitable for her second child. The mother found herself faced with the prospect of finding another school when almost every place was full. Most schools will willingly share their policies on preference with you. If the answer is not clear from the literature, ask the admissions office.

You will also want to know whether admissions decisions are made in the order in which applications are received or whether there is a screening process. The admissions office is the source for this answer, too. Many elementary schools, particularly private schools in small communities, admit children on a first-come, first-served basis. One school in an oil town in Texas admits only the first forty children whose parents show up on registration day. For many years this admissions policy worked very well, but after the oil boom the town's population doubled, and parents began getting in line at six o'clock in the morning to reserve places for their children. The school is considering starting to screen applicants. In Pasadena, California, one popular school had so many applicants that parents hand-delivered their applications to get them in on time.

Some schools respond to population shifts by expanding their facilities and adding class sections to accommodate the demand. Other schools use a variety of screening methods to select the children and families they feel will be most compatible with their program. Some schools prefer not to discuss the details of their screening procedures, while others may give parents a written guide telling them exactly what to expect during "a visitation assessment." Schools that follow this approach say that they have found that knowing exactly what goes on during the screening eliminates a lot of parental anxiety. Parents frequently ask me whether it is preferable to choose a school that screens applicants or one that uses a first-come, first-served approach. My answer is that no one method is necessarily better. A lot depends on where you live, on whether the community is homogeneous or heterogeneous, and on how well the school is equipped to handle individual differences. Schools that screen may end up with a narrower range of ability and learning styles. They are also more apt to have a parent body that agrees with their philosophy and goals.

•• The Admissions Process

The admissions process for private/independent schools is often more formalized than for "open" public schools. Moreover, unlike public schools, where requirements vary considerably on a state and even on a local basis, in the private/independent sector, while no two schools are identical, there are certain general guidelines that apply. The admissions process in private/independent schools frequently includes (1) an application, (2) personal recommendations or letters of reference, (3) a tour of the school, (4) an interview with the parents, (5) an interview with the child, (6) recommendations and reports from the early childhood school, and (7) some form of standardized testing. Schools often hold receptions or general information sessions in the evening for prospective parents. And some schools also visit early childhood classrooms to observe children working and playing in familiar settings.

In those places where there is a great deal of parental interest in private education and where there are many different schools to choose from, the admissions process can be complicated and very time-consuming for both parents and schools. This is because it is designed with two purposes in mind: (1) to give all candidates equal consideration, and (2) to help schools and prospective parents know as much about each other as possible before making a decision. If the admissions process is to work effectively, a commitment of time, energy, and interest is needed on the part of both parent and school.

••THE APPLICATION••

The application process usually begins with a telephone call to request an application and arrange for a tour of the school. It is a good idea to take notes during this initial conversation, since the details of the process may vary considerably from school to school within the same city. It is also a good idea to keep a copy of the application.

A small fee is usually required with the application to cover processing costs. In the case of financial problems, many schools will waive this fee. Applications are generally simple and straightforward, asking factual questions about the age and sex of your child, what schools, if any, the child has previously attended, and your home address and place of business. There is often a question about how the parent heard about the school. Some schools ask for names of people known to the school who can be used as references, and some ask for financial references. Schools may also ask about your educational background, whether you attended independent schools, and which ones.

Some schools, particularly those with a religious affiliation, may ask about your religion. Schools frequently ask about your home environment and child-care arrangements. Some, but by no means all, ask for written letters of recommendation. Occasionally, parents are asked to write a few paragraphs about their child's interests, about their life as a family, or about their goals for their child at school. There are no right answers to any of these questions. Be open and honest. If you try to mold your answers to fit what you believe the school wants to hear or to paint your child as someone diametrically opposed to what he or she actually is, and your child is accepted, you and your child could end up miserable and looking for another school next year.

Never send an essay, no matter how clever and eloquent, unless the application asks for one. Even if the school doesn't ask you to write an essay about your child, it is often a good idea to take a few minutes to think quietly about your child and jot down some of the things she likes and dislikes, some of the special things he says and does, things you love about her, things that drive you crazy, things you want to forget he ever did, things that you want to remember twenty years from now, things that make her sometimes exasperatingly but always irresistibly herself. These few moments of introspection will not only make it easier for you to talk intelligently about your child in the interview, but they will also help you to know whether or not a school is right for your child.

••School Reports••

Most ongoing schools ask for reports and teacher recommendations from early childhood schools. Some of these reports may be in the form of a checklist of developmental milestones and socialization skills. There may also be a space for teacher comments. All of the information in these reports will have been previously shared with you in conferences, so there should be no surprises. In fact, most early childhood reports tend to err in the direction of too much uncritical praise and too little constructive criticism. Teachers are so eager to stress the positive and avoid making any negative judgments about young children that all the children may end up sounding exactly the same—boringly perfect. When this occurs the school generally follows up with a more candid telephone conversation with the director.

••REFERENCES AND LETTERS
OF RECOMMENDATION••

Many schools ask for references or letters of recommendation from people who know you and your child well. If a school asks for two letters, it means two, not ten. More is not better in this case. Admissions directors are rarely impressed by unsolicited lists of the trustees you may know. When schools say they want letters from people who know you and your child well, they mean what they say. They don't want a letter from a celebrity or prominent person who doesn't know you or your child. Schools aren't interested in how many famous people you can convince to write letters; they are interested in finding out more about you and your child. They like letters with anecdotes that make you and your child come alive for them. They want to know if you will be a supportive, committed parent; if you are willing to give time and energy to your child's education; if you are open to advice and recommendations; if you will work in partnership with the school. If your friends haven't seen your child recently, invite them over for tea, a walk in the park, or a trip to the zoo with your child before you ask them to write a letter. The letter will be much more apt to present a real picture of your child.

Letters of recommendation should be honest; the writer should know both the child and the family well and really believe the statements he or she is making. Recommendations should also try to give through anecdotes and quotations a sense of the child as an individual. However, it is also good to remember that letters of recommendations do not, nor are they usually expected to, give a truly balanced picture of a child with all that child's strengths and weaknesses outlined in black and white. In a really competitive admissions process, any doubts or qualifications expressed about children or their families work against their admission to the school. A person with doubts either about a child's readiness to start school or about whether the child and the school would be a good match shouldn't write a letter of recommendation.

The letters from which I have taken the excerpts below were written by people who clearly know the children and their families well. They have seen the children at play and watched their interactions with family and friends. And they are enthusiastic about recommending the children and their families to the school.

I love playing games with Sara. She wishes intensely to play well, takes time to contemplate the intricacies, to direct, explain, and correct—entering enthusiastically into the competition but never threatened by it. She has humor, an almost intellectual ability to acknowledge subtleties and to challenge and encourage others to invent further.

Kevin spends a lot of his time building—a Lego castle done from a diagram—his own intricate creations with Tinkertoys. He loves jokes and making puns on words with his friends. He is also very fond of music and likes to try to pick out tunes on a toy harmonica.

I think of Vicky explaining to her friends the details of a game she has invented or cutting out wings for toy horses so they can fly like Pegasus. I think of her jousting matches with her sister riding through the yard on a toy horse and of the costume dramas she and her friends like to put on when we come to dinner.

Tommy's parents, Elizabeth and John, are both interesting and intelligent. Books are an important part of their lives. They are a close and supportive family keen not only to share their interests with Tommy but also to share his interests. They delight in lively family discussions on a variety of topics every night at dinner. Elizabeth and John never let themselves get too busy to talk with Tommy and his sister or to read them bedtime stories.

These excerpts are not intended to be used as samples or copied as form letters. They are merely examples of some of the things a school might be interested in knowing about a child or a family. But remember, as each child is different, so too is each good letter of recommendation.

••THE TOUR••

Each school handles informational tours slightly differently. Some tours are one-on-one, led by either a parent with a child in the school or a representative from the admissions office.

Other tours include four or five couples. Some schools want you to bring your child, others want just you and your spouse. In two-parent families, most schools expect both parents to make the effort to come. If only one parent shows up, a school may interpret this as a lack of interest in the child's education. Even when parents are divorced or separated, admissions people like to see both parents if this is at all possible. They also expect to make the arrangements with you, not with your secretary. Find out the name of the person you will be seeing. Be sure you have the time right, and try to plan your day so you don't have to run out in the middle for a meeting. Some schools give parents a tour before accepting an application under the assumption that only parents who are genuinely interested in the school will then go through the application process. Others insist that the application be submitted first, thereby hoping to avoid disrupting their program by taking around parents who are merely curious but have no real interest in applying. Tours usually last about thirty minutes. In addition to current parents and admissions officers, tours may also be given by teachers, older students, or even by the head of the school or of a division in the school.

If you have questions about the school or the program, by all means ask them on the tour, but don't feel you have to make up questions just to impress the other parents or the tour guide. Admissions directors tend to be sympathetic toward shy or nervous parents, but are seldom favorably impressed with those who try to dominate or take over in a group situation. If you have read all the material from the school carefully before the tour, you may well arrive with a list of questions in your head. I do not recommend that you refer to a written list since that can be distracting to the tour leader and may seem pretentious. Look interested and listen carefully to what the tour leader is saying and to the questions of the other parents. Do not be so eager to make an impression that you ask a question that has just been answered. Try to see your questions in relation to the tour, and don't ask about the gymnastics program while you are looking at the art room. Putting the tour guide on the spot with esoteric questions, asked mainly to show off your own knowledge, doesn't serve any useful purpose.

If you like the school after the tour, you might consider writing a short note saying how much you enjoyed seeing it and confirming that you feel you and your child would be very happy there.

••THE PARENT INTERVIEW••

Admissions officers generally like to meet with prospective parents so they can put faces to the names on applications and get a sense of whether or not the parents' philosophy and goals are compatible with those of the school. Sometimes the parent interview takes place right after the tour; sometimes it is scheduled for another day. Some schools talk with three or four couples together in a group, while other schools prefer to talk with parents on a one-to-one basis. Usually there is an opportunity to meet either the head of the school or the head of the division to which your child is applying. The very idea of having an interview causes anxiety in some parents. One mother told me, "The week before we were supposed to go for the interview I started having panic dreams. I dreamed I arrived at the interview, took off my coat, and found I was wearing blue jeans. Then when I tried to fill out the application my pen wouldn't work."

Try to relax about the interview. The purpose of the interview is not to make you feel uneasy or as if you are under a microscope. The admissions staff wants to get a sense of you as a family. They may question you about your interests and hobbies or ask you to describe your child. If you have taken a few minutes to really think about your child, as I suggested earlier, you will be ready for this kind of question and will be able to talk naturally and intelligently without either bragging or putting your child down. And you will not berate yourself later for a lack of preparation. One mother who hadn't done this came to me in despair after an interview and said, "After a few minutes of pleasant small talk, the director of admissions leaned back and smiled and said, 'Now tell me about Angela.' I was completely nonplussed and didn't have a clue what to do. I started muttering something about Angela being just an average sort of girl." This response led the admissions director to decide that the mother was not particularly involved with her daughter and had little understanding of her personality and learning style. The director later told me that while Angela seemed a perfectly acceptable candidate, she felt her mother would add

The Elementary School of Your Choice •• *185*

little to the school community and might be difficult to work with should any problems arise. Angela was not accepted.

Then there are the parents who insist on telling the admissions director over and over again in front of other parents how superior their son or daughter is. Don't try to impress the admissions director with tales of your undiscovered prodigy. If your child really does have unusual talents or abilities, the more appropriate time to discuss them is when you are trying to determine if the school's program will fit his or her needs.

Nor should you try to be someone you aren't to impress the admissions director. If you fool her into thinking you're something you're not, it will backfire and in the long run you will be unhappy at the school. "If you're conservative, be conservative, if you're glitzy, be glitzy. You don't have to go out and buy a new wardrobe or a new image. If you're a stockbroker, dress like a stockbroker, if you're an artist, dress like an artist." This is the advice admissions directors generally give.

And remember that, like all interviews, the parent interview is a two-way process. It is just as much a time for you to learn more about the school as it is for the school to learn more about you. Schools welcome questions when they are asked without antagonism. Parents have the right and responsibility to know the expectations and goals of a school and then to decide for themselves whether these expectations and goals are what they want for their child.

••THE CHILD'S INTERVIEW••

Most schools want to meet your child as well as you, and most children rather enjoy their interviews. One little girl told me, "I liked the school because there were nice things to do. They gave us a snack. The teachers were nice. The letter book was fun and I loved the plant they let me take home." My own daughter made friends with a little girl at an interview for kindergarten, asked to have a playdate afterwards, and the two have been fast friends ever since.

Try to schedule the interview for a time that will interfere as little as possible with your child's regular schedule. Don't cancel a playdate or force your child to miss a gym class. Try to find a time when both of you are relaxed and rested. Before you think about buying your child a new outfit for a school interview, remember it is more important for your child to be comfortable than to look like a fashion plate, and some children are more comfortable in old clothes than new ones. Ordinary school clothes are far more appropriate than party clothes. Finally, plan to arrive a few minutes early. Most schools have a place where you can relax and look at a book together.

••WHAT TO TELL YOUR CHILD ABOUT THE INTERVIEW••

Most children like to know what is going to happen. Find out in advance from the school how the interview will be structured and whether your child will be asked to go off alone with a teacher or do things in a group with other children. Then explain the process to him or her. It is important that children look forward to the visit, see it as a chance to do and see interesting things, and know you have met the people and think they are friendly and caring. Try to keep things as low-key as possible, but at the same time let your child know that you expect her to cooperate and participate to the best of her ability in the activities that the teacher suggests.

••What Happens at an Interview for Kindergarten

The interview process varies from school to school. Sometimes schools first see children in a group, then take individual children off to do things one-on-one with a teacher. In other schools children are interviewed individually, usually by the admissions director or a first-grade teacher. The interview usually includes a variety of directed activities such as solving puzzles, identifying letters, copying shapes, counting buttons, building staircases with Cuisenaire rods, catching balls, hopping on one foot, or matching words. Children may also be asked to write their name and tell when their birthday is or where they live. Often children are asked to daw a picture of themselves or their family. Schools are not looking for little Picassos or Georgia O'Keeffes; instead they are interested in your child's observational and cognitive skills. The degree of detail in the picture (the inclusion of body parts such as fingers, ears, and eyebrows; sense of proportion; clothing details) can tell a lot about your child's developmental level. This can also sometimes tell a lot about the child's self-concept and emotional development. But not always. One parent had been reading Greek myths with her son. The night before his interview, she read him the story of Ulysses and the Cyclops, and they looked at a book on cubism. At the interview he was asked to draw a person, but was not asked to talk about his drawing. After the interview he proudly presented his mother with a Cyclops drawn in the cubist style. Her heart sank as she asked him to tell her about his picture, and he said it was Polyphemus, the Cyclops, and that he had tried very hard to make him to look just like the funny pictures they had looked at the night before. The mother called the admissions director and told her what had happened. The admissions director realized that this was a case not of a child who didn't know how to draw a person but of a creative child and a family who cared enough to share their interests. The boy was admitted to the school.

Sometimes children are asked to tell a story or talk about a favorite book. This gives the teacher a sense of a child's vocabulary and use of language. That is, if the child agrees to cooperate. One mother recalls that as her son was describing his visit to a school, he mentioned that he had been asked to tell a story. "Oh, which one did you tell?" "I didn't tell one. I didn't feel like telling a story so I said I didn't know any," replied this child who had been read to every night since his birth. Sensing his mother's displeasure, he decided to remedy matters at the next interview. Unfortunately, he wasn't asked for a story—but he was determined to tell one anyway and followed the teacher around the room throughout the interview trying to get her to listen to his story.

The child's response to the interviewer is often key to how well the interview goes and how much the interviewer actually learns about the child. Rest assured, however, that most interviewers have had a lot of experience with young children and are generally adept at establishing rapport.

•• What Is Being Evaluated During the Interview?

Schools are usually interested in finding out how your child adapts to new situations, learns new tasks, follows directions, cooperates in group activities, and works independently. Evaluations may cover any or all of six major areas: language facility, perceptual-motor skills, learning style, cognitive abilities, social-emotional development, and self-concept.

1. Language facility
- •• receptive language: language as it is heard
- •• expressive language: naming, syntactic ability (getting words in the right order), grammatical ability
- •• understanding and remembering words, sentences, and ideas

2. Perceptual-motor skills
- •• vision and hearing—history of ear infections
- •• fine motor coordination: pencil grip, cutting, sorting, etc.
- •• gross motor coordination: hopping, skipping, throwing, and catching
- •• visual and auditory perception: ability to distinguish sounds and forms, matching similar shapes
- •• visual and auditory memory—long and short term
- •• visual-motor integration: copying shapes

3. Learning style
- •• attention span: ability to focus, maintain, and also shift attention
- •• impulsiveness: "jumping in" without thinking or stopping to plan
- •• sense of responsibility: Whom does the child blame for mistakes? Does child see self as responsible for successes and failures?
- •• cognitive style: Does the child tend to approach problems analytically or more intuitively? Does the child use manipulative materials or verbal strategies in problem solving?

4. Cognitive abilities
- •• intellectual potential
- •• verbal conceptualization
- •• problem-solving abilities
- •• readiness skills

5. Social-emotional development and maturation
- •• relationships with peers
- •• signs of emotional tension, problems with control, or unusually withdrawn behavior that could interfere with learning

6. Self-concept
- • anticipation of success in unfamiliar circumstances
- • willingness to take risks
- • level of anxiety and effect on learning[2]

Not every school will evaluate all these areas, and those that do will give differing degrees of importance to particular strengths or weaknesses, depending on their program and goals. A school that stresses group activities and projects will be more interested in social skills, while a school that puts a premium on academic excellence may be more interested in verbal dexterity. Children are not expected to be able to read or write anything other than their names. Don't send your daughter to the interview with a copy of *Alice's Adventures in Wonderland* or suggest that your son recite the names of all the planets. "Schools," in the words of one director, "are not looking for children who perform like trained monkeys." They are looking for children who are curious about their world and interested in learning.

•• Tests

Whether you send your child to public school or to private/ independent school, testing is an issue you will probably face. It has been estimated that American school children take more than 100 million standardized tests a year, approximately 44 million of which are admissions and intelligence tests. The federal government mandates that all children suspected of having a disability be screened to identify those with special needs. IQ tests are an admissions factor in many programs for gifted children. A number of school districts are screening children before they begin kindergarten, then again before permitting them to go on to first grade.[3] According to a 1984 NAIS study, three-quarters of private/independent schools do some formalized testing for kindergarten admissions, and 77 percent use published tests. One-fourth of the schools used IQ scores. Schools in the West generally place more value on cognitive skills, while New England schools tend to be more interested in social and emotional development. The most commonly used tests were the Draw-a-Person test, the WPPSI-R, the WISC-R, and the Gesell tests.[4] Some schools also use the DIAL-R, the Metropolitan Readiness Test, or the Jansky Index. While individual schools may use a variety of tests, these tests usually fall into two categories: readiness and screening, and IQ.

••READINESS TESTS AND SCREENING TESTS••
Readiness tests are often based on Gesell's developmental schedules. They usually include matching letters and words, picture recognition, auditory discrimination, letter and number identification, listening skills and comprehension, number concepts and quantitative reasoning, verbal concepts, and sense of object-symbol correspondence. Readiness tests typically last between twenty and thirty minutes and are used in part to determine whether children are ready to begin a more formal approach to reading and to number concepts.

Screening tests are used to assess a child's language development, cognitive learning, physical motor development, and personal/social development. They are used to identify both strengths and areas that need attention and development. If a screening test reveals problems, the child is generally referred for a more thorough diagnostic evaluation. Some schools may use only a portion of a particular screening test and instead of recording a numerical score may write a brief note to the parents about their child's performance, describing relative strengths and weaknesses.

As a result of information derived from readiness and screening tests, a school may make a number of recommendations. It may advise that a child wait a year to begin kindergarten or go into a transitional or pre–first grade class to work on prereading and prearithmetic skills instead of first grade. It may use the results to group children within a class. Or, in the case of a private/independent school, the admissions committee may decide that a child isn't right for the school. The use and possible abuse of readiness and screening tests is a subject of intense debate among educators. Advocates say that knowing children's developmental age rather than just their chronological age helps ensure that grade placement and schoolwork are matched to a child's actual ability. Opponents argue that tests can become self-fulfilling prophecies that lower expectations and self-esteem, and even make children feel like failures before they begin school. They fear that children who test poorly may be given a watered down curriculum that will put them on a less-challenging academic track.

The developers of the tests agree that they should never be used as the sole criterion for grade placement or the grouping of children. Development is never static, and as parents and teachers know, children can change dramatically from one day to the next. Readiness and screening tests are useful predictors only if they are used in concert with parent questionnaires and the skilled observation of children at work and play.

••IQ TESTS••

IQ tests, also known as intelligence tests, are designed to measure a child's ability to perform certain tasks in comparison with other children of a similar age. According to Ruth Ochroch, Ph.D., clinical professor of psychology and coordinator of assessment training in the doctoral program in clinical psychology at New York University, "IQ tests are not school subject related with the exception of the Kaufman Assessment Battery for Children which contains 6 achievement subtests out of a total of 16 subtests. Test developers also strive to be 'culture free.' " IQ tests are relatively good predictors of a child's success in school but poor predictors of later career or economic success. As we have come to realize the incredibly complex nature of intelligence, through the work of Howard Gardner at Harvard among others, we no longer see a child's current performance on an intelligence test as equivalent to that child's total intelligence. We also know that a child's IQ changes. A precocious child who scores 130 or higher at age four may well not turn out to be a prodigy at all but rather a bright-average child who had an early developmental spurt. On the other hand, the world is full of late bloomers whom parents and teachers alike despaired of at six or even seventeen who then proceeded to make their mark on the world at thirty, forty, fifty, or later. Children mature at different rates and experience growth spurts and plateaus at various times. Some educators, like Frederick Erickson at the University of Pennsylvania, find that "social status is so highly correlated with IQ that it casts suspicion on IQ scores as reflecting intelligence rather than socio-economic status."[5] Everyone agrees that the children who do best on IQ tests are those who have been read to, listened to, talked with, and taken on trips and expeditions.

There are several types of IQ tests. Some are administered to a group of children, in the same way other standardized tests are; others are administered individually. Group tests usually take between thirty minutes and an hour. While there is no reading on the kindergarten test, other levels do require reading and may consequently be invalid for a child who has a reading problem. (If your child has a reading problem, be sure to tell the tester before a group test is administered.) The most frequently given group tests are the Otis-Lennon Mental Abilities Test and the Cognitive Abilities Test (CAT). Individual IQ tests usually take around ninety minutes to complete. Because no reading is required, they are often a more accurate estimate of a child's ability. The most frequently given individual tests are the Wechsler Primary and Preschool Scale of Intelligence, Revised (WPPSI-R), the Wechsler Intelligence Scale for Children, Revised (WISC-R), the Stanford-Binet, Fourth Edition, and the Kaufman Assessment Battery for Children. A new revision of the WISC, WISC III, was published in September 1991. When tests are revised, the norms on which the scores are computed may change. According to Mary S. Kelly, Ph.D., of Teachers College, Columbia University, "Sometimes when IQ tests are renormed, individual children's scores may be lower on the new test than on the old, but this shouldn't represent any cause for concern."

IQs were traditionally computed by dividing a child's mental age (MA), that is, the sum of successfully completed items on the test, by the child's chronological age, then multiplying the quotient by 100. Today, IQs are derived from a distribution of subtest scores for each age level, with the average IQ being 100 and a standard deviation of 10 to 15 points. The top possible score on the Stanford-Binet, Fourth Edition, is 164, and on a WPPSI-R or WISC-R, 160.

The classification of IQ Scores on the Wechsler is as follows:

Very superior	130+
Superior	120–129
Bright average	110–119
Average	90–109
Low average	80–89
Below average	70–79
Limited	69 and below[6]

In addition to an overall IQ score, Wechsler tests yield separate verbal and performance scores. Various studies have shown that children from middle-class backgrounds usually score higher on the verbal than on the performance part of the test. This is particularly true in urban areas where children may have fewer opportunities to run outside and actively interact with their environment, and are instead more apt to observe and discuss it. However, a difference of ten to fifteen points between a child's verbal and performance scores may sometimes indicate the need for further investigation. The WPPSI-R, like the WPPSI, consists of ten main subtests and two supplemental ones. The main verbal subtests are Information, Comprehension, Arithmetic, Vocabulary, and Similarities. The supplemental verbal test is Sentences. The main performance subtests are Object Assembly, Geometric Design, Block Design, Mazes, and Picture Completion. The supplemental test is Animal Pegs. The WISC-R has similar subtests, but Geometric Design and Mazes are replaced by Coding and Picture Arrangements. WISC III has an additional supplemental test symbol search. The verbal tests measure vocabulary, abstract reasoning, factual knowledge, and commonsense reasoning. The performance tests measure non-verbal abstract reasoning, visual/spatial organization, sequencing, attention to visual details, and fine motor coordination. They are scored from 0 to 19. A score of 10 means a child is in the 50th percentile for his or her age. These subtests give a more detailed profile of a child's relative strengths and weaknesses. They indicate whether a child is more proficient at verbal or quantitative reasoning. They also indicate how visual, perceptual, and motor skills are progressing. Testers usually analyze variations and patterns of difference in a child's scores to understand more about individual strengths and weaknesses and learning styles. Unfortunately, according to Dr. Ochroch this has not always been the case in cities where there is a great deal of competition for placement in private schools, and sometimes the final numerical IQ is treated as though it were cast in stone. Some psychologists only provide the subtest scores at the school's insistence. The more sophisticated schools with their own school psychologists will ask for subtest scores. Because of the ten to fifteen point variability, many psychologists prefer to provide a range, that is, superior to very superior, or bright average to superior, for both the verbal and performance scales rather than a numerical IQ.

The Stanford-Binet, Fourth Edition, is divided into four areas:

verbal reasoning, abstract/visual reasoning, quantitative reasoning and short-term memory. A child receives a standard age score, or SAS, in each area and a full-scale, or test-composite, score.

The classification of IQ scales on the Stanford-Binet, Fourth Edition, is as follows:

Very superior	132+
Superior	121–131
High average	111–120
Average	89–110
Low average	79–88
Slow learner	68–78[7]

In large metropolitan areas with many private schools, those schools may arrange to have children tested at one central location and have the results sent to each school instead of making children go through six or eight different tests. One such testing center, the Educational Records Bureau (ERB) in New York, has been testing applicants for private/independent schools since 1966. The ERB is a nonprofit educational institution chartered by the board of regents in 1927. It also has offices in Wellesley, Massachusetts. More than a thousand schools, both in the United States and overseas, use ERB testing programs.

Parents in cities where the ERB administers tests often say to me, "My son just had his ERB. What is an ERB test?" In fact, the ERB is not a test. The ERB administers a variety of objective standardized tests to children, including achievement tests at older grade levels, and Wechsler and Stanford-Binet tests for kindergarten and first-grade admissions. The tests indicate a child's strengths and weaknesses and give a sense of the child's readiness for kindergarten or first grade. A child's verbal development, reasoning abilities, number concepts, small motor development, hand/eye coordination and perceptual skills are looked at in comparison with those of other children across the country in the same age group. A low score will not automatically result in a child being overlooked, and a high score in no way assures a child an automatic acceptance to any school. The results of these tests are not cast in stone. They do not predict whether a four-year-old will graduate Phi Beta Kappa from college, or even forecast a child's success in elementary school. In fact, according to Maxine J. Scherl, the associate director of the ERB, "The important thing to remember is that the testing represents the child's performance at a particular time in his or her life. It is not meant as a predictor of long-range potential. Children this young are still developing and may present a different profile on subsequent tests in future years."

All the schools with which I am familiar also stress their opinion that "any testing of children at this age cannot be viewed as a definite evaluation but only as a glimpse of your child's performance at a given moment on one particular day." Children's scores may be influenced by a variety of factors, including whether they had a nap that day, whether they are coming down with a cold, whether they have just had a fight with a sibling, or even whether their parents are feeling upset or anxious. Rosemary Lea, who has taught first-grade children for nearly thirty-five years, is convinced that she can tell as much about whether a child will be happy and successful in school by looking at him and talking to him as by testing him. "If he has some common sense, if he knows when his birthday is and where he lives, if he understands my humor, if he is willing to argue with me, if there is a sparkle and a smile, and a piece of steel in a shy one, then he will be happy here."

•• What Should I Do to Prepare My Child for Admissions Tests?

The best preparation begins the day your child is born. It is called "good parenting." It is loving your child and setting limits. It is helping your child develop confidence and a sense of self-esteem. It is reading to your child, and talking and telling stories together. It is going to the market together and picking out the vegetables for dinner. It is doing puzzles and playing games. It is watching the elephants in the zoo or going for walks in the woods. It is painting and making shapes with Play-Doh. It is doing mazes and building castles out of blocks. It is listening to music or looking at paintings in a museum. It is answering a million questions that all begin with "why." It is sharing your world and all the things that are important to you.

Do all of these things, but don't have your child tested for practice. Don't try to find a copy of the test or hire a tutor. My own experience in testing young children and in reading reports of other testers leads me to believe that this is self-defeating, expensive, time-consuming, and not in the best interest of your child. If you appear overly anxious about prepping your child for a test, your child will sense your anxiety, become anxious, and have difficulty concentrating and focusing on the test. Testers are looking for spontaneity, for the way children react to challenges. A child who has taken a test for practice may well respond with polite boredom rather than interest, and thus may end up with a lower score. A child who is tutored for the test may very well look up at the tester with a sweet smile and say, "Oh, I know how to do this, I do it with Miss Kay every Tuesday." A comment like this must be noted in the write-up of the test and the score may be invalidated. If by chance the tutoring should go undetected, the final result could be worse yet. Your child could be placed in an inappropriate school or grade and wind up with a diminished sense of self-esteem— feeling like a failure at six.

•• Assessing the Qualifications of the Tester

If a school requires that your child be given an IQ test as part of the admissions process, you will want to know that the person administering the test has been properly trained. Dr. Ruth Ochroch recommends that parents ask specific questions about the qualifications and experience of the person who will be testing their child. Make sure that the psychologist is licensed and is either a clinical or school psychologist. The only exceptions are testers working in public school systems. According to Dr. Ochroch, psychologists testing young children should have had training and experience in this area. This requirement is sometimes ignored, and tests may be administered by people with inadequate training. In addition to training and experience, Dr. Ochroch believes that testers should know young chidren and be able to establish a good rapport with them. Testers should also be patient and willing to take the time to bring out the best in a child rather than rushing through the exam mechanically because they are being paid by the test and want to give as many as possible as quickly as possible.

•• How Do Schools Decide?

As I noted earlier most schools give preference to certain groups. Next they usually consider the balance of their class. If a school is coed, there needs to be a good balance of boys and girls. Age is a factor. A school might accept a child who is slightly on the young side if it is also planning to accept several other younger children. Schools are also looking for a certain degree of economic, ethnic, and social diversity. No school wants everyone's father and mother to be a lawyer. Schools also look for diversity in personality types; they don't want a class full of either leaders or followers. Many schools would agree with the school in Georgia that wrote in its catalog, "Savannah Country Day seeks a diverse group of students. That's because we believe that the school is enriched as much by a student of average ability who has great personality or boundless spirit or special talent as by an academically gifted student. We also believe that our student body is enriched by children from different cultural, racial and ethnic backgrounds."[8]

Admissions people look for children who will thrive in their school. They want children who can handle their curriculum without undue stress. They want children who will be comfortable with the degree of competition and academic expectations. They want children who will fit in well with the other children. They want children who will benefit from their offerings in art, music, drama, and athletics, as well as academics. What schools are looking for in applicants of course varies widely from school to school, depending on the school's goals and expectations. Some have very definite opinions on the kind of child who will do well. A teacher at one such school said to me, "We have a specific type of child in mind. We look for a child who is first of all emotionally mature. This is a traditional pencil and paper school, not a school with lots of manipulative materials. This school is very demanding and it is necessary to be a pretty sophisticated five-and-a-half-year-old. We want a child who is linguistically agile." Other schools look for more intangible qualities such as a certain liveliness and curiosity. Some schools look for children with special talents, even if they have possible weaknesses in other areas.

In making admissions decisions, elementary schools look at families as well as children. Remember that most schools—

elementary as well as early childhood—want families who will support the school, who will understand it, and who will feel comfortable there.

Who decides? Admissions decisions in all but the smallest schools are generally made by an admissions committee. This committee is composed of the head of school, the head of the lower school, the admissions director, and sometimes one or two lower-school teachers. When I was a lower school head, our admissions committee consisted of myself, the headmaster, and the director of admissions. Our three first-grade teachers served in an advisory capacity.

•• The Wait List

The meaning of "wait list" varies from school to school. Some wait lists are cosmetic. That is, the school feels that your child is not academically suitable for its curriculum and has no intention of changing its mind. However, the admissions director may be reluctant to send a straightforward letter of rejection for some reason: perhaps someone close to the school, such as an alumnus/alumna or a trustee, has written a particularly enthusiastic letter of recommendation; perhaps the director of the early childhood school has been very supportive; perhaps an older sibling is at the school, or you or your husband went there.

Most wait lists, however, are not cosmetic. Most schools put children on wait lists only when they would very much like to have that child if there were room. Don't give up. Places do often open up. In our increasingly mobile society, someone's mother or father is quite likely to be transferred over the summer. When you call the school to accept the wait list, try to get some idea about its length and a realistic idea of your child's chances for acceptance. Be sure to expresss your enthusiasm. If it is your first-choice school, say so. Other things being equal, schools tend to want people who want them. If this is an ongoing school, talk to the director of your child's early childhood school. If he or she feels the school is really appropriate for your child and knows how much you want it, a few well-chosen words to the admissions director can be very helpful in seeing that your child is given top consideration for the first available spot. It also isn't a bad idea to ask an alumnus/alumna, a trustee, or the parent of a child in the school to say a few words on your behalf, but only if you know them well and feel they would speak with genuine enthusiasm. A halfhearted recommendation from a friend of a friend or someone you met once at a cocktail party that damns with faint praise does more harm than good.

•• Coping with Rejection

If you receive a rejection letter from a school, there is usually very little you can do. The admissions staff has made up its mind and that's that. Parents, of course, respond differently to these letters. Some strike back. One mother I know had her daughter tested by a psychologist, who then wrote a letter stating how superior the child was to the school that had rejected her. The school thanked the psychologist for the information and politely declined to reverse its decision. Another parent used social and political pull to get her son into a school in Virginia. Unfortunately, the school was too academically rigorous and competitive for the boy. The "whole experience turned out to be a disaster," and according to his mother, the boy left after a year. It has been my professional experience that if a parent succeeds in convincing a school to reverse its decision, it is usually to the child's detriment, and the parents sooner or later regret it.

Try to keep in mind, hard as it may seem at the time, that often a school is the best judge of whether or not your child will thrive there. If your child is rejected by a school, it's best to put it behind you with the realization that no matter how much you thought you liked that school, it probably wasn't the right one for your child. Begin to look seriously at your other options. The one exception to this rule is when the school tells you that it feels your child is a little young for its program and suggests you apply again next year. If you like the school, by all means wait and apply the following year. Before you decide to accept another school that doesn't mention age, remember that if your child is young for one kindergarten, he or she is probably young for the others as well, and the first school is really doing you a favor by being honest.

Also beware of the school that doesn't have any space at your child's grade level but offers a place in the next grade because that's where they have an opening. One mother who accepted such an offer found her daughter faced with having to repeat a grade a few years later, not because she couldn't keep up academically, but because the social pressure of being the youngest was overwhelming: "The other girls were wearing bras and talking about boyfriends and Sarah was still a little girl playing with Barbie dolls and sleeping with stuffed animals." Don't jeopardize your child's future by jumping at the solution that seems easiest at the moment without carefully considering the longer-term impact.

Being rejected can sometimes lead you to the discovery of viable new options. A mother from a small city in Michigan told me that initially she felt devastated when her son didn't get into a private school. She was forced to look at the local public school, and discovered everything she had liked in the private school and more: small classes and wonderful teachers, plus an enclosed nature area with a Japanese garden filled with pheasants and wood ducks and wild turkeys. She was delighted, and so was her son.

Finally, remember there is no one school that will make or break your child's future academic career. There is no one best school. The best school is always the one that is right for your child now, not tomorrow. In the next two chapters, we will look at your part in your child's life at school beginning with your role as your child's first teacher.

PART III

Your Role in Your Child's Education

·· ·· ·· ··
E L E V E N
·· ·· ·· ·· ·· ·· ·· ·· ·· ·· ·· ··

Parents as Their Child's First Teachers

Our young sons and daughters start to school this fall. It's going to be sort of strange and new to them for awhile, and I wish you would sort of treat them gently.

You see, up to now they have been "King of the hill" . . . and boss of the backyard . . . and mother has always been near to soothe any wounds and repair hurt feelings.

But now things are going to be different.

Very soon they are going to walk down the front steps, wave goodbye and start out on the great adventure . . . an adventure that might take them across continents, across oceans . . . an adventure that will probably include tragedy and sorrow. . . . To live their life in the world they will have to live in, will require faith and love and courage.

FROM THE *FREE TRADER,*
TRI-LAKES EDITION

As a child I thought getting ready for school meant a plaid dress, a pair of squeaky new shoes, and a pencil case filled with freshly sharpened pencils. I was wrong. Getting ready for school really began the day I was born. Getting ready for school was learning to smile and to hold a cup, to talk and to walk, and to go up and down stairs by myself. It was listening to my mother read nursery rhymes and *Winnie-the-Pooh,* learning to love the sound and rhythm of language. It was making friends and knowing how to comfort a friend when something went wrong. It was the gradual awareness that when my mother went out to do an errand, she wasn't gone forever; she would come back to love me and to teach me about the world. Getting ready for school was learning that it was all right to ask "why" a thousand

·· ·· ·· ··

times a day. It was finding out that the world was full of questions and puzzles waiting for answers, and that there were books and people out there to help me find the answers. It was learning the things I could do by myself and knowing that if I needed help I could ask for it. It was the sense of joy and accomplishment that came from learning to dress myself, to hang by my knees, or to write my name—and to exclaim, "I did it!"

It is important to remember that we are our children's first teachers. This isn't always as easy as it sounds. As Burton White, founder of the Harvard Preschool Project, once said, "You get more information with your new car than you do with your new baby."[1] In an attempt to address parents' need for information, the Missouri Department of Elementary and Secondary Education together with four school districts began an innovative program in 1981 called "Parents As First Teachers," based on White's research at Harvard. Its goal was to provide parents with practical child-development information and appropriate resources. Children taught themselves but parents provided a safe, enriched environment and helped the children expand their original ideas and language skills. An independent evaluation of the project in 1985 found that "the superiority of the project children was substantial and dramatic in nearly all linguistic, intellectual and school related areas. . . ."[2] School officials anticipate a positive impact on the children's lives, including less need for remedial instruction. They also believe that the development of trust between parents and educators, which is an essential part of the program, will lead to an ongoing close relationship between home and school that will benefit the children. Various studies have supported this view by showing that the most successful early childhood intervention programs work closely with parents.

What does this research mean for middle-class parents and their children? It reinforces my belief that, quite simply, you are an important, ongoing partner in your child's education. It means that no matter how wonderful the school you choose for your child is, you can't expect the school to educate your child without your help. And there are a number of important ways that you can help.

1. Let your children know that you value them for what they are, not just what they do. Jerome Kagan, a Harvard professor of developmental psychology, finds that this "need not involve a lot of physical affection: it depends on what is natural to you. Just communicate in your eyes that your child is valuable."[3]

2. Encourage your child to become a "doer" rather than always a watcher. The head of a lower school in a large city recently said to a group of third-grade parents, "Your urban children are all very verbal but they are not 'doers.' They may lack exposure to practical mathematical concepts such as measuring, making change, estimating and making comparisons. These experiences can easily be made available in an urban environment. Opportunities to build and assemble things can be provided. City children need to throw and catch balls, and to run and jump and climb, all of which can be done in the local park or in front of a building. Doing develops critical thinking."

3. Help your children to feel good about themselves. Praise them for their efforts and accomplishments. A child with a positive self-concept will get along more easily with peers and have more confidence to experiment and try new ideas.

4. Help your children to experience success by giving them opportunities to master such important childhood skills as pouring their own milk, making a peanut butter and jelly sandwich, using scissors, jumping rope, throwing, catching and kicking a ball, or climbing a tree. When children expect to succeed because they have experienced success in the past, they are more likely to succeed in the future.

5. Teach your chidren not to be afraid of failing. Tell them that you don't expect them to do everything right all the time and show them by your reaction to their mistakes that you mean what you say. Let them see you and other adults make mistakes sometimes. A teacher I know was asked at a parent's evening to identify the most important thing she taught her class. She responded after a moment's thought, "I teach them how to fail," and went on to explain that learning to know and accept the possibility of failure gives children the freedom and the power to go beyond the answer book to test hypotheses of their own, to experiment, and to invent.

6. Try to set realistic goals for your children and not let them sense your disappointment when they have trouble living up to your expectations.

7. Give your children lots of opportunities to play with other children. Research at Duke University, Vanderbilt University, the University of Washington, and Pennsylvania State University indicate that children who do not have social intelligence—that is, who can't interpret the feelings and intentions of playmates—can have academic as well as social difficulties later on in school.[4]

•• The Superbaby Trap

One of the hazards facing children today is having an overanxious parent. These parents are often dismayed to discover that just as there are no instruction manuals for babies, there are also often no correct answers to questions and problems. They are used to demanding perfection and getting it, and so they seem to want a similar perfection in their children. Perfection for these parents may mean not only the perfect little physical specimen our parents asked for, but a child who must be first in everything throughout life. Early childhood teachers complain that parents drag their toddlers from gym class to swimming to violin lessons to French for tots, leaving them no time to be two-year-olds. The children, they find, are often exhausted and cranky. Of course, the desire for precocious children is not new. Cultural historian Philippe Aries reports in his book, *Centuries of Childhood,* that cases of child prodigies were fairly common from the fifteenth to the seventeenth centuries.[5] More recently, pianists such as Liszt, Joseph Hofman, and Leopold Godowsky were playing by the age of four, and Vladimir Horowitz is reputed to have said that he started playing late—at the age of five.[6] What is new today is not the rare child who becomes a genuine prodigy, but the ever-increasing number of children who are being inappropriately pushed by overly ambitious or misguided parents, as well as by the numerous commercial enterprises that foster the competition.

When my own son was small, I succumbed, despite both my better judgment and my experience as a teacher, to the advertised enticements of an early reading program. After a week of sitting patiently on the floor showing flash cards to a squirmy toddler, I relegated them and the guidebook to the top shelf of a closet and we went back to reading Dr. Seuss and Winnie-the-Pooh. My son later learned to read at school in first grade. My daughter, on the other hand, who was never exposed to the benefits of flash cards, picked up reading on her own at the age of three by figuring out the signs in taxis and buses. It is not always easy for even the most well intentioned parents to ignore the lure of promised academic precocity for their children. However, as Kerstin Rhodie, a former colleague of mine at St. Bernard's who has taught several generations of young children, said to me, "You can't make a tooth grow by wanting it to grow. It is the same with children. If parents are anxious about a child's progress, they will transmit this anxiety to the child and the anxiety will only increase the difficulty. Every child has an internal time clock, and when that child is ready to do something it will be done."

Try not to put pressure on your children to do things they are not ready to do or make them compete in ways they're not yet ready for. Just because the boy who lives down the block is riding a bicycle or playing ice hockey doesn't mean your child is ready or interested in doing these things. Pushing children to do things too soon doesn't help them to master skills, it only creates frustration for both parent and child. Don't worry if your child hasn't started to read before kindergarten or even first grade. No matter what you may have heard or read, the other children are not all reading when they start school. Rest assured that if you have done the things I suggested, unless there is a learning disability that requires special help, your child will learn to read at school when he or she is ready. If, on the other hand, your child is ready to read and demanding to be taught, pointing at words and asking what they say, give that child the help he or she asks for. Just don't push your children into reading or anything else before they are ready.

Much of the frenetic search for early perfection in our children may in the end prove counterproductive. David Perkins, a senior research fellow at the Harvard Graduate School of Education, has found that one aspect of adult creativity "involves the ability to cut across traditional boundaries and make unexpected connections. . . . Gutenberg got the idea for making the first printing press from watching the operation of a wine press."[7] Psychologist Erik H. Erikson holds that in "play age," or preschool, children, what is being learned is "a sense of initiative and purpose in life, as well as a sense of playfulness and creativity."[8] Harvard professor of psychology Ellen Langer argues that "what you do when you put yourself in a play situation is look for novelty, and when you're involved with something novel, you're necessarily mindful."[9]

This is not to say that all classes for preschoolers are bad but rather that we should use some common sense and discretion. Obviously overscheduling a toddler or even a ten-year-old to the point of exhaustion is a bad idea. However, if the alternative to French for tots is not daydreaming in a tree house or sailing toy boats in a stream, but rather an hour or two in front of a television or Nintendo set, go for the French. But before you sign your child up for any program, take a close look at your reasons. Are you doing it because you think you ought to or because you think you and your child will enjoy it? Do you see it as a hassle or potential fun? Try to target your child's interests, not your own preconceptions about "important" knowledge. Follow up on interests your son has shown instead of the ones you wish he had. If your daughter spends the day using your bed as a trampoline and your living room sofa as a vault, then a gym class would probably be more appropriate for her than Mozart for Toddlers. If your child loves to paint, sign up for an art class. Just don't insist on doing everything all at once because that's what your friends are doing.

There are times, though, no matter how much we care and how well we think we know our children, that we don't really know the things that have an impact on them, the things that nudge that special spark of creativity along. Recently my daughter Diana was asked to write a composition about her favorite place. She disappeared into her room with a pad and pencil. And when she reappeared I discovered that her favorite place wasn't a toy store or a museum or an art studio or even a gymnasium, but a rock:

I like to go exploring in the woods behind my country house in the Adirondacks. One day I went through the woods near the woodshed and I found a rock. It was very flat. So I named it Flat Rock.

After that I went there every day early in the morning.

When I got there I would sit and feel the morning sun soak in through the trees on my bare legs. On cold days I'd feel the frost around me. Sometimes I'd go and read a book. Sometimes I'd creep up there after dinner and watch the light get dimmer and dimmer.

When it was summer I would pick some flowers and make a circle around Flat Rock with them. I would pretend that I was a princess and little piles of rock would be all the people scurrying here and there. I would be on a balcony looking over the rim.

In the fall I would pick pine cones for tepees and twigs for Indians. I'd use Flat Rock as the battle field and the trees for hideouts.

I would also use Flat Rock as a friend when I was frustrated, troubled, mad, or lonely. I'd come and talk to Flat Rock for hours just as if it were a real person.[10]

I learned a lot about my daughter and about eight-year-olds from reading that composition. Sometimes I wonder if Huck Finn didn't know something that we have forgotten. Perhaps it's not the computer or the math lab or Mozart for Kids or the reading-readiness kit that our children need but tree houses and rafts on the river and flat rocks in the woods behind the house. And the curriculum we teach our children isn't reading, writing, and arithmetic, or even the languages of computers. It's preparing our children to stand on their own two feet and think for themselves.

Our children's interests and knowledge reflect both the experiences we give them and our own attitudes toward these experiences. Psychologists find that our children are keenly aware of our attitudes, both the conscious and the unconscious ones. Professor Kagan said recently, "If you want your child to care about intellectual inquiry then be that way. [If] you want your child to be idealistic, be that way. You want your child to be against war, you don't have to worry about buying toy soldiers, that is quite irrelevant. In your behavior, behave as though you are against war and you'll get the child you want."[11] Our children learn to see the world through our eyes before they see it through their own. They learn our values not only through the words we speak but also by the things we do and the things we don't do. Helping our children to understand our values and our world, to know the things that are important to us and our expectations for them, to know why we do the things we do and live the way we do—these are the most important things we can do to get our children ready for school.

Getting Your Child Ready for School

1. Try to share your world and your experiences with your children. Take your children to the store with you to buy orange juice and to the bank to cash a check. Eat dinner together. Turn off the TV and talk.

2. Talk to your children about what you're doing and why you're doing it. Share your interests with your children. Take them to the office with you occasionally; show them where you work and what you do. When you go on walks together, talk to them about the animals you see or about the changes in the seasons; point out the squirrels getting ready for winter and the geese migrating south.

3. Try to really listen to your children. Don't listen to the news, read the newspaper, check the latest stock quotations, or comb the dog's hair while they are talking. Look your children in the eyes and really listen to what they are saying. Encourage them to share things with you, to tell you their hopes and dreams as well as their sorrows and angers. Try to let them know that you are there for them when they need you.

4. Encourage your children to make choices. Let them decide whether they will wear the blue sweater or the green one, whether they will have grapes or apples for dessert.

5. Set reasonable limits for your children and enforce them as consistently as possible. It is confusing for a child to be allowed to bounce on the sofa one day but not the next, to not know when you mean what you say and when you don't.

6. Encourage your children to explore, to experiment and question. George Z. Tokieda, a science teacher at the Brearley School in New York City, talked about some of the ways parents can help spark scientific curiosity in children without buying expensive equipment or signing up for courses:

In the same way that Archimedes made the bathtub famous, you and your children can use your bathtub as an experimental laboratory to make many discoveries about density, buoyancy, volume, mass, and displacement—concepts which explain all about floating and sinking. As you walk down the sidewalk you can be paleontologists and look for fossils in the walls of buildings. . . . You can be skyline astronomers and watch daily and seasonal changes. . . . Over what building does the sun travel each day? Is it the same height each day over your building? Does the sun shine down the same street at the same time each day? In which direction is it moving along the streets as we go into winter? . . . Stop off at the playground for a "class" in "Playground Physics." The seesaw is a wonderful way to introduce leverage. . . . Be sidewalk ecologists and go on a moss hunt as you walk along. . . . Adopt a favorite patch and watch it change through the seasons. . . . Take a little piece home and start a terrarium in one of those wonderful plastic salad containers.[12]

7. Try to make music and art a part of your children's lives. Sing to your children and with them. Provide records and tapes to listen to and encourage them to make their own. Take your children to museums and concerts. Regardless of whether they play an instrument or paint when they are older, this will give them the background for a later understanding and appreciation of the arts.

8. Encourage your children to do things for themselves at the appropriate age: to feed and dress themselves, to bathe themselves and brush their teeth, to clean their rooms and help with household chores. Children develop a feeling of control and a sense of self-esteem when they can say, "I did it. I did it all by myself."

9. Make time to play with your children. Play board games, card games, and old favorites such as Simon says and hide-and-seek. Play catch and kick a soccer ball around. Build snow caves in the winter and sand castles in the summer. Children need to know how to enjoy being part of a family.

10. And last but not least, read to your children. Read many different kinds of books, books about nature, and about astronomy. Read biographies and mysteries and adventure stories, nursery rhymes and fables, poetry and mythology. Show your children the worlds of adventure and mystery that lie between the covers of a good book. Don't worry about whether the book is too hard or too easy, you will know whether it is right for your children by the way they react. Get your children a library card and take them to the library with you. Browse through bookstores together. But above all, let your children see you read. Every time your children see you engrossed in a book, it reinforces that reading really is important to you and not just something you tell them to do because it's good for them like eating oatmeal.

•• Visual/Perceptual and Fine Motor Activities

A number of parents have asked me over the years for suggestions on ways they can give their children more practice with fine motor activities and help sharpen visual/perceptual skills. If you sense that your child's fine motor skills are not developing as rapidly as they should be or that your child seems to be having trouble with visual/perceptual tasks in school, kindergarten teachers recommend trying some of the following activities at home. The necessary equipment can be bought at most toy and art supply stores; some of it can be made at home.

Clay and Play-Doh
Cutting and pasting
Dot-to-dot picture books
Pegboards: Children copy geometric patterns with colored pegs on a board
Parquetry blocks: Children copy geometric designs with colored blocks
Beads for stringing
Sewing cards
Pickup sticks
Dominoes
Board games: Candyland, Checkers, Chutes and Ladders, Lotto, Bingo, Chinese Checkers
Puzzles
Card games: Go Fish, Old Maid, Slap Jack, Snap, War, Concentration
Memory games
Ring toss

If you decide to try these activities, remember not to push your children or force them to do things before they are ready. If your child dislikes one activity or finds it frustrating, try something else. If the activities aren't enjoyable for you and for your child, the purpose is defeated.

•• The First Day of School

My father, who is eighty years old, remembers his first day of school. He spent most of it locked in the closet for getting in a fight with the principal's son. Fortunately we don't lock children in closets anymore, but our children may still have their own set of worries and anxieties. One fifth grader remembers that for the first half of first grade he didn't know where the bathroom was at school, so he spent most of the time when he was supposed to be learning to read worrying about whether he could wait until he got home to go to the bathroom. Some preschool age children think that going to school is a one-time event and don't realize they have to go back after the first day. One mother solved this problem by putting up a chart for her son with stars to indicate which days he went to school.

While we can't always anticipate all our children's concerns, we can help them to deal with these concerns by being there when they need us and encouraging them to talk to us. Most children like to know what to expect from new experiences, and we can help our children make the adjustment to school by giving them a sense of what to expect. Many parents find the following suggestions helpful in preparing their children for their first day of school.

Advance Preparation

1. Try to visit the school with your child either in the spring or at the end of the summer. One mother told me that she and her son visited the school he was planning to attend and talked about it together: "We talked about the things he would get to do—the paintings and collages and all, and about the kids he would meet. We talked about it a lot together and we talked to other children who lived in the building and were going to school there too."

2. Try to find out which teacher your child will have and ask if you can set up a brief meeting. A few schools ease the transition from home to school by arranging for teachers to come to visit children at home the week before school starts. My own children's early childhood teachers came to visit every year. They sat on the floor with my children building with Legos and talking about the things they would be doing at school. Some kindergarten and first-grade teachers write a short letter to each of their students welcoming them to school. Many schools hold open houses for parents and children so they can meet their teachers and get used to their classrooms before school begins. Some schools hold these sessions in June so teachers can give out pamphlets with suggested summer activities and can make specific individualized suggestions to parents on ways they can help their children feel ready for school in September. Other schools have special orientation programs that bring new students into school for a day before classes begin so they can learn where everything is and how to use the cafeteria.

3. Find a children's book about starting school and read it with your child. There are a number of good books on starting school: Sesame Street has one, and there is also one in the Berenstain Bear series. *Will I Have a Friend?* by Miriam Cohen, illustrated by Lillian Hoban, is another excellent choice. Your local library or bookstore will probably have several choices: even your supermarket may have a few. One book I found in a supermarket, *Amanda's First Day of School,* is a story about a bear named Amanda who is too excited to go to sleep the night before school starts, or even to eat her breakfast in the morning. The book touches on many of a young child's concerns and ends on a reassuring note.

4. Some schools put out special handbooks for parents about starting school. Find out if your child's school has a parent handbook, and if it does, read it and discuss relevant points with your child. The federal government publishes a helpful booklet titled "Plain Talk About When Your Child Starts School." It is available free of charge from the Consumer Information Center, Pueblo, Colorado 81009.

5. If possible, arrange for your child to have a playdate with one or two of the children who will be in the same class. If you are new to the community and don't know any of the children, you can usually get the names of some children in the neighborhood by calling the school.

Guidelines for the First Day

1. Give your children a sense of control over the process of starting school by letting them decide whether they will wear the red shirt or the blue shirt, give them the opportunity to select their own lunch box, and encourage them to help you get their lunch ready.

2. Have everything ready the night before school starts, including the clothes your child has selected.

3. Sometimes it is comforting for a child to take a favorite toy tucked away in a backpack. Before you suggest this to your child, however, be sure the school permits children to bring toys from home.

4. Take your child to school on the first day, even if it means taking a vacation day. I have seen children in tears because all the other children had a parent there and they didn't! (See chapter 6, "Separation.")

5. Be sure to be on time to pick your child up. If you are even one minute late your child may feel abandoned.

When I asked one eight-year-old if she remembered how she had felt when she started school, she responded thoughtfully, "I used to think I can't wait to go! But then when the time came to go I wasn't so sure about going. I didn't want to leave Mommy." One little boy wrote, "On my first day at kindergarten I was shy. On my second day I wasn't shy at all. On the third day I made friends." Many of the other children I spoke to also remembered first feeling shy or scared or embarrassed, then excited about making a friend or discovering that school was fun. It is important for parents to remember that all these feelings are normal and very typical.

Finally, it is good to remember that while starting school is an important event in your child's life, it is not really comparable to landing a person on the moon or discovering the North Pole. Even if something does go wrong on the first day, all is not lost. As one teacher who has seen several generations of children start school said to me, "It is easier if children get off to a good start in school, but if they don't there are many routes to success in school, and not all start on the first day."

In the next and last chapter, we will look at what it means to be part of a school community. We will explore ways you can help your children find success at school by being an effective partner in their education.

•• •• •• ••
T W E L V E
•• •• •• •• •• •• •• •• •• •• •• ••

Parents and Schools: A Partnership

School learning is not an isolated cognitive operation. It builds on preschool relationships between parents and child which have promoted a given level of development and academic learning readiness. . . . Good relationships between home and school can serve to motivate students to achieve at the level of their ability in school.

JAMES P. COMER, M.D.,
DIRECTOR OF THE SCHOOL
DEVELOPMENT PROGRAM,
CHILD STUDY CENTER,
YALE UNIVERSITY

"What is your child doing in science this week?" the science teacher asked the parents perched on small yellow chairs in an elementary school classroom on a recent October evening. There was a moment of silence, a few self-conscious coughs, and then one or two hands were tentatively raised. The teacher explained why it is important for parents to know what their children are studying; the parents nodded in agreement. Some asked the next morning at breakfast about levers, centrifugal force, the bonding habits of baboons, or gravity on Jupiter. A few followed up with a trip to the zoo, the planetarium, and the public library, or helped set up a home-based experiment to reinforce what their children were doing in school. Their children will learn that what they are doing in science is important and worthy of their parents' interest. But not all parents have the time to do all these things every week. Teachers realize that parents have other responsibilities, and they do not expect parents to put their lives and careers on hold while they go to

•• •• •• ••

the zoo to help their child research the life-style of the Malaysian tapir. However, even the busiest, most driven parents can find time to ask questions and show an interest in their child's activities—and a little interest on a parent's part can go a long way. Researchers at Johns Hopkins University have shown definitively that parents' involvement in their children's education almost guarantees that their children's achievement level will increase.[1]

Gene I. Maeroff, senior fellow at the Carnegie Foundation for the Advancement of Teaching, charged recently that many parents turn over too much responsibility to schools and consequently know little about what their children are studying or even how they are doing. Parents, he finds, often fail to take advantage of the feedback offered by schools, and after the first few grades, "parent conferences and open school nights in some places get as much attendance as a lecture on antelopes at the public library."[2] If parents want to help their children find success in school, they need to make the time to meet with teachers, observe classes, and review homework assignments. According to Diane Ravitch, adjunct professor of history and education at Teachers College and Chester E. Finn, Jr., professor of education and public policy at Vanderbilt University, coauthors of "What Do Our 17-Year-Olds Know?" "Children learn pretty much what the important adults in their lives make a point of seeing that they learn . . . children are not likely to learn about the Declaration of Independence or the Great Depression, or the voyage of Odysseus, or the uncertainties of Hamlet unless adults see to these things in a purposeful way."[3] Parents cannot expect to turn a child over to a school and have that child returned twelve or thirteen years later stamped with an official seal of approval like an electrical appliance. If you want your child someday to be "welcomed into the company of educated men and women," you must be actively involved in that child's school from the first day of school.

·· The Ten Most Important Things You Can Do to Help Your Child in School

There are a number of important steps you can take from the very beginning to help ensure that your child has a successful experience in school.

1. Let your child know that school is important to you. Be sure your child gets to school on time in the morning. Take vacation dates seriously: if you book flights the day before vacation starts or return two days after vacation ends, your children are going to get the message that vacation takes priority over school. Show an active interest in what your child is doing in school, and be ready and willing to help. If your four-year-old son needs cranberries because his class is making cranberry sauce for Thanksgiving, be sure he has those cranberries; if your nine-year-old daughter needs a book on cougars for a research project, take her to the library to get that book. Find out what your child is studying and try to send in books or pictures to enrich the curriculum. When my son was in kindergarten and the class was studying foreign cultures, a family from Portugal dressed up in traditional Portuguese clothes, sang Portuguese folk songs, and brought in Portuguese treats for snacks. At another school, one of the parents, an Olympic kayaker, brought her kayak to school and talked with the children about kayaking. When I was teaching, a mother arranged for the class to meet the authors of a book the children were reading. You don't have to have an exotic skill or special talent to contribute. Most parents can find something interesting to share with their children's class, even if it is only helping to make Jell-O or sending in a jump rope for *J* week in kindergarten.

2. Get to know your children's teachers, and build up the kind of rapport that makes communication easy. Try to take your children to school and pick them up whenever possible. This provides a nice tie between parent and school and gives you a chance to pass on important pieces of information to the teacher. Get to know other teachers in the school. Find out who the best teachers are. If your school permits parents a choice in teacher selection, take advantage of that opportunity. Remember, though, that no one teacher, no matter how good, is always the best teacher for every child. Arrange a meeting with your children's teachers before the end of the year to discuss their progress, share thoughts on the kinds of assignments that they respond well to, and the type of class atmosphere that seems to help them to thrive. The teachers may not assign your child to the class you request because they must also keep in mind the balance of the class as a whole, but they will know that you care about your child's education and will probably give extra thought when placing your child in a class for next year.

3. Get involved in your child's school. There are many ways to be involved. Start by attending all the activities the school offers: parents' nights, panel discussions, and lectures. Elementary schools always need volunteers to help in the library, chaperone class trips, sell tickets for the raffle, and bring treats for the class party. Children like to be able to say, "My mom is working on the book fair" or "My dad's doing safety patrol today." When you contribute time, your children will feel you are really part of their experiences and their lives. You might decide to volunteer to be a class representative or become active in the PTA. Be sure to vote for the school board (every registered voter can vote). Go to school board meetings and be an active participant. Consider running for the community school board yourself. If there are problems in your child's school, learn how to work for change within the system.

4. Be your child's advocate. Don't let your child get lost in a bureaucracy. Find out who does what in your child's school. Find out where the power lies and who makes what important decisions. In some schools, individual teachers make most of the decisions about the children they teach and administrators deal primarily with scheduling and logistical problems. In other schools, administrators know the strengths and weaknesses of each child and play a major role in all key decisions; in still other schools, the head of school is the only real source of power. In some of the best schools, major decisions are often arrived at by consensus, with teachers, administrators, and heads of school all working together.

5. Communicate with the school. Be sure to let your child's teacher know when changes or upheavals occur in your household. School directors, principals, and teachers bemoan those parents who come in and say, "Oh, by the way my husband and I have been in Hong Kong for the last month, we got divorced last week, we adopted a new baby in September, my husband has been in the hospital for the last two weeks—have you noticed any change in Timmy?" As a school administrator and teacher, I always told parents early in the school year to be sure to let us know when anything out of the ordinary happened at home; even the death of a guinea pig or a goldfish can have great significance for a six-year-old. Now as a parent I am even more aware of how important that advice was.

6. Read! I've said it before but it merits saying again. Good reading skills and comprehension are key to success both in school and afterwards. Even jobs that are not normally associated with reading now require the ability to understand and process complex written material. An electrician spends 120 minutes a day reading technical references, blueprints, schematics and a secretary spends 168 minutes on reference books, lists, letters, handbooks.[4] Reading to a child means more than turning pages. It means losing yourselves in a book together. It means talking about motivation, wondering why characters make the choices they make. It means asking questions and pondering hidden meanings. It means understanding the sound and rhythm of language in poetry. And don't stop reading to your children just because they learn how to read themselves. Keep right on reading together until and even after they are old enough to enjoy Dickens and Tolstoy.

7. Have dinner with your children. Again I've said this before but it merits repetition. While work schedules may not permit a family to sit down together every night for dinner, it is certainly possible for most families to do so at least several times a week.

8. Try to see that your child has a decent breakfast and an adequate amount of sleep at night. As a teacher, I was always amazed by the number of third graders who seemed to be up watching the ten o'clock news. Children who are hungry or sleepy in class aren't getting the education they deserve.

9. Set reasonable goals for your children's achievement in school, goals that challenge but don't overwhelm them. Discuss these goals with your children. Let your children know that you don't expect perfection but you do expect their best. Show your children that you take their homework seriously (see section on homework). Daniel B. Taylor, a former senior vice president of the College Board, has expressed the opinion that one of the reasons Asian-American children are the highest-scoring group on the SATs is that their parents "value their children's education so much that they inculcate the centrality of that education into every aspect of their everyday lives."[5]

10. Remember that you are responsible for your children whether you are physically present or not. If you can't be around yourself when your children come home from school, try to see that they have access to someone of your educational level. Your choice of a caretaker for your child is as important as your choice of a school. As one teacher said to me, "Intellectual curiosity can wilt away without someone to talk to—someone who can answer your questions or lead you on the road to discovery."

•• Some Things to Avoid

As you take these steps to help your child find success at school, remember that though you are acting as your child's advocate, you and the school are partners, not adversaries, in your child's education. And try to avoid being openly confrontational or casting yourself in the role of opponent.

1. Try to see the teacher as an ally, not someone who is out to get your child or to blame you for everything that isn't going right. Try to think of yourselves as partners and assume that any feedback from the teacher is meant to be constructive even if you don't agree with it.

2. While it is part of your role to speak up for your child and even to be politely persistent when you feel an important issue is at stake, it is counterproductive to be overly aggressive or demanding. The head of one lower school tells about the parent who cornered her in a shoe store, demanding to know how her child was doing. Every time that parent came to school, the unanimous reaction was, "Oh, not her again."

3. Don't go over the teacher's head unless you are forced to. If a problem arises, discuss it with the teacher first. Many problems can be solved by parents and teachers just sitting down together and talking.

4. Try not to give your child mixed messages about school. If children hear you criticizing a teacher or the way a subject is being taught, they may conclude that the teacher doesn't know what he or she is doing and they don't have to listen. This is very confusing to a child.

5. Don't expect your children to behave the same way at school as at home. Children who are very confident and outspoken at home may be shy and standoffish at school, or vice versa.

6. Don't get in the habit of making excuses for your children. If your children forget their homework and you always bring it to school for them, your children will fail to learn responsibility for their own work.

7. Do not talk about how special your child is to other parents and teachers; remember that every parent's child is special to that parent. Boasting is just as irritating once your child is in school as in the admissions process.

8. Don't make your child feel conspicuously different from the other children without good reason. If all the other children are wearing play clothes to school, don't send your children to school in a party outfit. An adult friend of mine still remembers the embarrassment she felt at being sent off to sleep-away camp in her "Doctor Dentons." After discovering that no other seven-year-old was still wearing "Doctor Dentons," she hid them in the bottom of her trunk and slept in her underwear all summer. Sounds trivial, doesn't it? Yet it was anything but trivial to the child.

This does not mean to say you should abdicate parental responsibility and give in on questions involving health or principle. You don't have to give in to every new fad in clothing or buy the latest designer sneakers. By all means see that your child wears boots in the rain and a hat and gloves when it's below freezing.

9. Don't have your child tutored or tested without telling the school. In a partnership you don't make important decisions without telling your partner. If you believe your child is having the kind of difficulty that warrants outside help, make an appointment and talk to the school. Perhaps they have experts on staff who could do the testing or tutoring. This could be an advantage for your child because communication would be easier with the class teacher. It would also be more convenient and probably less expensive.

10. Don't use parents' night as a forum to talk about your child. This not the time to share anecdotes about your children or discuss any academic or social problems. Save this for a parent/teacher conference.

Finally, if something does go wrong at school, try not blame yourself. Remember, there are a few things that are ultimately beyond our control. If we do the best we can for our children, that is all we can reasonably expect of ourselves.

•• For Working Parents

Working full-time need not interfere with being involved parents. Jerome Kagan, a profesor of developmental psychology at Harvard, reminds us that "the idealistic youth that all of us have praised, the ones who stood in Tiananmen Square against the tanks—90 percent of them were in day-care centers from 6:30 or 7 A.M. to 6 at night. Their parents worked six days a week, twelve hours a day . . . yet there's no evidence that these youth are more aggressive, more delinquent, or more prone to psychosis. . . . There isn't a certain amount of time you have to be with your child."[6] These young people, of course, come from a different culture, but I still believe their experiences are relevant to the children of working parents in the United States.

The fact that you are working does not mean that the school will see you as an indifferent or bad parent. Studies have shown that working parents spend as much time as nonworking parents reading and playing with their children.[7] There are many ways you can be positively involved in your child's school experience: offer to come to school for an assembly and talk to the children about what you do, consider arranging for a class to visit your place of work and see firsthand how a job is done, take a vacation day if necessary to chaperone a class trip or attend a school open day.

One mother working full-time as a pediatrician put her children in a school two blocks from her office so that she could pick them up from school and could run over to the school to help out in the library if a patient canceled an appointment. Another mother told me that she had given up entertaining and seeing friends so she could devote herself to her family and to her career. Some parents put in long hours during the week in order to have weekends free for their families. Many parents who can't be home when their children return from school set aside time for a telephone chat every afternoon. Others have told me about the special notes they leave for their children to read when they get home in the afternoon. Dr. T. Berry Brazelton suggests that parents "concentrate on getting close to their children as soon as they walk in the door, then everything that follows becomes family time—working, playing, talking."[8]

Often families seem to benefit from having two working parents. Lois Hoffman, a professor at the University of Michigan, has demonstrated that working mothers who feel confident and fulfilled in their jobs bring that sense of competence home to their children.[9] In most cases, whether working full-time has a positive or negative impact on a child often depends on a parent's attitude. Brazelton finds that "if parents feel a sense of competence, they're going to be freer to look for it in a child. . . . If they're all tied up in knots, they're not going to see beyond their own issues to the child's issues."[10]

•• Communication Between Home and School

Schools have a variety of ways of keeping parents informed and involved with their children's lives at school. Some schools have weekly newsletters in early childhood school and kindergarten. Some schools send home informal notes periodically during the year. A kindergarten teacher explained, "We might be working on the color red at school. I would send home a letter asking parents to talk to their children about things that are red. We might ask them to send in red snacks. If we were studying concepts such as vertical and horizontal, we would ask parents to point out that trees are vertical and fences are horizontal as they drive down the road." Other schools invite parents to visit classes on open school days or to come to school to have lunch with the children.

·· Talking to Your Children About School

It is important for you not only to know the things your children are doing in school but also to have a sense of how they feel about them. Asking children for information can be very frustrating. Children are not generally receptive, in the words of one principal, when "they are grilled at home about what they did in school." It is always better to ask children open-ended questions to draw them out rather than ones that can be answered yes or no and then dismissed. One idea to promote sharing that has worked well in a number of families is for everyone, adults included, to tell at dinner something they learned today that they didn't know yesterday. It doesn't necessarily have to be academic: it can be how to head a soccer ball, or how to do a cartwheel or back walkover in gymnastics, or how to resolve a conflict peacefully. Another idea is for everyone to bring a word they found in their reading and discuss it.

Try to chat with your children about school instead of asking for an evaluation or quizzing them about what they got wrong on a test the minute they walk in the door. By all means ask about the test, just don't do it before you've given them a hug and kiss and let them tell you about the baseball game or the new hamster. Sometimes, as I used to remind the parents of my third graders, there may be a period when your children see school as private and don't want to talk about it. Don't worry, this phase usually passes. Instead of asking "What did you do in school today?" try asking your child what he or she liked best or least. I sometimes ask, "What was the funniest thing that happened today?" With a kindergarten or preschool age child you might try asking, "What things did you do at school that are like things we do at home?"

Let your children realize they can bring home the bad news as well as the good news without having to relive their feeling of failure. If things aren't going well, try to find out why and be supportive. If your child comes home and says, "I hate school" or "The teacher is mean to me," ask your child to tell you what actually happened, what the specific problem seems to be, and what can be done to correct it. A child's statement "I hate school" may not have anything to do with the curriculum or the teacher but may mean instead that your son had a fight with his best friend. "The teacher is mean to me" may mean that your daughter wasn't allowed to sit next to her best friend during a spelling test.

No matter how awkward the time your child chooses to talk may be in terms of adult schedules, it is important to really listen. Children are very sensitive about how much of their parents' attention they actually have. A first-grade teacher told me of a child who had taken an important problem to her mother but said afterwards, "Mommy looked at me but she didn't listen."

Try also to make time for the closeness that comes from quiet moments together—the moments that make words easier when they are needed: the Sunday afternoons when you are snuggled up together in a big chair in front of the fire reading *Charlotte's Web* or *The Secret Garden* or sitting on the porch for a moment together as you watch the sun set.

•• Homework

If your child is just starting kindergarten, homework may seem a distant problem off somewhere in the mysterious world of junior high and beyond. It is not, however, really all that far away; some kindergarten teachers assign five minutes or so of homework to get children used to the idea, and most first-grade teachers expect a child to read every night at home. Homework generally increases gradually every year until by fifth or sixth grade children may be spending up to an hour and a half or two hours a night on homework. Schools vary greatly in the amount of homework they assign at different grade levels, so don't worry if your child has slightly more or less homework than friends in other schools.

The important point is that you have a clear understanding of the homework policy at your child's school. Teachers give homework so that children will have the opportunity to practice what they have learned in class. Good homework assignments are not just busywork, they encourage children to expand on what they have learned and to do some exploring on their own. Teachers believe that homework helps children develop responsibility and independence as well as organizational skills. There is a correlation, particularly in math and science, between the amount of homework children do and academic achievement.

Educators and psychologists find that when parents seem ambivalent about homework or treat it lightly, children are more likely to have difficulty doing it. There are a number of steps you can take to help your children develop good homework habits.

1. Plan a regular time every night for homework.

2. Turn off the television while your child is doing homework. It is impossible for most children to concentrate with a ball game on a television in the next room.

3. See that your child has a quiet, well-organized workplace with good light and all the necessary equipment such as a dictionary, ruler, pencils, and erasers.

4. Be sure your child reads the directions and understands the assignment.

5. Check to see that assignments are complete and reasonably neat. If you are not sure about standards here, call the teacher and discuss your concerns.

6. Try to be available to answer questions and give support but don't do your children's homework for them. If parents give too much direct help, teachers may be led to believe children understand concepts when in fact they are still confused.

7. Don't overschedule your children with after-school activities; children vary greatly on how much they can handle, but always be sure your child understands that school comes first.

8. Set clear limits on television and telephone time. Most schools also ask that children not attend parties on school nights.

9. Teach your children to estimate how long an assignment will take and then to compare their estimate with the actual time required. This is an excellent way to help children learn to plan their time.

10. If your child is confused about an assignment or doesn't seem to understand a new concept, let the teacher know right away before your child falls behind.

•• Playdates

Play is as important as studying for children. There is an important correlation between social skills developed through play and academic achievement in school. Researchers have found that kindergarten children who are rejected by their peers often do worse on readiness tests than children with better social relationships.

For many of our children, playing with friends means "playdates" arranged and scheduled by parents. Much as we may long for the carefree spontaneity of a bygone era when we ran out the door to play with our friends, it is important to face the demographic realities of the 1990s. In many communities, we must set up playdates in order for our children to play with other children after school. Friends are important at any age and perhaps never more so than in the early years at school. Children who are worried about not having any friends will have little energy left for learning to read and write. New friendships with classmates are often formed, and previously made friendships cemented in after-school play.

•• Parent-Teacher Conferences

Many schools schedule a parent-teacher conference in lieu of a written report for children in early childhood school and kindergarten. In the early years of elementary school, written reports are frequently supplemented with conferences. By fifth or sixth grade, conferences may take place only when either the teacher or the parent suspects a potential problem. The purpose of a conference is to provide an opportunity for parents and teachers to learn more about a child, to try to construct a portrait of the child at home as well as at school, and ultimately to help the child feel and be successful in school. Ideally, conferences increase mutual understanding and trust between parents and teachers.

However, it is important to realize that both parents and teachers bring a considerable emotional investment to the conference table. One teacher who recently became a parent said to me,"I realize now that there is no such thing as an objective parent, and there shouldn't be. That's not your role. It makes it easier for me now to deal with parents knowing that, and it's easier for me to avoid taking it personally when a parent seems defensive or unrealistic about a child." I will never forget a conference I had early in my own teaching career. A boy in my class was having serious trouble with the work, and I suspected he might have a learning disability. I asked his mother to come in for a conference and gave her what I felt was a clear and rational description of the problems I saw in class. In the middle of my description she burst into tears. I was bewildered; I had not said anything either untrue or cruel. But I was twenty-one years old, and had no children and no real understanding of the emotional investment she was bringing to the conference. I was describing an academic problem in class, but she was hearing "There is something wrong with your son" and thinking "I can't stand that, because he's my son and I love him and he has to be perfect."

The emotional investment is not always one-sided. Teachers are often more likely to be told what's wrong than what's right in their classrooms, and in some schools they may receive little encouragment or positive feedback from supervisors and administrators. Teachers also have egos that may be fragile at times, causing them to see your concerns as challenges to their competence and intelligence. A good conference is not a confrontation; it is an honest exchange between parent and teacher in an attempt to help a child find success in school.

Conferences are usually most effective when both parents and teachers have taken the time to do a little advance preparation. Before a conference, take a few minutes to sit down and think over how things have gone over the last couple of months. What books or projects has your child seemed excited about? Have any assignments been particularly difficult? Does your child seem to understand the homework assignments? Are they being done with a minimal amount of help? It is often a good idea to make a list of questions or topics you want to cover. Be sure to tell your child that you are having a conference with the teacher and ask if there is anything he or she would like you to bring up.

If possible, both parents should go to a conference together not only to show the teacher that you are interested in your child's education but also because it is helpful to have someone to compare notes with afterwards. Often parents hear different things in the same conference. A mother told me that after their first parent conference her husband said, "Miss Jones thinks

Jennifer is wonderful, perfect." This mother, however, had heard Miss Jones talking instead about the things they were working on with Jennifer at school, and Jennifer's progress in problem areas. To the mother, this was the teacher's way of pointing out where Jennifer was weak and needed additional work. Both parents had heard part, but not all, of what the teacher was trying to get across.

In a conference, teachers often start by discussing the areas in which a child is doing particularly well, then move on to talk about other areas where they see a need for improvement. When teachers mention areas that need strengthening, be sure to ask for suggestions on ways you might follow up on what the school is trying to do. Try also as you listen to get a sense of your child's learning patterns: some children learn best visually, others orally; some children get the whole picture quickly and then have trouble remembering details, others focus well on details but have trouble putting the whole picture together. Knowing your child's learning style will help you play on his or her strengths when your child studies at home.

The more openly you and your child's teachers are able to discuss your child's strengths and weaknesses, the more useful the conference will be for both of you. There are some general rules to keep in mind before and during a conference to ensure a mutual sharing of information.

1. Try to begin the conference on a positive note. You might want to mention an assignment or activity your child has particularly enjoyed. One teacher told me about a conference that never got on a constructive track after a parent's first remark was "We're spending all this money to send Peter to private school and we just don't understand why he isn't learning anything."

2. Try to broaden your concern and take it out of the realm of your particular child. Rephrase your questions when necessary. For example, if you want to find out your child's achievement level in relation to her peers and the school does not like to compare children, do not ask, "'Is she the best in reading or math." Instead, try asking if she is having more trouble or less with a subject than the other children in the class. The teacher is more apt to understand you and supply you with what you need to know to help your child.

3. Be sure you understand the relative importance of what the teacher is telling you. Is it an interesting observation, something she just wants you to be aware of but not do anything about at the moment, or is it a serious problem that requires immediate action? Do not hesitate to ask for clarification here. Sometimes it is helpful for a parent to ask the teacher whether what he is describing is something all children do at this age. And if so, whether in his experience children tend to grow out of it.

4. If you think the teacher is using inappropriate or unchallenging material in the classroom, instead of saying this outright in a way that will put the teacher on the defensive, try instead asking why this material is being used and what the teacher hopes to accomplish with it. You might also say that your child has shown great interest in Vikings or number theory or animal habitats, for instance, and ask for suggestions to further this interest.

5. If there is to be a follow-up to the conference such as diagnostic testing or tutoring, make sure you and the teacher are in agreement on exactly what the follow-up will involve, when it will take place, and who will be responsible for arranging it.

6. At the end of the conference, always ask if there is something you can do at home to reinforce what your child is doing at school.

•• Report Cards

Most schools send parents written report cards two to four times a year describing their chidren's progress in school. Report cards vary widely in format, ranging from checklists to short essays. Many schools do not use letter grades until fourth or fifth grade. It is important for you to understand that report cards are not a definitive statement on your child's achievement and potential; they are merely an account of how one teacher sees your child at one point in time. If you don't understand what a teacher is trying to say or if you believe that a comment is way off the mark, follow up with a conference.

Report cards can be a source of anger or misunderstanding between parent and school. Part of the problem derives from differences in the way parents and teachers approach report cards. Parents are interested in knowing as much as possible about the progress of one very special child. Teachers, on the other hand, must accurately describe twenty-five or more different children; if the teacher is a science or music teacher, he or she may have to report on close to one hundred children. There is no time scheduled for report writing during the school day, and consequently, teachers often spend hours doing them in the evening or over the weekend. Some teachers are better than others at translating their observations in the classroom into meaningful comments for parents.

Another potential problem inherent in report cards is that parents and teachers may use certain words and phrases in different ways. For instance, the phrase "is improving" may indicate a weak area that the teacher is working on with the child and "continues to make steady progress" may mean things were a little shaky at first but are getting better. Teachers do not try to mislead parents, but because they have been trained to look for the positive, to focus first on a child's strengths rather than weaknesses, they may inadvertently give parents a mistaken sense of their children's abilities. Teachers are not always aware that parents may misunderstand their comments. Misunderstandings can be particularly troubling for parents later on when grades appear and they find themselves trying to reconcile a C with the optimistic comments of the previous year. When you read a report written in a narrative style, pay attention both to what is being said and what is not being said; look for points the teacher is trying to highlight and areas or skills she doesn't mention.

••Sharing Report Cards with Children••
Report cards are addressed to parents and often are written in a language and style more readily comprehensible to adults than children. It may not be appropriate to read a narrative-style report card word for word to a child in kindergarten or first grade, but it is certainly appropriate to discuss all the important points and recommendations with your child. Be sure to rein-

force your interest in your child's progress and your willingness to help in any areas where there is difficulty. Try to focus on what your children have learned in class and what they hope to do differently next term rather than on any negative comments.

••GRADES••

Grades are usually introduced in fourth or fifth grade. Initially they are often more of a barometer of a child's interest and effort than a guide to ability or potential. Later on, in the upper years of elementary school, grades become more important—but not nearly as important as many parents believe. So far, research has failed to show any direct correlation between a child's grades in elementary school and that child's later success in life. On the other hand, how you and your child react to the grades can be very important. If children begin to see themselves as "failures" or "stupid," their future achievement may be in jeopardy.

••School Records

Schools vary in what they keep in children's records. Some schools' files are filled with information on every aspect of a child's school career, while other schools elect to keep only the bare minimum. A child's official school file—the file that follows the child on to the next school—usually contains, in addition to basic information on the child's age and parents' names and address, report cards, testing records, accounts of disciplinary actions, and attendance and health data. All the information in this official file is available to parents on request. The 1974 Federal Family Educational Rights and Privacy Act, also known as the Buckley Amendment, gives parents "the right to inspect and review any and all official records, files and data directly related to their children." If you wish to review your child's cumulative record, make an appointment to see the guidance counselor, division head, or principal.

Schools sometimes also keep unofficial records that contain notes on conferences and teacher discussions as well as confidential parent information and in-house academic or psychological evaluations. These notes are not part of the official record and are not shown to anyone outside the school. Even within the school, they are available only on a need-to-know basis and are usually kept in an administrator's office for professional reference only.

•• When Things Go Wrong at School

Despite all your best efforts, sometimes things won't turn out the way you had hoped. It is important that you be able to recognize the signs that something is wrong. A mother told me about a dream her son related to her: "Mommy I had this dream. I was riding a bicycle up this ladder and everybody else was in cars. No matter how hard I tried to keep up they kept getting farther and farther ahead." The boy had recently begun saying he didn't want to go to school and had seemed unusually quiet and withdrawn. His mother noticed that he seemed to have trouble making decisions, even to the point of being unable to decide which candy bar he wanted at the corner store. The boy was smart and very verbal, but almost a year younger than many of his classmates. The mother shared her concern with the school. After a thorough evaluation and much discussion, it was determined that he wasn't able to cope with the pressure to keep up with the older children. A mutual decision was made that the boy would repeat second grade. While repeating is controversial and not a generally accepted solution to difficulties at school, in this particular case it was effective. The boy went on to become an honors student, and is now a sophomore at Harvard.

As your children move through the elementary years there are some red flags to watch out for and which you should not ignore:

1. An unwillingness to go to school
2. An expressed fear of school
3. Acting out
4. Unusual anxiety or tension
5. Unhappiness
6. Crying a lot
7. Not wanting to play
8. Aggression or increased fighting
9. Sadness or withdrawal
10. Complaints of a variety of physical symptoms with no apparent cause. Headaches, abdominal pain, vomiting, and constant eye blinking can all be signs of stress in a child.

Parents and Schools: A Partnership •• 237

If you notice any of these in your child's behavior, ask your child what's going on, but don't expect to get the whole answer right away. It may take weeks to get to the source of the problem. If any of the signs persist for more than a day or two, call the teacher and find out how your child seems at school. The problem could be that your child has been put in a reading or math group where the pace is too swift or it could mean your child is coming down with the flu. It could also mean your child is in the wrong grade, or even the wrong school. Don't jump to conclusions; just try to find out what's going on so that you can take appropriate action. Remember, changing schools is a major event in a child's life and not something to be undertaken lightly. It is always best to try to find a solution in the school where your child is currently enrolled.

•• Success in School—Ours and Our Children's

Many of us still have vivid memories of our first encounters with school. These memories may or may not be relevant to our own children's education, and yet they can exert unconscious pressure on our decisions about our children, influencing the kinds of schools we choose, our relations with teachers, and even our reactions to our children's earliest successes and failures. Some of us as adults have fond memories of these early years, memories that we may hope to relive through the experiences of our children. Other adults have memories that are still painful; like the father who recalled that on his first day of school he felt he "was somehow not up to snuff, not as good as the other kids" and who felt all through school that he was "on the ragged edge." Try to remember that it is your children who are going to school, not you, and try not to relive your own successes and failures through them. Because you played on the soccer team or were elected class president, learned to read at an early age, or failed math, it does not follow that your son must play on the soccer team, your daughter must be elected class president, and that either one will be an early reader or fail math.

We should try to see our children as separate individuals who must ultimately experience their own successes and failures. If we are able to do this, perhaps we can bring a wisdom and sense of perspective not only to our children's own triumphs and tragedies but also to our response to them. Dr. Lee Salk, professor of clinical psychology in pediatrics at Cornell University Medical College, has said, "Every child has the makings to be successful in something but it may not be what the parent has in mind." To help our children achieve their potential, we must first, according to Dr. Salk, "know our children well, recognize their strengths and weaknesses, and learn to be responsive to them." As parents we must be careful not to expect perfection in everything all the time. A child who has trouble writing may find success in science or on the soccer field. Every child needs to succeed in something, but no child needs to succeed in everything.

Conclusion

"**K**nowledge is power" is a slogan that used to be emblazoned on the facades of public schools. The implication was that this knowledge and the power to which it could eventually lead were available by means of an education accessible to all children. Is this true today? Can a child get the education needed to be successful later on from the neighborhood school, or does it have to come from a "name brand" school? Is the education that was good enough for us also good enough for our children?

Even though we know better, it can be difficult when we become parents if we live in certain communities not to get caught up in what is sometimes called the "craziness of the school thing"—an anxiety spawned by the belief that there is a secret educational track on which we must somehow get our children started as soon as they can walk and talk. But the real question is not whether a school is public or nonpublic, or even whether it is seen as prestigious, but whether it is an effective school for your child. Many adults have told me that it was the nurturing, supportive approach to education that they found at their early schools that gave them the confidence and encouragement to go on to college and to flourish there. I believe that as parents we should worry less about getting our children into a "hot school" or started on a particular academic track and instead pay more attention to developing initiative, self-confidence, and competence. We should try also to instill a sense of discipline and give our children an appreciation for the old-fashioned American work ethic. Our goal should be to find a quality academic environment that is a good fit for our child—an environment that will foster these traits and nurture our .

children's talents. We may find that academic environment, as we have seen, in a wide variety of settings, including our neighborhood school.

An effective school must provide a quality education, but it must also be right for your child. If you are really worried about where your young children will go to college or what they will be doing when they are thirty-five, send them to a school that is right for them as they are now. Send them to a school where they can develop self-confidence and a love of learning, where they can develop at their own pace in their own way.

But remember that children, unlike electrical appliances, don't come with guarantees and neither do schools. The best school in the world will have its share of failures, and even poor schools will have their successes. A lot depends on your child and a lot depends on you. We must try not to expect too much too soon. We must remember that our children need time. They need time to talk and time to listen. They need time to curl up with a book with no questions to answer or book reports to write. They need time to memorize poetry because they like the sound of it, not because it is due on Tuesday. They need time to be silly and babyish. They need time to waste and time to create. They need a little time off from analysis and evaluation. They need time to play at your feet or to be by themselves. They need time to be children.

•• •• •• •• •• •• •• •• •• •• •• ••

Appendix

•• •• •• ••

••ORGANIZATIONS AND RESOURCE CENTERS

GENERAL INTEREST
COALITION OF ESSENTIAL SCHOOLS
EDUCATION DEPARTMENT, BOX 1938
BROWN UNIVERSITY
PROVIDENCE, RI 02912

ELEMENTARY SCHOOL CENTER (ESC)
2 EAST 103RD STREET
NEW YORK, NY 10029

ERIC CLEARINGHOUSE ON EARLY CHILDHOOD
   EDUCATION
COLLEGE OF EDUCATION
UNIVERSITY OF ILLINOIS
1310 SOUTH 6TH STREET
CHAMPAIGN, IL 61820

HIGH/SCOPE FOUNDATION
600 NORTH RIVER STREET
YPSILANTI, MI 48197

•• •• •• ••

NATIONAL ASSOCIATION FOR THE EDUCATION OF YOUNG
   CHILDREN
1834 CONNECTICUT AVENUE, NW
WASHINGTON, DC 20009

NATIONAL ASSOCIATION OF CHILD CARE RESOURCE AND
   REFERRAL AGENCIES
ROCHESTER, MN
TEL. (507)287-2020

NATIONAL COMMITTEE FOR CITIZENS IN EDUCATION
   [NCCE]
410 WILDE LAKE VILLAGE GREEN
COLUMBIA, MD 21044

NATIONAL PTA
700 NORTH RUSH STREET
CHICAGO, IL 60611

INTERNATIONAL READING ASSOCIATION
P.O. BOX 8139
800 BARKSDALE ROAD
NEWARK, DE 19714

UNITED STATES DEPARTMENT OF EDUCATION
400 MARYLAND AVENUE SW
WASHINGTON, DC 20202

RELIGIOUS SCHOOLS
FRIENDS COUNCIL ON EDUCATION
KAY EDSTENE, EXECUTIVE DIRECTOR
1507 CHERRY STREET
PHILADELPHIA, PA 19102

JEWISH EDUCATION SERVICE OF NORTH AMERICA
730 BROADWAY
NEW YORK, NY 10003

NATIONAL CATHOLIC EDUCATIONAL ASSOCIATION
1077 30TH STREET NW, SUITE 100
WASHINGTON, DC 20007

NATIONAL ASSOCIATION OF EPISCOPAL SCHOOLS
ANN GORDON, EXECUTIVE DIRECTOR
815 SECOND AVENUE
NEW YORK, NY 10017

UNITED PARENT TEACHERS ASSOCIATION OF JEWISH
   SCHOOLS
426 WEST 58TH STREET
NEW YORK, NY 10019

PRIVATE/INDEPENDENT SCHOOLS

COUNCIL FOR AMERICAN PRIVATE EDUCATION
1625 EYE STREET NW, SUITE 412
WASHINGTON, DC 20006

NATIONAL ASSOCIATION OF INDEPENDENT SCHOOLS
   (NAIS)
18 TREMONT STREET
BOSTON, MA 02108

REGIONAL ASSOCIATIONS

INDEPENDENT SCHOOLS ASSOCIATION OF THE CENTRAL
   STATES
THOMAS REED, PRESIDENT
1400 WEST MAPLE AVENUE
DOWNERS GROVE, IL 60515

INDEPENDENT SCHOOLS ASSOCIATION OF THE
   SOUTHWEST
RICHARD W. EKDAHL, EXECUTIVE DIRECTOR
P.O. BOX 52297
TULSA, OK 74152

PACIFIC NORTHWEST ASSOCIATION OF INDEPENDENT
  SCHOOLS
SR. SANDRA THEUNICK, PRESIDENT
FOREST RIDGE SCHOOL
4800 139TH AVENUE SE
BELLEVUE, WA 98006

SOUTHERN ASSOCIATION OF INDEPENDENT SCHOOLS
JOHN H. TUCKER, JR., PRESIDENT
NORFOLK ACADEMY
1585 WESLEYAN DRIVE
NORFOLK, VA 23502

INDEPENDENT SCHOOLS ASSOCIATION OF NORTHERN
  NEW ENGLAND
RICHARD L. GOLDSMITH, EXECUTIVE SECRETARY
P.O. BOX 265
BRIDGTON, ME 04009

INDEPENDENT SCHOOLS ADMISSIONS ASSOCIATION OF
  GREATER NEW YORK (ISAAGNY)
1010 PARK AVENUE
NEW YORK, NY 10028

PARENTS LEAGUE OF NEW YORK
115 EAST 82ND STREET
NEW YORK, NY 10028

PARENTS COUNCIL OF WASHINGTON, DC
GRACE MULVIHILL, PRESIDENT
7303 RIVER ROAD
BETHESDA, MD 20817

MINORITY RECRUITMENT
A BETTER CHANCE, INC. (ABC)
419 BOYLSTON STREET
BOSTON, MA 02116

PREP FOR PREP
GARY SIMONS, EXECUTIVE DIRECTOR
163 WEST 91ST STREET 10024

EARLY STEPS
ANGELA FLEMISTER, EXECUTIVE DIRECTOR
1047 AMSTERDAM AVENUE
NEW YORK, NY 10025

MINORITY HOTLINE—(800)343-9138
RANDY CARTER AT NAIS

INDEPENDENT SCHOOL ALLIANCE FOR MINORITY
  AFFAIRS
MANASA HEKYMARA
110 SOUTH LA BREA
SUITE 265
INGLEWOOD, CA 90301

ASSESSMENT
EDUCATIONAL RECORDS BUREAU (ERB)
3 EAST 80TH STREET
NEW YORK, NY 10021

EDUCATIONAL RECORDS BUREAU (ERB)
BARDWELL HALL
37 CAMERON STREET
WELLESLEY, MA 02181

EDUCATIONAL TESTING SERVICE
PRINCETON, NJ 08542

SPECIAL CONCERNS

AMERICAN MONTESSORI SOCIETY
BRETTA WEISS, NATIONAL DIRECTOR
150 FIFTH AVENUE
NEW YORK, NY 10011

ASSOCIATION OF WALDORF SCHOOLS OF NORTH AMERICA
C/O ANNE CHARLES
17 HEMLOCK HILL
GREAT BARRINGTON, MA 01230

ASSOCIATION FOR CHILDREN WITH LEARNING
 DISABILITIES (ACLD)
155 WASHINGTON AVENUE
ALBANY, NY 12210

INDEPENDENT EDUCATIONAL CONSULTANTS ASSOCIATION
BOX 125
FORESTDALE, MA 02644

AMERICAN ASSOCIATION FOR GIFTED CHILDREN
15 GRAMERCY PARK
NEW YORK, NY 10003

CENTER FOR THE STUDY AND EDUCATION OF THE
 GIFTED
BOX 170
TEACHERS COLLEGE, COLUMBIA UNIVERSITY
NEW YORK, NY 10027

NATIONAL ASSOCIATION FOR GIFTED CHILDREN
4175 LOVELL ROAD, SUITE 140
CIRCLE PINES, MN 55014

THE ORTON DYSLEXIA SOCIETY
724 YORK ROAD
BALTIMORE, MD 21204

Notes

1. Changes and Challenges

1. U.S. Department of Labor, Bureau of Labor Statistics, Division of Labor Force Statistics (Washington, D.C.: March 1990).

2. Alison Leigh Cowan, "Women's Gains on the Job: Not Without a Heavy Toll," *The New York Times*, 21 Aug. 1990. (Based on a Times poll June 20–25, 1989.)

3. U.S. Bureau of the Census, *Current Population Survey 1989* (Washington, D.C., 1989).

4. Andrew Stein, "In N.Y.C., Streets of Terror," *The New York Times*, 21 May 1990.

5. U. S. Bureau of the Census, *Consumer Income Series* (Washington, D.C.: April 1990 & Sept. 1990, page 60, Number 167 & 168.

6. Dennis Hevesi, "Increasing Percentage of High School Graduates Enroll in Colleges," *The New York Times*, 22 April 1990.

7. U. S. Department of Education, National Center for Education Statistics, Office of Education Information Branch (Washington, D.C.: December 1990).

8. Laura Mensueros, "Moving Targets." *Education Life*, 18 April 1990.

9. Peter Passell, "So Much for Assumptions about Immigrants and Jobs," *The New York Times*, 15 April 1990. (As quoted from George J. Borjas, *Friends or Strangers* [New York: Basic Books, 1990].)

10. Felicia R. Lee, "New York City's Schools See Crime Rising in Lower Grades," *The New York Times*, 24 April 1990.

11. Beverly Baker, Fullerton Police Department and the California Department of Education, Winter 1990, *The Network News*, September/October 1990.

12. Allan Shedlin, Jr., "Acting for Children in a 'Crossfire' World," *Education Week*, 14 Nov. 1990.

13. Ernest L. Boyer, "Education Goals: An Action Plan," National Governors Association, Winter meeting, 25 Feb. 1990.

2. The Roots of Early Childhood Education

1. Rita Kramer, *Maria Montessori* (New York: G. P. Putnam's Sons, 1976).

2. Samuel J. Braun and Esther P. Edwards, *History and Theory of Early Childhood Education* (Belmont, CA: Wadsworth Publishing Co., 1972), 103.

3. Jean Piaget, *To Understand Is to Invent: The Future of Education* (New York: Grossman, 1973).

4. William Goodwin and Laura A. Driscoll, *Handbook for Measurement and Evaluation in Early Childhood Education* (San Francisco: Jossey-Bass Publishers, 1980), 3.

5. Head Start Bureau, published data, Washington, D.C.

6. *Infant and Toddler Child Care Act*, H.R.3, 101st Cong., June 20, 1990. (Head Start legislation)

7. Home Start, Follow Through, The Ypsilanti Early Education Program, HOPE (Home-oriented Preschool Education Project) in Appalachia, West Virginia, BEEP (Brooklyn Early Education Program), The Kramer School Project in Little Rock, Arkansas, The New Parents as Teachers Project in Missouri.

8. *Early Childhood Education: What Are the Costs of High Quality Programs?* (Washington, D.C.: U.S. General Accounting Office, GAO/HRD-90-43BR, January 1990).

9. Edward F. Zigler, "Formal Schooling for Four-Year-Olds? No," in *Early Schooling: The National Debate* edited by Sharon L. Kagan and Edward F. Zigler (New Haven: Yale University Press, 1987), 39.

10. Howard Gardner, *Frames of Mind: The Theory of Multiple Intelligences* (New York: Basic Books, 1983), x.

11. Ibid., 246.

12. Carol Lawson, "For Architect of Child Care, Small Gains," *The New York Times*, 22 June 1989.

3. The Basic Ingredients of a Good Early Childhood Program or School

1. Ellen Galinsky and Judy David, *The Preschool Years* (New York: Times Books, 1988), 413.

2. Fred M. Hechinger, "Can Dewey Offer Relevant Wisdom on Working with the Whole Child of the 90's?" *The New York Times*, 18 July 1990.

3. Harriet K. Cuffaro, "The Developmental Interaction Approach," in *Education Before Five*, ed. Betty D. Boegehold et al (New York: Bank Street College, 1977), 47.

4. Ellen Ruppel Shell, "Now, Which Kind of Preschool?" *Psychology Today*, December 1989, 56.

5. Amy Stuart Wells, "For Montessori, a Revival and a Return to Roots," *The New York Times*, 27 June 1990, Education section.

6. Ibid.

7. Alison Clarke-Stewart, *Daycare* (Cambridge: Harvard University Press, 1982), 85.

8. "Accreditation Criteria and Procedures." Position Statement of the National Academy of Early Childhood Programs, A Division of the National Association for the Education of Young Children, Washington, D.C., 1984.

9. J.R. Berrueta-Clement et al., *Changed Lives: The Effects of the Perry Preschool Program on Youths through Age 19* (Ypsilanti, MI: High/Scope Press, 1984).

4. A Parent's Dilemma: What to Look For, How to Choose

1. Nadine Brozan, "Dalton Easing the Toddler Rat Race, Closes Its Nursery," *The New York Times*, 22 May 1989.

2. Ellen Galinsky and Judy David, *The Preschool Years* (New York: Times Books, 1988), 415.

3. "Accreditation Criteria and Procedures." Position Statement of the National Academy of Early Childhood Programs, a Division of the National Association for the Education of Young Children, Washington, D.C., 1984.

4. Ibid.

5. *Early Childhood Education: What Are the Costs of High Quality Programs?* (Washington, D.C.: U.S. General Accounting Office, GAO/HRD-90-43BR), January 1990.

5. Getting In: A Parent's Guide to Admissions

1. Julie Hazzard, *Early Childhood Programs: State Efforts 1989* (Denver, CO: Education Commission of the States, 1989).

2. *Harvard Gazette*, 4 Nov. 1988, 5.

6. Parents and Children: Ready or Not

1. Louise Bates Ames, Clyde Gillespie, and Frances L. Ilg, *The Gesell Institute's Child From One to Six: Evaluating the Behaviour of the Preschool Child* (New York: Harper & Row, 1979), 21.

2. Ibid, 22.

3. Jane M. Healy, *Your Child's Growing Mind: A Parent's Guide to Learning from Birth to Adolescence* (Garden City, NY: Doubleday, 1987), 24.

4. Louise Bates Ames and J. A. Chase, *Don't Push Your Preschooler* (New York: Harper & Row, 1973), 164.

5. Ames, et al, *The Gesell Institute's Child*, 28.

6. Boyd R. McCandless, *Children: Behavior and Development*, 2nd ed. (New York: Holt, Rinehart and Winston, 1967), 159.

7. B. M. Caldwell et al, "Infant Care and Attachment," *American Journal of Orthopsychiatry* 1970: 40, 397–412; J. C. O'Connell, "Children of Working Mothers: What the Research Tells Us," *Young Children: Research in Review* 1983: 38, 63–70; Sandra Scarr, *Mother Care/Other Care* (New York: Warner Books, 1984), 19.

8. John Bowlby, *Attachment and Loss, Vol. II. Separation: Anxiety and Anger* (New York: Basic Books), 1980.

9. Kathe Jervis, ed., "Separation: Strategies for Helping Two to Four Year

Olds" (Washington, D.C.: National Association for the Education of Young Children, 1984).

10. Penelope Leach, *Your Baby and Child From Birth to Age Five* (New York: Alfred A. Knopf, 1978), 197.

11. Ellen Galinsky and Judy David, *The Preschool Years* (New York: Times Books, 1988), 383.

12. Robert A. Furman, "Experiences in Nursery School Consultations," *Young Children*, November 1966, 84–95.

7. Starting Your Child in Elementary School

1. Gordon J. Klopf, Allan Shedlin, Jr., and Esther Zaret, *The School as Locus of Advocacy for All Children* (New York: Elementary School Center, 1988).

2. National Center for Educational Statistics (monograph), Education Branch, Office of Educational Research and Improvement (Washington, D.C.: U.S. Department of Education, 1990).

3. *A Nation at Risk* (Washington, D.C.: Government Printing Office, 1983), 1.

4. William Snider, "Department Expands Its Conferences to Promote Choice," *Education Week*, 6 Sept. 1989.

5. Edward B. Fiske, "Wave of Future: A Choice of Schools," *The New York Times*, 4 June 1989.

6. Education Commission of the States Clearinghouse. Denver, CO: December 1990.

7. Joe Nathan, "Progress, Problems, and Prospects of State Choice Plans." Available free of charge from the Planning and Evaluation Service, Office of Planning, Budget, and Evaluation, U.S. Department of Education, 400 Maryland Ave., SW, Room 3127, Washington, D.C. 20202-4244.

8. Rudy Perpich, "Choose Your School," *The New York Times*, 6 March 1989.

9. Sally Reed, "A Look at America's Great Schools," *Instructor*, Fall 1986: 7.

10. Ibid, 5.

8. Educational Options

1. Jeffrey S. Gurock, ed., *Ramaz: School, Community, Scholarship and Orthodoxy* (Hoboken, NJ: KTAV Publishing House, 1984), 50.

2. Charles O'Malley, Office of Private Education, U.S. Department of Education, Washington, D.C., December 1990.

3. Valerie E. Lee and Carolee Stewart, "National Assessment of Educational Progress: Proficiency in Mathematics and Science 1985–86," in *Catholic and Public Schools Compared: Final Report* (Washington, D.C.: National Catholic Educational Association, 1989); Helen M. Marks and Valerie E. Lee, "National Assessment of Educational Progress: Proficiency in Reading 1985–

86," in *Catholic and Public Schools Compared: Final Report* (Washington, D.C.: National Catholic Educational Association, 1989).

4. "What Is the Difference between 'Private' and 'Independent' Schools?" *NAIS Profile* (Boston: National Association of Independent Schools, 1990).

5. Ibid.

6. *The Harvard Education Letter* 7 (January/February 1991):7.

7. Ibid.

8. Ibid.

9. Anne Chapman, *The Difference It Makes: A Resource Book on Gender for Educators* (Boston: National Association of Independent Schools, 1988), 17.

10. Valerie Lee, "What Works Best? The Relative Effectiveness of Single-Sex and Coeducational Schools" (Paper delivered at the NAIS Conference, New York, NY, March 1991).

11. Peter Schmidt, "Three Types of Bilingual Education Effective, E.D. Study Concludes," *Education Week* 10 (February 20, 1991): 1.

12. Leila Badran, "The Gift of an Additional Language Can Make the Difference," *Parents League Review* (New York: Parents League of New York, 1991), 99.

13. Martha Mendelsohn, "Your Child and a Second Language: As Easy as Uno, Deux, Drei," *New York Family*, Summer 1990, 17.

14. M. Edith Rasell and Lawrence Mishel, "Shortchanging Education: HOW U.S. SPENDING ON GRADES K–12 LAGS BEHIND OTHER INDUS-TRIAL NATIONS," *Briefing Paper* (Washington, D.C.: Economic Policy Institute, 1989).

15. National Education Association. *Estimates of School Statistics 1989–90* (Washington, D.C., April 1990).

16. John C. Esty, Jr., "Independent Schools: What, Whither, and Why," *Teachers College Record* 92 (Spring 1991).

9. Finding the Right Fit

1. Richard J. Coley and Margaret E. Goertz, *Research Report: Educational Standards in the 50 States* (Princeton, NJ: Educational Testing Service, 1990).

2. Nebraska State Board of Education, "What's Best for 5-Year-Olds?" (Ypsilanti, Michigan: The High/Scope Press, 1986), 4. (Reprinted in High Scope Resource.)

3. Anne Bridgman, "Educator Urged to Emphasize Significance of Early Schooling," *Education Week,* 5 Feb. 1986, 18.

4. Martin Haberman, "The Nature of Multicultural Teaching and Learning in American Society," *Peabody Journal of Education* 65 (Spring 1988):101.

5. Debra Viadero, "Battle over Multicultural Education Rises in Intensity," *Education Week*, 28 Nov. 1990.

6. The National Institute of Education, *Becoming a Nation of Readers: The Report of the Commission on Reading* (Washington, D.C.: U.S. Department of Education, 1985), 1.

7. Ibid, 7.

8. Ibid, 8.

9. *What Works. Research About Teaching And Learning* (Washington, D.C.: U.S. Department of Education, 1986), 21.

10. *Becoming a Nation of Readers,* 37.

11. Ibid, 39.

12. Ibid, 44.

13. Jeanne Chall, *Learning to Read: The Great Debate*, rev. ed. (New York: McGraw Hill, 1983).

14. *Becoming a Nation of Readers*, 76–77.

15. Survey Commissioned by the American Association of University Women, *Education Week,* 6 Feb. 1991, 7.

16. Robert Rothman, "Psychologist's Cross-National Studies in Math Show U.S.'s Long Road to 'First in the World.' " *Education Week,* 13 March 1991, 6.

17. Ibid.

18. Peter West, "Math Groups Urge Changes in Teacher Preparation," *Education Week,* 13 March 1991, 5.

19. *What Works. Research about Teaching and Learning*, 23.

20. Tom K. Phares, *Seeking—and Finding—Science Talent: A 50 Year History of the Westinghouse Science Talent Search* (Pittsburgh: Westinghouse Electric Corporation, 1990), 41.

21. Gene J. Maeroff, *The School Smart Parent* (New York: Henry Holt & Co., 1989), 273.

22. Ibid, 272.

23. Herbert Kohl, "Computers in School: Beyond Drill," *The Great School Debate* (New York: Simon & Schuster, 1985), 213.

24. David Rockefeller, Jr., "The Arts in American Education," *Today's Education,* April–May 1978.

25. Coley and Goertz, *Research Report.*

26. "Accreditation Criteria and Procedures," Position Statement of the National Academy of Early Childhood Programs, a Division of the National Assocation for the Education of Young Children (Washington, D.C., 1984).

10. Getting Your Child into the Elementary School of Your Choice

1. Julie Hazzard, *Early Childhood Programs State Efforts 1989* (Denver, CO: Education Commission of the States, 1989).

2. *Elementary School Admission* (Boston: National Association of Independent Schools, 1986), 22.

3. Hazzard, *Early Childhood Programs.*

4. Barbara B. Judy, *Kindergarten Admission Procedures in Independent Schools with Suggested Guidelines* (Ann Arbor, MI: University Microfilms, 1984), 172.

5. Daniel Goleman, "An Emergency Theory," *The New York Times Education Life,* 10 April 1988.

6. David Wechsler, *Manual for Wechsler Intelligence Scale for Children*

Revised (New York: Psychological Corp., 1974); idem, *Wechsler Preschool Primary Scale of Intelligence Revised Manual* (New York: Psychological Corp., Harcourt Brace, 1989).

7. R. L. Thorndike, E. P. Hagan, and J. M. Sattler, *Technical Manual: Stanford-Binet Intelligence Scale, Fourth Edition* (Chicago: Riverside Publishing Company, 1986).

8. The Savannah Country Day School Catalog, January 1988.

11. Parents as Their Child's First Teachers

1. Mildred M. Winter, "Parents as First Teachers," in *A Better Start: New Choices for Early Learning*, ed. Fred M. Hechinger (New York: Walker & Company, 1986), 93.

2. Burton L. White, *Educating the Infant and Toddler* (Lexington, MA: D. C. Heath & Co., 1990), 179.

3. "A Conversation with Jerome Kagan," *Harvard Gazette*, 22 Sept. 1989, 6.

4. Daniel Goleman, "Study of Play Yields Clues to Success," *The New York Times*, 2 Oct. 1990.

5. Philippe Aries, *Centuries of Childhood: A Social History of Family Life* (New York: Vintage Books, 1962), 222.

6. Harold C. Schonberg, "Vladimir Horowitz: Thunder, Lightning and Awe," *The New York Times*, 12 Nov. 1989, II, 1:3.

7. William J. Cromie, "Perkins: Teaching People to be Creative Means Understanding a Complex Process," *Harvard Gazette*, 29 Sept. 1989, 7.

8. Daniel Goleman, "Erikson, in His Own Old Age, Expands His View of Life," *The New York Times*, 14 June 1988, C1.

9. Ken Gewertz, "Langer Looks at Mindful Living," *Harvard Gazette*, 24 Nov. 1989, 9.

10. Diana Townsend-Butterworth, Jr., "Flat Rock," unpublished story, November 1990.

11. "A Conversation with Jerome Kagan." Harvard Gazette, 22 Sept. 1989, 6.

12. George Z. Tokieda, "At a Snail's Pace," *Parents League Review*, New York 1989.

12. Parents and Schools: A Partnership

1. Gene I. Maeroff, "School Smart Parents Strengthen Education," *Education Week*, 25 Oct. 1989, 32.

2. Ibid.

3. Diane Ravitch and Chester Finn, Jr., "What Do Our 17-Year-Olds Know?" *Columbia: The Magazine of Columbia University*, December 1987: 23.

4. *Why Reading Counts* (Newark, DE: International Reading Assocation, 1989).

5. Daniel B. Taylor, "Asian-American Test Scores: They Deserve a Closer Look," *Education Week*, 17 Oct. 1990, 23.

6. "A Conversation with Jerome Kagan," *Harvard Gazette*, 22 Sept. 1989, 5.

7. Sandra Scarr, *Mother Care/Other Care* (New York: Warner Books,1984), 27.

8. T. Berry Brazelton, "Working Parents: How to give your kids what they need," *Newsweek*, 13 Feb. 1989, 67.

9. Ibid.

10. Fred Clement, "Dr. Spock's Successor," *Princeton Alumni Weekly*, January 28, 1987.

•• •• •• •• •• •• •• •• •• •• ••

Bibliography

•• •• •• ••

Books for Parents

Early Childhood

Boegehold, Betty D., Harriet K. Cuffaro, William H. Hooks, and Gordon J. Klopf, eds. *Education Before Five. A Handbook on Preschool Education.* Developed by The Bank Street College of Education. New York: Bank Street College of Education, 1977.

Brazelton, T. Berry. *Toddlers and Parents. A Declaration of Independence.* New York: Dell Publishing Co., 1974.

Brenner, Barbara, *The Preschool Handbook: Making the Most of Your Child's Education.* Bank Street's Complete Parent Guide. New York: Pantheon Books, 1990.

Clarke-Stewart, Alison. *Daycare.* The Developing Child Series. Cambridge: Harvard University Press, 1982.

Elkind, David. *Miseducation: Preschoolers at Risk.* New York: Alfred A. Knopf, 1987.

Galinsky, Ellen, and Judy David. *The Preschool Years: Family Strategies That Work—from Experts and Parents.* The Bank Street College of Education. New York: Times Books, 1988.

Hechinger, Fred M. *A Better Start: New Choices for Early Learning.* New York: Walker and Co., 1986.

Kagan, Sharon L., and Edward F. Ziegler, eds. *Early Schooling: The National Debate.* New Haven: Yale University Press, 1987.

Provenzo, Eugene F., Jr., and Arlene Brett. *The Complete Block Book.* Syracuse, N.Y.: Syracuse University Press, 1983.

White, Burton L., Ph.D. *Educating the Infant and Toddler.* Lexington, Mass.: D.C. Heath, 1988.

White, Burton L. *The First Three Years of Life.* Rev. ed. New York: Prentice-Hall, 1985.

Zigler, Edward F., and Edmund W. Gordon, eds. *Daycare.* Scientific and Social Policy Issues. Boston: Auburn House, 1982.

•• •• •• ••

Elementary

Bazarini, Ronald. *Boys: A Schoolmaster's Journal.* New York: Walker and Co., 1988.

Chall, Jeanne. *Learning to Read: The Great Debate.* New York: McGraw-Hill, 1967.

Cohen, Dorothy H. *The Learning Child: Guidelines for Parents and Teachers.* A Bank Street College of Education Book. New York: Schocken Books, 1988.

Farnham-Diggory, Sylvia. *Schooling: The Developing Child.* Cambridge: Harvard University Press, 1990.

Fideler, Elizabeth F. *A Parent's Primer: What You Need to Know about Your Child's Elementary School.* New York: Irvington Publishers, 1988.

Nemko, Martin, and Barbara Nemko. *How to Get Your Child a Private School Education in a Public School.* Rev. ed. Berkeley: Ten Speed Press, 1989.

Sobol, Tom, and Harriet Sobol. *Your Child in School: Kindergarten through Second Grade.* New York: Arbor House, 1987.

Spodek, Bernard, ed. *Today's Kindergarten: Exploring the Knowledge Base, Expanding the Curriculum.* New York: Teachers College Press, Columbia University, 1986.

General Issues

Adler, Mortimer J. *Paideia Problems and Possibilities: A Consideration of Questions Raised by the Paideia Proposal.* New York: Macmillan, 1983.

Amabile, Teresa M. *Growing Up Creative: Nurturing a Lifetime of Creativity.* New York: Crown Publishers, 1989.

Ashton-Warner, Sylvia. *Teacher.* New York: Simon & Schuster, 1963.

Balaban, Nancy. *Starting School: From Separation to Independence.* A Guide for Early Childhood Teachers. New York: Teachers College Press, Columbia University, 1985.

Bloom, Benjamin S., ed. *Developing Talent in Young People.* New York: Ballantine Books, 1985.

Brazelton, T. Berry. *To Listen to a Child: Understanding the Normal Problems of Growing Up.* Reading, Mass.: Addison-Wesley, 1984.

Chapman, Anne. *The Difference It Makes: A Resource Book on Gender for Educators.* Boston: National Association of Independent Schools, 1988.

Elkind, David. *The Hurried Child: Growing Up Too Fast Too Soon.* Reading, Mass.: Addison-Wesley, 1981.

Gardner, Howard. *Frames of Mind: The Theory of Multiple Intelligences.* New York: Basic Books, 1985.

Gilligan, Carol, Nona P. Lyons, and Trudy J. Hanner, eds. *Making Connections. The Relational Worlds of Adolescent Girls at Emma Willard School.* Cambridge: Harvard University Press, 1990.

Healy, Jane M. *Your Child's Growing Mind: A Parent's Guide to Learning from Birth to Adolescence.* Garden City, N.Y.: Doubleday, 1987.

Kagan, J. *The Nature of the Child.* New York: Basic Books, 1984.

Leach, Penelope. *Your Growing Child: From Babyhood through Adolescence.* New York: Alfred A. Knopf, 1989.

Oakes, Jeannie, and Martin Lipton. *Making the Best of Schools: A Handbook for Parents, Teachers, and Policymakers*. New Haven: Yale University Press, 1990.

Oppenheim, Joanne, Betty Boegehold, and Barbara Brenner. *Raising A Confident Child*. The Bank Street College of Education. New York: Pantheon Books, 1984.

Pogrebin, Letty Cottin. *Growing Up Free: Raising Your Child in the 80's*. New York: McGraw-Hill, 1980.

The New York Hospital-Cornell Medical Center Department of Psychiatry, with Mark Rubinstein. *The Growing Years: A Guide to Your Child's Emotional Development from Birth to Adolescence*. New York: Simon & Schuster, 1987.

Silberstein-Storfer, Muriel. *Doing Art Together*. New York: Simon & Schuster, 1982.

Trelease, Jim, ed. *The New Read-Aloud Handbook*. Penguin, 1979.

Assessment

Ames, Louise Bates, Clyde Gillespie, Jacqueline Haines, and Frances L. Ilg. *The Gesell Institute's Child from One to Six: Evaluating the Behavior of the Preschool Child*. New York: Harper & Row, 1979.

Boehm, Ann E., and Mary Alice White. *The Parents' Handbook on School Testing*. New York: Teachers College Press, Columbia University, 1982.

Ilg, Frances L., Louise Bates Ames, Jacqueline Haines, Clyde Gillespie. *School Readiness: Behavior Tests Used at the Gesell Institute*. Rev. ed. New York: Harper & Row, 1978.

Special Concerns

Ames, Louise Bates. *Is Your Child in the Wrong Grade?* Rosemont, N. J.: Modern Learning Press, 1966.

Brazelton, T. Berry. *Working and Caring*. Reading, Mass.: Addison-Wesley, 1987.

Clarke, Louise. *How to Recognize and Overcome Dyslexia in Your Child*. Baltimore: Penguin, 1974.

Colfax, David, and Micki Colfax. *Homeschooling for Excellence*. New York: Warner Books, 1988.

de Hirsh, Katrina. *Predictive Reading Failure*. New York: Harper & Row, 1966.

Friedrich, Elizabeth, and Cherry Rowland. *The Parents' Guide to Raising Twins*. New York: St. Martin's Press, 1983.

Gardner, Richard A. *The Boys and Girls Book About Divorce with an Introduction for Parents*. New York: Bantam Books, 1970.

Kappelman, Murray. *Raising The Only Child*. New York: New American Library, 1975.

Krementz, Jill. *How It Feels to Be Adopted*. New York: Knopf, 1982.

Krementz, Jill. *How It Feels When Parents Divorce*. New York: Knopf, 1984.

MacCracken, Marry. *Turnabout Children: Overcoming Dyslexia and Other Learning Disabilities*. New York: New American Library, 1986.

Osman, Betty B. *Learning Disabilities: A Family Affair.* New York: Warner Books, 1979.

Sanger, Sirgay. *The Woman Who Works, The Parent Who Cares.* New York: Harper & Row, 1988.

Scarr, Sandra. *Mother Care/Other Care.* New York: Warner Books, 1984.

Smith, Sally L. *No Easy Answers: The Learning Disabled Child at Home and At School.* Toronto: Bantam Books, 1981.

Turecki, Stanley, and Leslie Tonner. *The Difficult Child.* New York: Bantam Books, 1985.

Vail, Priscilla L. *The World of the Gifted Child.* New York: Walker and Co., 1979.

————. *Smart Kids with School Problems: Things to Know and Ways to Help.* New York: E. P. Dutton, 1987.

Private/Independent School Guides

New York Independent Schools Directory. Published by The Independent Schools Admissions Association of Greater New York in cooperation with Parents League of New York, Inc., published annually. Available by mail from Parents League of New York, Inc., 115 East 82nd Street, New York, NY 10028.

Private Independent Schools 1990. The Bunting and Lyon Blue Book. Wallingford, Connecticut: Bunting and Lyon Inc., published annually.

The Handbook of Private Schools. Boston: Porter Sargent Publishers, Inc., published annually.

Books to Read to and with Your Children

This is a list of some of the books I have enjoyed reading aloud, first with my lower school students, and later at home with my own children. It is a very personal list and is in no way intended as a definitive list of books for children. I have purposely omitted some of my favorites because I feel they are more enjoyable when read silently. Some of the books are part of a series: if you like the first one you will want to try more in the series, or other books by the same author. This list is merely intended as a beginning; your local librarian or bookstore will be an excellent source for additional suggestions. I have put an asterisk in front of some of the shorter books that are geared to very young children, but I have not listed books by age level because I believe good books span a variety of ages. Your children will let you know if a book is too long or too difficult for them by their expressions as they listen. If your audience begins to squirm or look bored, put the book away and try another one. Never read a book aloud to your children that you don't enjoy yourself. Reading aloud should be a pleasure you and your children share long after they are able to read to themselves.

Banks, Lynne Reid. *The Indian in the Cupboard.* New York: Avon Books, 1984.

Bates, Katharine Lee. *Once Upon A Time: A Book of Old-Time Fairy Tales.* New York: Rand McNally, 1921.

Baum, L. Frank. *The Wizard of Oz.* Illustrations by Evelyn Copelman. New York: Grosset & Dunlap, 1956.

*Berenstain, Stan and Jan. *He Bear She Bear.* New York: Random House, 1974.

Bond, Michael. *A Bear Called Paddington.* Illustrated by Peggy Fortnum. New York: A Yearling Book. Dell, 1968.

Brink, Carol Ryrie. *Caddie Woodlawn.* New York: Macmillan, 1935.

*Brown, Margaret Wise. *Goodnight Moon.* Illustrated by Clement Hurd. New York: A Harper Trophy Picture Book, Harper & Row, 1977.

*Brown, Margaret Wise. *The Runaway Bunny.* Pictures by Clement Hurd. New York: A Harper Trophy Book, Harper & Row, 1977.

Burnett, Frances Hodgson. *A Little Princess.* New York: Yearling, Dell Publishing Co., 1975.

————. *The Secret Garden.* Illustrated by Tasha Tudor. New York: J. B. Lippincott, 1962.

*Burton, Virginia Lee. *The Little House.* Boston: Houghton Mifflin, 1978.

*Cohen, Miriam. *Will I Have a Friend?* Illustrated by Lillian Huban. New York: Macmillan, 1967.

Dahl, Roald, *Matilda.* Illustrated by Quentin Blake. New York: Viking Penguin, 1988.

————. *The BFG.* Illustrations by Quentin Blake. New York: Puffin Books. Viking Penguin, 1984.

D'Aulaire, Ingri, and Edgar Parin. *Book of Greek Myths.* Garden City, N. Y.: Doubleday, 1962.

*de Brunhoff, Jean. *The Story of Babar.* Trans. by Merle Haas. New York: Random House, 1966.

Henry, Marguerite. *Misty of Chincoteague.* Illustrated by Wesley Dennis. Rand McNally, 1947.

*Heyward, DuBose. *The Country Bunny and the Little Gold Shoes.* Pictures by Marjorie Flack. Boston: Houghton Mifflin, 1939.

*Hoban, Russell, *Bread and Jam for Frances.* Illustrated by Lillian Hoban. New York: Harper & Row, 1964.

Kaye, M. M. *The Ordinary Princess.* New York: Simon & Schuster, 1986.

*Knight, Hilary. *The Owl and the Pussy-Cat.* based on the poem by Edward Lear. New York: Macmillan, 1983.

Konigsburg, E. L. *From the Mixed-up Files of Mrs. Basil E. Frankweiler.* New York: A Yearling Book. Dell Publishing Co., 1967.

Krementz, Jill. *A Very Young Gymnast.* New York: Knopf, 1978 (See also other titles in series).

Lewis, C. S. *The Lion, the Witch and the Wardrobe.* With pictures adapted from illustrations by Pauline Baynes. New York: Macmillan, 1970.

Lindgren, Astrid. *Pippi Longstocking.* Trans. by Florence Lamborn. Illustrated by Louis S. Glanzman. New York: Puffin Books, Penguin, 1977.

MacDonald, George. *The Princess and the Goblin.* Illustrated by Jos. A. Smith. New York: Grosset & Dunlap, 1985.

Milne, A. A. *Winnie the Pooh.* New York: E. P. Dutton, 1926.

Nesbit, E. *Five Children and It.* With Illustrations by H. R. Millar. New York: Puffin Books. Penguin, 1959.

*Piper, Watty. *The Little Engine That Could*. Illustrated by George and Doris Hauman. New York: Grosset & Dunlap, 1930.

*Potter, Beatrix. *The Tale of Peter Rabbit*. New York: Frederick Warne & Co., 1986.

Prokofiev, Sergei. *Peter and the Wolf*. Adapted from the Musical Tale. Illustrated by Erna Voigt. Boston: David R. Godine, 1980.

*Rey, H. A. *Curious George*. Boston: Houghton Mifflin, 1941.

Riordan, James. *Tales of King Arthur*. New York: Rand McNally, 1982.

*Scarry, Richard. *Richard Scarry's Animal Nursery Tales*. New York: Golden Press, 1975.

*Sendak, Maurice. *Nutshell Library*. Includes *Alligators All Around; An Alphabet; Chicken Soup with Rice; A Book of Months; One Was Johnny: A Counting Book; Pierre*. New York, Harper & Row, 1962.

*———. *Outside Over There*. New York: Harper & Row, 1981.

*Seuss, Dr. *And to Think I Saw It on Mulberry Street*. New York: Vanguard, 1937.

*———. *Horton Hatches the Egg*. New York: Random House, 1940.

*Slobodkina, Esphyr. *Caps for Sale*. New York: Scholastic Inc., 1968.

*Steig, William. *Sylvester and the Magic Pebble*. New York: Simon & Schuster, 1969.

The Random House Book of Poetry For Children. Selected and introduced by Jack Prelutsky. Illustrated by Arnold Lobel. New York: Random House, 1983.

The Real Mother Goose. Illustrated by Blanche Fisher Wright. Chicago: Rand McNally, 1916.

Thompson, Kay. *Eloise*. Illustrated by Hilary Knight. New York: Simon & Schuster, 1969.

The Aesop for Children. With Pictures by Milo Winter. Chicago: Rand McNally, 1919.

The Arabian Nights. Illustrated by Earle Goodenow. New York: Grosset & Dunlap, 1946.

The Iliad and The Odyssey. The Heroic Story of the Trojan War. The Fabulous Adventures of Odysseus. Adapted from the Greek Classics of Homer by Jane Werner Watson. Pictures by Alice and Martin Provensen. New York: Golden Press, 1956.

Thurber, James. *Many Moons*. New York: Harcourt, Brace, 1943.

Tolkien, J.R.R. *The Hobbit or There and Back Again*. Rev. ed. New York: Ballantine Books, 1937.

*Waber, Bernard. *Ira Sleeps Over*. Boston: Houghton Mifflin, 1972.

*Wells, Rosemary. *Peabody*. New York: E. P. Dutton, 1983.

White, E. B., *Charlotte's Web*. Pictures by Garth Williams. New York: Harper & Row, 1952.

———. *Stuart Little*. Pictures by Garth Williams. New York: Harper & Row, 1945.

Wilder, Laura Ingalls. *Little House on the Prairie*. Pictures by Garth Williams. New York: Harper & Row, 1971.

Williams, Margery. *The Velveteen Rabbit or How Toys Become Real*. Illustrations by William Nicholson. Garden City, N.Y.: Doubleday, 1958.

Index